# A GENERAL HISTORY OF ENGLAND
## 1832-1960

# A GENERAL HISTORY OF ENGLAND

## 1832-1960

BY

### W. A. BARKER, M.A. CANTAB.
HEADMASTER OF THE LEYS SCHOOL,
SOMETIME FELLOW OF QUEENS' COLLEGE, CAMBRIDGE

### G. R. St. AUBYN, M.A. OXON.
ASSISTANT MASTER AT ETON COLLEGE

AND

### R. L. OLLARD, M.A. OXON.
SOMETIME SENIOR LECTURER AT THE ROYAL NAVAL COLLEGE, GREENWICH

SECOND EDITION

A. & C. BLACK LTD
4, 5 & 6 SOHO SQUARE LONDON W.1

FIRST PUBLISHED 1953
SECOND EDITION 1960

MADE IN GREAT BRITAIN
PRINTED BY UNWIN BROTHERS LIMITED
WOKING AND LONDON

# PREFACE

## TO SECOND EDITION

IN this edition we have added a short chapter on recent developments in the Commonwealth and in Foreign Affairs. The changes since 1945 have been so vast as to require a book to themselves. To write it was out of the question; to ignore the period entirely was easy, but equally unsatisfactory. We hope that our brief sketch, for all its obvious inadequacy, will enrich the reader's understanding of the preceding century.

Some passages in other chapters have been re-written with the same end in view, and we have done our best to clear up obscurities and to correct errors of fact, judgement and expression. The bibliography has also been extended.

W. A. B.
G. R. St. A.
R. L. O.

# PREFACE

## TO FIRST EDITION

THIS book is written on the same principles as its predecessor, *A General History of England 1688–1832*. We have taken the history of Foreign Policy, Society, the Constitution, the Empire and the Church down to 1950. But to pursue a continuous narrative of domestic politics, or to attempt an evaluation of Literature and Thought, after the First World War would be presumptuous and probably of little use.

As in our first volume, we have included in the text the dates of many of the people mentioned, in order to help the reader keep his bearings. In any case everyone's dates are given in the index. We have also provided a list of Prime Ministers, an analysis of the British Commonwealth, a selection of books for futher reading, a genealogical tree of the Royal Family and a glossary to which readers should refer when they find a word they do not understand.

Our colleague, W. A. Barker, has been in America during the writing of this volume. Although he has fortunately been able to send us certain chapters, it would be unfair to hold him responsible for the imperfections of the book as a whole.

We would like to thank Mr. P. G. Henderson and Mr. K. V. Rose for reading our proofs and for making many valuable suggestions. We are also most grateful to Mr. C. R. N. Routh for helping with the maps in both volumes, and to Mr. A. A. Rouse for his useful criticism. We wish to express our warmest thanks to Mrs. H. Hartley, who has helped in a hundred ways and whose hospitality has made even proof-reading a pleasure.

*St. Catherine's, Argyll*

R. L. O.
G. R. St. A.

September 1952

# CONTENTS

# CONTENTS

# CONTENTS

## MAPS

## CHAPTER I

# VICTORIAN ENGLAND, 1837–1901

## 1. Early Victorian England, 1837–1865

To most people living in the stormy, unsettled years of this century the word "Victorian" suggests order, tranquillity and plenty—an age in which people ate enormous meals and raised vast families on a steadily increasing income; an age in which houses were over-furnished and ugly; an age of starchiness and respectability, of long sermons and tall hats, an age when new ideas were frozen into silence by the deadening power of convention. Solid comfort in the home and complete stability in the country sum up this common conception of the Victorians.

There is much truth in all this, but, taken as a whole, the picture is not a good likeness. Certainly the Victorians themselves would be astonished and indignant at it. They regarded their age as one of revolutionary change in practically every department of life and prided themselves on their eager acceptance of new ideas. Progress was their watchword; the nineteenth century seemed to them one of the supreme epochs in history when the mind of man was throwing down barriers that had stood for centuries and finding on all sides new worlds to conquer. And indeed a comparison of England at the Queen's death with what it was at her accession gives every support to this view. To take but a few examples; in 1837 the fastest method of travel was by stage-coach averaging about ten miles an hour; hospitals were few and filthy; the great bulk of the people received no education; the Universities cared little for learning and less for teaching; there was no regular civil service; promotion in the army was still by purchase and there was no regulation of the conditions or employment or hours of work in the factories[1] and mines. By 1901 Britain was covered with a network

[1] The Factory Acts of 1802 and 1819 only stopped employers from buying pauper children to work as slaves, and the Act of 1833, which was the first measure to regulate conditions of work had only four Government Inspectors to enforce it.

of railways which reduced all journeys to a matter of hours; a vastly increased number of hospitals was staffed by a trained and efficient nursing service; Oxford and Cambridge were worthy of their fame; the civil service was the admiration of the world; the army had been thoroughly reformed and the working man was protected by a code of Factory Acts, Mines Acts and the like. The transformation is almost incredible. Those sixty years had seen more changes than the preceding six hundred.

The rate of change was so swift that it is difficult to fix any exact point at which the everyday life of England altered decisively. Nevertheless there is an obvious distinction between the Early Victorian and Late Victorian periods, and in politics the dividing line was drawn by Bagehot at the death of Lord Palmerston in 1865. This division of the reign has been accepted in the great work on Early Victorian England edited by G. M. Young and will be followed in this book.

In 1845 Benjamin Disraeli, the future Prime Minister, published a novel entitled *Sybil—or The Two Nations*. The meaning of the sub-title is explained in the following dialogue:

"Say what you like," says Egremont (the hero of the book), "our Queen rules over the greatest nation that ever existed."

"Which nation?" asked the stranger, "for she rules over two."

Egremont was silent, but looked inquiringly.

"Yes", resumed the stranger after a moment's interval. "Two nations; between whom there is no intercourse and no sympathy; who are as ignorant of each others' habits, thoughts and feelings, as if they were dwellers in different zones, or inhabitants of different planets; who are formed by a different breeding, are fed by a different food, are ordered by different manners, and are not governed by the same laws."

"You speak of—" said Egremont hesitatingly, "THE RICH AND THE POOR."

Readers may perhaps wonder what special significance the author meant to be attached to this. Extremes of wealth and poverty had existed side by side in England from time immemorial. What was new or dangerous about the Rich and the Poor? The answer is to be found in the political awakening of the working class. The French

Revolution had shaken European society to its foundations and the re-establishment of the *ancien régime* on the Continent at the Congress of Vienna was felt by many Englishmen to be unjust and by all to be insecure. In the thirty years that followed Waterloo all Europe listened anxiously for the first distant rumblings of revolution. Because England was politically the most mature of all nations she was more acutely aware of this danger and more active in finding out the remedy. Disraeli's phrase "the Two Nations" may seem theatrical but it was not far from the truth. Rich and Poor were conscious of themselves as two separate and potentially hostile groups. The old personal ties of master and man had been much weakened by the growing scale of industry. Men and women were herded into the poisonous squalor of the new towns to work for an employer who was barely a name to them.

The working-class standard of living during the Early Victorian period was meagre in town and country alike. It was not until the sixties that the factory workers decisively outnumbered the agricultural labourers and not until the eighties that England began to import a great part of her food. Throughout the early years of the reign everything depended on the success or failure of the harvest at home. If the weather was bad, the countryman went hungry and the reduced diet of the townsman weakened his resistance to the diseases which flourished in the overcrowded, undrained slums. In the good years, farm workers earned enough to feed themselves and their families, and the worker in industry, whose wages were higher, had a little money over to spend on furniture and other household necessaries. Things which we regard as essential were then looked upon as luxuries and except for drink, which was very cheap, the ordinary working man could afford no extras. This is a generalization, but apart from fluctuations caused by the weather, conditions varied from place to place and from trade to trade. In agriculture, for instance, the standard of life of labourers in the western counties like Somerset and Dorset was notoriously lower than elsewhere, rarely rising above starvation level even in the best years. In industry the depths of poverty were reached by the Irish immigrants who crowded the slums of Liverpool and the hand-loom weavers whose long, agonizing struggle to compete with the machine-loom was foredoomed to failure. On the other hand the foundry-workers of the midlands and the cutlers of Sheffield earned enough to feed and clothe their families decently and could even afford such a luxury as a cottage piano.

So much for wages. The diet of the working man consisted largely of wheat bread and a little meat, except in Ireland and Scotland where the people were so poor that they lived almost exclusively on potatoes and oatmeal. Towns and villages near the sea could supplement this monotonous fare with fish, and the countryman usually grew vegetables and kept chickens. For the townsman fruit and green vegetables were in the early years of this period something of a rarity, though the development of the railways gradually improved matters. In times of real scarcity both town and country dweller resorted to poaching which in those days of savage Game Laws was a much more desperate affair than it is now. Battles between armed gangs of poachers and patrols of keepers were common and deaths were not infrequent.

The houses of the poor were as a rule damp, overcrowded, unventilated and undrained. In the country these evils were mitigated by a good natural water supply and by the fresh air. But in the towns the undrained sewage often seeped into the drinking water and cholera resulted. The unpaved, undrained slums in which men brought up their families, the roaring, suffocating factories in which they worked, the reeking gin palaces where they went for oblivion and the smoke-darkened sky under which they lived, combine to form a picture of human existence as hellish as any of which we have record. Yet this is not to say that conditions were worse than the worst of previous ages. The rate of infant mortality, for instance, was lower in the new towns than it had been in the slums of London in the early decades of the eighteenth century. What made these miseries so much more terrible than anything that had gone before was that, for the first time, their existence was widely recognized. They were on such an enormous scale that they forced themselves on the mind and conscience of society. The condition of the industrial working-class had not worsened, but was at last recognized for what it was. The pages of the Reports of Royal Commissions— Blue Books as they were called—detailed the circumstances of squalor and beastliness in which a great part of the nation lived. Novels like Dickens' *Bleak House* and Disraeli's *Sybil* told the same story in a vivid and powerful manner and reached an immense public. The Early Victorians were aware of the evils and the wretchedness at the base of their society as no generation had been before them. In an age of rapid change they had much to worry about; but about the question of the poor—the "condition of England question" as Disraeli called it—they worried most of all.

The old approach to the problem of social distress—the fitful dispensing of soup and jellies, "poor peopling" as Florence Nightingale contemptuously called it—was obviously inadequate though it remained a fashionable amusement among well-to-do ladies. The government must do something. But what? The Early Victorian statute book provides the answer. Attempts at regulating conditions of work were made in the Factory Acts of 1833 and 1847. The first limited the working day to ten hours and mitigated the worst evils of child labour; but it applied only to textile factories and the means of enforcing it were insufficient. The Act of 1847 extended the ten-hour day to all industries and regulated more strictly the employment of women and young girls. By 1850 the Saturday half-holiday was established and the working man could escape to the country or the football field for a breath of fresh air.

If things were bad in the factories, in the mines they were indescribable. The Mines Report of 1842 revealed that, in some districts of the midland coalfield, women were being used as human pit-ponies in conditions that revolted the conscience of England. In many pits the ventilation doors on which the safety of the miners depended were left in charge of small boys who sat for hour after hour all alone in the dark caverns of the earth. The Mines Act of 1842 prohibited the employment of women underground in any circumstances and made the age of ten the earliest at which a boy might work below the surface. In the passing of the Mines Act and the Factory Acts already mentioned the most tireless worker was Lord Ashley, later Earl of Shaftesbury (1801–1885). Towards the end of the eighteenth century Burke had written that society rested on two principles—the spirit of religion and the spirit of a gentleman. To one who personified these ideals Early Victorian England owed the establishment of a code of labour laws of which only the merest outline has been given here.

Such were the first steps taken to relieve the conditions under which the poor man worked. The conditions in which he lived had already received some attention from the Government. In 1818 Commissioners had been appointed to inquire into the various charities in which the country abounded, such as almshouses and endowments for the distribution of free food and drink. The task of finding out what these foundations were, what their purpose was and how far it was carried out, was so enormous that it was not finished until 1837. The report disclosed a mass of slackness, abuse and misappropriation. Old men and women lived in dirty alms-houses on a diet not far removed from starvation whilst the Warden and Trustees stood themselves sumptuous dinners at the founder's expense. In some cases the almshouses had been allowed to tumble down and their income had been appropriated by the trustees. Even in cases where the original purpose of the foundation was being carried out satisfactorily the value of the endowment had often increased with time and the surplus, instead of being used for charity, went to provide a handsome salary for the man in charge. The diffi-culties of a conscientious man in this awkward position form the plot of Anthony Trollope's novel *The Warden* published in 1855. The worst of these malpractices withered in the glare of publicity. In 1835 the Charity Commission was established with powers to reform those who could not reform themselves and to apply money which had been left for obsolete or socially undesirable purposes to better use.

A much less popular measure was the New Poor Law of 1834. The Speenhamland system was thoroughly bad; bad for the employer because it enabled him to use the rates to pay a large part of his wages bill and bad for the workman because it made a pauper of him and took away his self-respect. The new Act stopped out-door relief absolutely and set up new workhouses run on uniform lines throughout the country. In many ways, no doubt, these new "Unions"[1] were an improvement, but the bleak, inhuman spirit in which they were run stirred up a wave of popular hatred. Husband

---

[1] So called from the fact that one workhouse was provided for a "union" or group of parishes.

and wife were separated from each other and a hundred petty regulations made them more disliked than the no less horrible but more easy-going institutions they replaced. Moreover, removal of outdoor relief brought the threat of the workhouse much nearer to a great number of people, for wages did not at once adjust themselves and there was a period of terrible misery until they rose to a level at which a man could support his family. But in spite of its defects and of its lack of imagination the New Poor Law marked a great advance. At last there was a centralized national system for dealing with the problem of poverty. The Poor Law Board sitting in London might be harsh and stupid, but at least it had created a nation-wide organization which a later age might easily put to a more liberal and intelligent use.

The squalor of the new towns was, as we have seen, due not least to the lack of sanitation, of a pure water supply, and of properly paved and lighted streets. The great landmark here is the Municipal Reform Act of 1835. Up to this time the old medieval institutions of township and borough had survived unaltered, but the idea of a corporation, so natural to the medieval mind, was imperfectly understood in the centuries which followed. Who owned the property of a corporation? Was it the members of the corporation? If so, was it wrong for them to spend the corporation's income on enormous banquets for themselves and in feathering their nests generally, for in practice this was what was usually done? The answer to these questions is given by F. W. Maitland, the greatest of English legal historians:

"Our law, if I am not mistaken, had never dictated to the boroughs what they should do with their property: it had trusted to their honour. If, observing all constitutional forms, holding duly convened meetings and so forth, the corporators divided among themselves the income or the land of the corporation, they were, I believe, unpunishable and their acts valid. But whatever may have been the law, we surely feel that in William IV's reign it was scandalous that the corporators of a great town should think, or act as though they thought, that the property of the corporation, or such remnants of it as had not been squandered, was their property: was their property morally, or . . . *bona fide*."

This was the spirit which animated the Municipal Reformers. The Act of 1835 swept away all the old close[1] corporations and replaced them with bodies elected by all the ratepayers. The new corporations were made responsible for sanitation, water supply, the upkeep and lighting of streets and were empowered, but not compelled, to create and maintain local police forces.[2] London was specifically excepted from the provisions of the Municipal Reform Act because on paper it had a democratic and popular constitution. The real reason was that its power and prestige were so great that it could not be unceremoniously lumped in with the generality of provincial towns. The work of the Act was carried a stage further by the Public Health Act of 1848. This set up a Public Health Board with power to enforce the standards laid down by law on the local corporations and to grant them money if they were too poor to carry out their obligations. If no competent local authority existed, the Health Board was empowered to create one. This system of maintaining a uniform level of social service through local bodies which are supervised and, if necessary, aided by a centralized national authority is the master weapon forged by the Early Victorians to fight their social problems and is still in use today. First employed in the administration of the New Poor Law it was extended to health and later to education. It is an administrative triumph and the credit for it is due entirely to the disciples of Jeremy Bentham (1748–1832) of whom the greatest was Edwin Chadwick (1800–1890). These men, the second generation of Utilitarians (see Chapter II), created the modern Civil Service and their example of industry, intelligence and incorruptibility has influenced and still does influence the English way of life more deeply and more profitably than that of many whose names are better known.

But Lord Ashley in the Commons and the Utilitarians in the Civil Service were not the only allies of the working man. The cholera epidemics of 1831 and 1854 drew no distinction between

[1] So-called because membership of the corporation and the right to elect its officers were severely restricted by out-of-date qualifications. The close corporation was the local counterpart of the Parliamentary rotten borough.

[2] By an Act of 1856 all counties were compelled to keep up a regular police force.

rich and poor though naturally the mortality was greater among those who lived in crowded and unhealthy conditions. The threat of disease, like the threat of revolution, played on the fears of the governing classes; the novels of Charles Dickens appealed to their pity and humanity, the Evangelical Movement and the Anglo-Catholic Revival to their consciences. A run of good harvests, the rapid development of the railways and the enormous volume of British foreign trade led to a steady increase in the national income and a gradual but real improvement in the working-class standard of life. But there was never much to spare; a wet year or the blight in the Irish potato crop could still cause bitter hardship. It was not until the steamships of the Late Victorian period made American grain easily available that the spectre of famine disappeared.

If the advance of the working classes during the Early Victorian period was slow, that of the professional classes was spectacular. The increase in wealth, the reforming spirit at work in the Church and in the public schools, the development of science and the breaking down of the barriers of patronage in the civil and military service of the State offered limitless opportunity to men of talent and education. Just as the Reformation had opened to laymen paths hitherto closed to all but the clergy, so the Early Victorian period opened to all men of ability careers which had previously been the closed preserve of the aristocracy. Like the Reformation, this was a European and not simply an English affair. The "career open to the talents" was one of the slogans of Napoleon's Empire and its adoption in Europe was a tribute to his brilliant success as an administrator; in England it was largely the work of the Utilitarians.

In this new situation the public schools, which had altered little in the preceding century, were ripe for reform. The hour brought forth the man. In 1828 Dr. Arnold was appointed Headmaster of Rugby. The changes he made have become the fundamental principles of the modern public school. The formation of character was his first aim and to achieve it he introduced the prefectorial system which gave the older boys a taste of responsibility and the younger a taste of discipline. Not that he neglected the intellectual side of education: the Classics were better taught under Arnold than in any public school of his time, and history and modern languages

9

found, for the first time, a small but significant place in the curriculum. Above all he was determined that his boys should leave Rugby instructed Christians and the chapel, generally regarded as a Temple of Boredom and occasionally violated by hooliganism,[1] became the hub of the school life. So successful were Arnold's methods that they were soon imitated in the older schools and in the many new ones which were founded during the Victorian Age.

The Universities of Oxford and Cambridge were in at least as bad a state as the public schools. The great majority of Fellows and Heads of Houses were clergymen with no knowledge of the world and no interest in the vast new fields of learning which were being explored. Professors no longer delivered the public lectures for which they were paid and Fellows were admitted without undergoing the formality of an examination. In one Oxford College, however, there were signs of better things. Under Dr. Copleston, who was Provost from 1814 to 1828, Oriel had revived the practice of examining for Fellowships and had gathered in its Senior Common Room a band of men remarkable for their ability and for the seriousness with which they took their duties. Gradually other colleges began to follow suit. But the cause of University Reform was forgotten after 1833 in the fierce religious controversy caused by the Oxford Movement (see Chapter XIV). At Cambridge the collision of High and Low Church parties was less severe and there was a steady movement towards reform. The appointment of the Royal Commissions in the fifties was a decisive step. Examinations for Fellowships were widely adopted and the monopoly of the clergy was broken. The system of "Founder's Kin", by which those who traced their descent from the founder or his family could claim a Fellowship, was abolished. Though until 1854 a man could not go to Oxford unless he was a member of the Church of England, the chief barriers had been thrown down by the Early Victorians and all was clear for a new Renaissance of English learning. The example of the new University of London (founded in 1836) which was non-sectarian, did much to alter the constitution of the older Universities and its concentration on economics, politics

[1] As at Eton where the boys used to let rats loose among the Fellows as they walked in procession up the aisle.

and the physical sciences extended the scope of higher education.

Except for the Church which is dealt with in Chapter XIV the older professions altered comparatively little during the Early Victorian period. The army remained much what it had been in the eighteenth century. The Duke of Wellington, who resisted all attempts at reform, was Commander-in-Chief from 1827 till his death in 1852. The Crimean War (1853–1856) exposed the antiquated and inefficient organization of the army at a hideous cost in life and suffering. Public opinion was aroused. But the defenders of the old system were strongly entrenched at the War Office and it was not until the Late Victorian age that their resistance was overcome. Roughly the same is true of the navy except that reform and re-organization were forced on the service not by the Crimean War but by the modernization of the French Navy under Napoleon III and the consequent fear of invasion. Nevertheless the Early Victorian period did see some changes in the methods of officering and manning the fleet. Up to 1855 there had been no system of continuous engagement for the ratings. When a ship paid off at the end of her commission (usually two or three years) the men were discharged. If another ship happened to be commissioning they could, if they wished, re-engage for another commission, but more often they had had enough of the navy for the time being and dispersed to their homes. The disadvantages of this system lay in the time taken to man a ship and the strong inducement to the better type of rating to take up a steady job in civilian life. The introduction of engagements to serve for ten years and a regular system of payment made the service happier and more efficient. For officers, conditions were even more unsatisfactory. In peacetime there were not enough ships in commission to provide appointments for more than about a third of the officers on the active list. Competition for appointments was intense and "interest"[1] was the first condition of success. As there was no system of compulsory retirement, a capable officer who lacked "interest" might spend fifty years as a half-pay lieutenant without getting a ship and it was a common thing to find Admirals and Captains of eighty or

---

[1] For a definition of this all-important word, see Glossary.

more. The only solution to the problem was to cut down the number of officers to a figure roughly equal to the number of appointments available. This was eventually achieved in the late fifties and a compulsory retiring age was fixed for each rank. This reform of the system of promotion attracted more men of ability into the service and made it harder for incompetents to rise on "interest" alone.

But it was not in the older professions that the widest prospects were opened to men of talent. The Indian Civil Service was recruited entirely by competitive examination after 1853 and by 1855 the various government departments at home began somewhat gingerly to follow this precedent, a process not completed till Gladstone's great ministry of 1868–1874. Apart from the government service, the tremendous expansion of English trade and industry was creating a whole new class of managers and business men. Peel and Gladstone, the two greatest Prime Ministers of the century, both sprang from this new section of society. The combination of the special qualities of this class, self-reliance, energy, adventurousness, and a strict code of personal morals, with the grace and cultivation of the landed aristocracy is the very heart of Early Victorian society and the secret of its greatness.

The social habits and amusements of the age differed greatly from those of the preceding century. Dress, for instance, was more sober and more uniform. The flowered waistcoat, the brightly coloured coat, the knee-breeches and silk stockings which make eighteenth-century portraits so delightful had given way to trousers, dark tail-coats and the general air of restrained formality which characterizes modern morning dress. Gay colours and individuality in dress were resigned to women. The clothes of the aristocracy were at first sight indistinguishable from those of the middle class and, by the late Victorian age, from the Sunday best of the prosperous working man. The use of powder on the hair was discontinued, except for footmen in the houses of the great, and the taking of snuff became less aristocratic and more common. Tobacco, which had been out of favour in polite society since the seventeenth century, was rapidly coming back, though no gentleman would smoke in public or in the presence of a lady. People still ate on the substantial scale of the eighteenth century but with noticeably less grossness. Wine still flowed abundantly at the tables of the well-to-do but drunkenness was far less common. In this refinement of manners the influence and example of Queen Victoria's court had perhaps the greatest share, as it certainly had in making the family the focus of social life.

The happy family life of the Queen and Prince Albert was in remarkable contrast to the hatreds between father and son and the squabbles between brother and brother which had seemed an invariable characteristic of the Hanoverians. Victoria's court was the model of morality and the domestic virtues became fashionable. In the eighteenth century upper-class parents showed, as a rule, little affection or interest in their children whose upbringing was in consequence a haphazard affair. All this was now altered; children were brought up with a strictness which we should find over-whelming had it not been softened with affection. Even after childhood had been left behind, the family tended to take its pleasures in common. In the evenings they would gather round the piano for part songs, or cluster round the fire to hear their father read aloud the latest instalment of a novel by Dickens or Trollope. Inter-woven with the development of family life was the change in the position of women. The emphasis now placed on the family had much improved their standing: they were treated with more respect and in the all-important matter of marriage were generally allowed to decide for themselves instead of being expected to follow their parents' wishes with instant obedience. But the logical conclusion that, in the event of their not marrying, they should be allowed to choose their own way of life had not yet been reached. Consequently women like Florence Nightingale (1820–1910) who felt themselves called to follow a career looked on the family as an institution designed to thwart the development of character and talents and to keep people (especially women) from the jobs they were cut out to do. It was not the least of her astonishingly varied achievements that her own efforts and example opened the door of a professional career to her sex.

The Early Victorian Age has been dealt with at some length because of its unique importance. The problems it faced were acute and the answers it tried to find were full of vigour and invention. Energy, spirit, eagerness, gusto are the qualities which predominate though they are usually controlled by a deep moral seriousness or what we should call conscientiousness. The Late Victorian period for all its richness cannot rival its predecessor and many of its achievements were reached by proceeding along lines already laid down.

## 2. The Late Victorian Age, 1865–1901

Shortly before his death in 1865 Lord Palmerston, the Prime Minister, had remarked to a friend, "Oh, there is really nothing to be done. . . . We cannot go on adding to the statute book *ad infinitum*". This statement explains why his death is the dividing line in politics between Early and Late Victorian. The forces of reform that we have seen at work in the Early Victorian period had not spent themselves. Within three years of Palmerston's death Gladstone had begun his great ministry: the army was comprehensively reformed; the new system of entrance by competitive examination was extended to cover the whole civil service; education was extended and to some extent subsidized by the State. In these and a hundred other ways the life of society was changing; but great as these changes were they had already been mapped out by the Early Victorians. The blueprints had been drawn; they were now being translated into reality. The impact of reform on the life of the country has been generally discussed in the Early Victorian section of this chapter. The purpose of these few pages is to single out the qualities in the Late Victorian Age which were not evident in its forerunner.

Wealth was the most obvious characteristic of the Late Victorian period. Throughout the nineteenth century the country grew steadily richer; the poor man's condition became, if not enviable, at least tolerable enough to quiet fears of revolution; but the rich man became very rich indeed. Comfort and luxury, so long looked down on as degenerate, found their way into the homes of the well-to-do. Gone were the cold baths and cold houses of the Early Victorians. The geyser and the radiator introduced a new standard of domestic comfort. The increase in wealth and in the number of things it could buy tended to make the age harder, more selfish and more indifferent to the things of the spirit than the earlier period. There is a change from the anxiety and self-questioning of the Early Victorians to the complacency and self-satisfaction of the next generation. Glitter and vulgarity, the decay of the standards of self-discipline and self-restraint became more pronounced as society became fonder of money and less conscious of duty. As the reign drew towards its end the fashionable world looked more to the Prince of Wales, the future Edward VII, than to the ageing Queen, and it cannot be said that his example was inspiring. Money, comfort and pleasure were the chief pre-occupations of his somewhat shallow nature.[1] The decadence of the Edwardian age which may be reckoned as starting some ten years before the Queen's death adds something by contrast to the grandeur of the Victorian.

The general relaxation of standards was not without some good effects. The plays of Oscar Wilde and the comic operas of Gilbert and Sullivan show that the Late Victorians had at least the virtue of being able to laugh at themselves. The propriety of the earlier age had sometimes been carried to excess and the easiness, freedom and wit of the later period charm where seriousness and sternness would chill. Certainly women had more chance of leading their own lives and in both the important and the trivial affairs of life the age was nothing if not tolerant. Religious tests were removed at Oxford and Cambridge; the social taboo on smoking was set aside and the taste for cigarettes which the English soldiers had acquired from the French in the Crimean war gained ground rapidly.

Among the greatest change which the later Victorian age witnessed was the development of sport on scientific and professional lines. Village cricket had been popular since the beginning of the century but it was not until 1880 that the first County Championship was played. Public interest was intense and individual cricketers won a nationwide fame hitherto reserved for politicians and members of the Royal Family. The greatest of all was W. G. Grace (1848–1915) whose striking appearance and personality would have left a name behind even if his skill as a batsman had not. Rugby Football only dates from 1823, but its popularity was immediate and by the

[1] During a visit to Windsor in 1908, Margot Asquith wrote: "Our King devotes what time he does not spend upon sport and pleasure ungrudgingly to duty."

end of the century clubs like Guy's and Blackheath had fifty years of proud tradition behind them. Football had been the national sport of Englishmen since the days of Elizabeth. In 1863 the Football Association was founded and the final of the F.A. cup has remained the most important event of the footballing year. The new industrial towns took the same sort of corporate pride in the excellence of their teams as their medieval predecessors had taken in the beauty and magnificence of their public buildings. The Victorians applied the scientific method to games as to much else. Even fox hunting ceased to be the informal, amateurish pursuit it had been in the seventeenth and eighteenth centuries when squires hunted their own packs over their own estates. The enclosure of so much open land in the eighteenth century created a demand for a hunter that could take hedges and fences in its stride. The breeding of horses and hounds became a highly specialized and expert business. None but the richest landowner could afford to maintain a first-class pack or had acres broad enough to do justice to their speed and staying power. In consequence country gentlemen banded themselves together to form the hunts we know today. This passion for sport in all its branches which the nineteenth century did so much to develop has made Englishmen the despair of revolutionaries.

If the Late Victorian Age had within it the seeds of decadence it nevertheless brought forth abundantly the fruits that the Early Victorians had laboured to plant. The teachings of religion and the standards of morality might in some circles be laughed at but they were, in the main, still the stars by which men tried to steer. Perhaps the Late Victorians were spending the moral capital they had inherited from their fathers; but, be that as it may, there can be no doubt that the merits of that age far outweigh its shortcomings. The vigour and soaring energy of the early part of the reign were failing but there still remained an atmosphere of honesty, common sense, reasonableness, good humour and, above all, tolerance which make it seem from our day as remote and as desirable as the remembered island of Ithaca seemed to Ulysses on his wanderings.

## CHAPTER II

# LITERATURE AND THOUGHT IN THE EARLY VICTORIAN AGE

No age has ever been so conscious of its ideas and beliefs as the Early Victorian. The background of religion and morality against which the play of English life had been acted since the Reformation was swaying dangerously, though it was not precisely clear from what quarter it was threatened; rather, from the raucous shouts and resounding thumps backstage, it seemed that a fight had broken out among the sceneshifters in the middle of a performance; and the principal actors hurried up to the footlights to declare, in spite of nervous backward glances, their confidence in the stability of the scenery. It was this sense of being attacked from all sides at once that made the Early Victorians so uneasy and so uncertain of themselves. They had to find an intellectual defence for ideas which their forebears had taken for granted. No attempt will be made here to define these generally accepted ideas which have been sufficiently indicated in the previous volume. This chapter will concern itself with the new, unsettling, movements of the human spirit which were making so much stir.

In the hubbub and confusion three main themes of criticism soon became distinctly audible, the Romantic, the Utilitarian and the Scientific. These were the dynamic forces of the age and between them can claim credit for most Victorian achievement, whether in thought or in art or in action. So great indeed is their importance that it will be simplest to devote a section of this chapter to each.

## 1. The Romantic Movement

Romanticism means first and foremost a refusal to accept things as they are. A Romantic is, almost by definition, a rebel; he is passionately concerned with things as they ought to be and impatient with the injustice and stupidity of the world of his own day. Pope's famous phrase "Whatever is, is right" sums up the confidence and complacency of the eighteenth century from which the

Romantics were reacting. The pioneers of the movement were the poets, Byron, Keats, Shelley, Wordsworth and Coleridge, of whom only Wordsworth survived into Queen Victoria's reign. All, except perhaps Keats, had been deeply influenced by the ideas of the French Revolution. The horrors of the guillotine and the militarism of Napoleon caused a revulsion of feeling which split the movement in two. Byron and Shelley still regarded Pitt and Castlereagh and Wellington as the props of a corrupt, decaying and oppressive system at least as detestable as that which Napoleon had tried to create. Byron's famous attack on Wellington at the beginning of the Ninth Canto of *Don Juan* puts this point of view with great force:

> Though Britain owes (and pays you too) so much,
> Yet Europe doubtless owes you greatly more:
> You have repair'd Legitimacy's crutch,
>     A prop not quite so certain as before:
> The Spanish, and the French, as well as Dutch,
>     Have seen, and felt, how strongly you *restore*;
> And Waterloo has made the world your debtor
> (I wish your bards would sing it rather better).
>
> You are "the best of cut-throats":—do not start;
>     The phrase is Shakespeare's, and not missapplied:—
> War's a brain-spattering, windpipe-slitting art,
>     Unless her cause by right be sanctified.
> If you have acted *once* a generous part,
>     The world, not the world's masters, will decide,
> And I shall be delighted to learn who,
> Save you and yours, have gained by Waterloo?
>
> Never had mortal man such opportunity
>     Except Napoleon, or abused it more:
> You might have freed Europe from the unity
>     Of tyrants, and been blest from shore to shore:
> And *now*—what *is* your fame? Shall the Muse tune it ye?
>     *Now*—that the rabble's first vain shouts are o'er?
> Go! hear it in your famished country's cries!
> Behold the world! and curse your victories!

Like Fox before him Byron challenged the traditional view of British policy towards Europe. Later in the century the same theme was strongly argued by the Manchester Radicals Cobden and Bright. Speaking at Birmingham in 1858 Bright said:

"The more you examine this matter the more you will come to the conclusion which I have arrived at, that this foreign policy, this regard for 'the liberties of Europe', this care at one time for 'the Protestant interests', this excessive love for 'the balance of power' is neither more nor less than a gigantic system of out-door relief for the aristocracy of Great Britain."

Byron's ideas thus led logically to the pacifism and anti-imperialism which played so great a part in the formation of the Liberal Party and found in Mr. Gladstone their most powerful champion.

Byron and Shelley further startled opinion by their open contempt and hostility towards Christianity. To a great extent their objections were political, because almost everywhere in Europe the Church was on the side of reaction and oppression. But the most searching doubts which agitated the Early Victorians were those which concerned religion: it was on this topic, above all others, that they were most sensitive to criticism; and the poets, no less than the philosophers and the scientists, contributed to the unsettling of traditional belief.

Wordsworth (1770–1850) and Coleridge, on the other hand, exerted a conservative influence; Coleridge especially, as in later life he turned the brilliant powers of his mind from poetry to philosophy and investigated the principles of Toryism with profound understanding and insight. Wordsworth, whose genius had always responded most deeply to the beauties of nature, took less and less interest in politics. His acceptance of the Laureateship in 1843 from the hands of the Tory Peel was regarded by some of his former friends as a betrayal. Browning's poem *The Lost Leader* which begins:

Just for a handful of silver he left us

Just for a riband to stick in his coat

was a bitter commentary on Wordsworth's defection.

Both Coleridge and Wordsworth had a religious cast of mind, though their faith was unorthodox. What they had in common with Byron, Shelley and Keats, apart from their early sympathies with the liberal side in politics, was a desire to get away from the strict, neat verse forms of the eighteenth century and the cool, clear, complacent view of life it expressed. Pope and his followers had confined themselves to what they and their readers could understand; their approach, in a word, was rational. The Romantics on the other hand were fascinated by whatever was inexplicable, haunting, mysterious, awe-inspiring in nature or in art. Those emotions and experiences which they could least analyse seemed to them the very stuff of poetry. The difference of theme demanded a difference of form. Gone were the regular and restrained metres of the eighteenth century; in their place a new richness of rhythm and melody, a new sense of colour, brought life, spirit and movement into English poetry once again.

Perhaps the most influential of all the Romantics was Sir Walter Scott (1771-1832). As a poet he secured instant popularity and was regarded in his own lifetime as the equal, if not the superior, of Byron. But his novels, which he only started to write in middle life, have won him immortality. Few writers have rivalled his gift of story-telling and in his own particular field, the historical novel, he stands alone. What is even more remarkable than his purely literary achievement is the moral influence of his work on the educated classes of England and Scotland. Broadly speaking the qualities which Early Victorian society admired and those it condemned correspond with the moral ideas inculcated in Scott's novels. Scott, like Burke, was deeply impressed with the ideals of medieval society—chivalry, courtesy and loyalty—and, again like Burke, found their modern equivalent in the idea of a gentleman.[1] This veneration for the old feudal ideals marks a change from the enlightened self-interest which was the main principle of eighteenth-century society. In a way it was the re-statement of the Tory view of life as against Whig individualism and *laissez-faire*. The high-minded teaching of Scott's novels gained force from his own example: he practised what he preached. His *Life*, written by his son-in-law Lockhart, is an inspiring record of upright and unswerving endeavour.

[1] Compare Tennyson's ludicrous description of a hero of chivalry: "Like modern gentleman of seemliest port."

The message of the Romantics was taken up by Ruskin (1819–1900). To say exactly what he stood for is not easy. In the course of his long life he maintained many opinions, not all of which can be reconciled with one another; but in all his utterances the Romantic spirit can be heard: in his hatred of commercialism, in his love for wild landscapes and unplanned beauty; in his preference for the Ages of Faith over the Age of Reason; in the high colours and dancing rhythms of his own prose style.

The Romantic movement was, in the last analysis, the protest of the heart against the head. As such it was guilty of some obvious follies. The false, theatrical sentiment of the Gothic novel at which Jane Austen pokes fun in *Northanger Abbey*; the bogus ruins which country gentlemen built to lend an air of romance to their estates; the attempt to re-introduce the architectural style of the early middle ages in the construction of railway stations and hotels: all these now strike us as ludicrous. But set beside the achievement of the Romantic movement they are of little account. The revival of English poetry, the deepening and broadening of both Radical and Conservative political thought, above all, the rejection of the complacent materialism that threatened to rob England of her soul: these were the elements of incalculable value that the Romantics contributed to the Early Victorian age.

## 2. *The Utilitarians*

The Utilitarians are sometimes called by two other names, Philosophic Radicals and Benthamites. An examination of these names is the best introduction to the men and ideas they describe. Radicals they were to a man, in the sense that all of them believed more or less strongly in democracy, and all were in favour of sweeping change. The adjective "Philosophic" is no less apt, for they founded their beliefs entirely on reason, not on moral or religious principle. Their philosophy was simple: the aim of life is pleasure and we call actions good or bad according as they tend to produce pleasure or pain. The end for which society must strive is, therefore, the greatest happiness of the greatest number. How is this to be achieved? Nothing easier: simply let every man pursue his own happiness and everyone will be happy, because the happiness of all is identical with the happiness of each. A man who seeks his own good, seeks also the good of society. Owing to the natural harmony of interests, selfishness is the truest expression of public spirit.

From this it follows that all public and private charity and all attempts by the government to ease the lot of the poor are mischievous. Once the government, or anyone else, starts to interfere with the free operation of the natural laws of economics, the whole machine is thrown out of gear. Complete and absolute *laissez-faire* is the only policy. But first of all the ground would have to be cleared of obstructions caused by the stupidity and short-sightedness of England's past and present rulers. The first necessity was to reform the constitution which enabled a small privileged class to run the country exclusively for their own narrow, sectional interests. Clearly a democracy would be more likely to govern in the interests of all. The Reform Act of 1832, which owed its passage largely to the efforts of the Philosophic Radical, Francis Place (1771–1854), was a step in this direction. The second need was to educate the working man so that he would pursue his happiness in a rational way, recognizing that the happiness of all could only be attained by each man looking out for himself and refusing to combine into Trades Unions and similar organizations for benefiting one class at the expense of another. Finally, the law would have to be comprehensively reformed. In this connection the test to be applied was utility—that is, a law should only be retained if it could be shown to be useful. Hence the name Utilitarian.

The third name by which these thinkers were called, Benthamites, indicates the pre-eminence among them of Jeremy Bentham (1748–1832). Among his claims to recognition it is not the least that he was able to give a centre to the movement which bears his name and to co-ordinate the thoughts of different men into one coherent system. The Utilitarians were a small band but their unity was largely due to Bentham's intellectual power and personal charm. He was a queer mixture of the crank and the man of affairs. As an original thinker on questions of law, politics and philosophy, he was venerated throughout Europe and the New World. Long after he was dead the great reformers of the nineteenth century were working along the lines he had laid down. Yet he wasted years of his life and most of his money in designing model prisons, factories and schools; he abandoned the admirably clear English style of his youth for a pedantic, top-heavy Latinized verbiage of his own devising; and in his attempt to provide a scientific analysis of human motives and conduct he threw common sense to the winds. Not only did he refuse to admit any distinction between pleasure and happiness; he would not allow that pleasure could be of different kinds. According to his theory the pleasure obtained from drinking a glass of beer and from reading one of Shakespeare's sonnets was the same sort of pleasure, differing only in degree. The crowning touch of absurdity was added by his "felicific calculus"—that is, a formula for determining with scientific accuracy the exact amount of pleasure to be derived from every type of action.

Bentham's house was the headquarters of the Utilitarians. Although shy and retiring by nature, he was always accessible to his disciples. Among his most frequent visitors were Ricardo (1772–1823), the economist and member of parliament, Francis Place, whose contacts with Radical organizations throughout the country made him so formidable a power behind the scenes, and James Mill, a high official of the East India Company, together with his son, John Stuart Mill (1806–1873), whose fame was to eclipse his father's. Bentham, Place, Ricardo, the elder Mill and a few more were the founders of Utilitarianism and the prophets of the movement.

They were succeeded in the Early Victorian era by what may be termed the second generation of Utilitarians, who modified the teaching of their elders in several important respects. The truth was that Bentham's system contained an inner contradiction. If the principle of the natural harmony of interests was true, then clearly there was no need for governmental interference in the life of the nation, in other words no need for law. The science of law, according to Bentham's teaching, was the science of restraints. These restraints were necessary to secure a harmony of interests, to stop the minority from disturbing the majority in their rational pursuit of pleasure. Law is, in fact, intended to produce an artificial harmony of interests. But if people's interests are naturally in harmony they need no artificial harmonizing. The second generation of Utilitarians had to choose between these two principles and essentially it was a choice between *laissez-faire* and government control. Ought the State to interfere more in the life of the nation or less? The young men came down on the side of increased State control.

This change of approach can be seen in the Utilitarian attitude towards the colonies. Bentham had accepted the opinion of Adam Smith (1723–1790), the great *laissez-faire* economist, that colonies were an encumbrance to the mother country to be got rid of at the earliest opportunity. The younger Benthamites,[1] notably Gibbon Wakefield (1796–1862) and Charles Buller (1806–1848) took a more realistic view. So far from getting rid of her colonies, Britain was founding new ones and the colonial empire offered an unrivalled field for experiments in political and economic reform. These men played a large part in colonial development. Charles Buller accompanied Lord Durham on his famous mission to Canada in 1838 and helped to draw up that great report which contains the essential ideas of Dominion Status and marks the beginning of the change from Empire to Commonwealth. Wakefield in Australia invented a new technique of colonization. Hitherto new countries had been opened up by selling land to immigrants at the lowest possible price. The result was that the land was occupied by poor people without enough money to develop it properly. Consequently the crops were scanty, the colonists remained poor and could not afford to buy manufactured goods from the mother country. Wakefield's scheme was to sell the land at a high price and use the money thus gained to increase the supply of labour and capital available for its cultivation. Thus the colony would be more prosperous, the land would support a larger population, and British manufacturers would acquire a new market for their goods. Such arguments as these were unanswerable and before the end of his life Bentham himself became a convert to the new view.

At home the influence of the younger Utilitarians on the reform of the civil administration and the development of the social services has been emphasized in Chapter I. Their achievement is perhaps best illustrated by the career of Sir Edwin Chadwick (1800–1890) of whom G. M. Young in his *Portrait of an Age* writes:

---

[1] Also known as the Radical Imperialists. See page 233.

"Born in 1800, in a Lancashire farmhouse where the children were washed all over, every day, the mainspring of Chadwick's career seems to have been a desire to wash the people of England all over, every day, by administrative order." He was the driving force on the Poor Law Commission, he served on the Royal Commission which investigated child labour in factories and resulted in the Ten Hours Bill, he took the initiative in setting up two successive Royal Commissions on Sanitation and finally became a member of the first Public Health Board. Throughout his long and busy official life he kept up a ceaseless flow of pamphlets and articles on political, social and economic subjects and was an untiring advocate of competitive examination for entry into the Civil Service of which he was himself so distinguished a member.

The second generation of Utilitarians were practical reformers rather than political thinkers but they did include one philosopher. John Stuart Mill, though he always continued to call himself a Utilitarian, changed the whole direction of the movement. Individual liberty, which Bentham had regarded as of minor importance, seemed to him the supreme political good. Thus, although a democrat and a champion of votes for women, he remained fearful of the tyranny of the many over the few and opposed the principle of "one man, one vote".

To assess the work of the Utilitarians is impossible, for the forces of social change that they set in motion have not yet come to a halt. Nearly all the institutions of the modern state bear the imprint of their hands. Their moral belief, equating good and evil with pleasure and pain, may seem to us a somewhat stunted thing. But in their rational criticism of obsolete laws and methods of administration they supplied the Early Victorians with the tools of reform and taught them how to use them.

### 3. Science and Religious Belief

In the nineteenth century science advanced with such bewildering rapidity on so broad a front that no general survey of its development can be attempted in a work of this size. Moreover, it was in those days, more settled than our own, true that science knew no frontiers. To confine ourselves to the British Isles would make the story incoherent. That the British contribution to the general advance of European chemistry and physics was not unworthy of the country-men of Newton is evident if we do no more than mention the names of Davy (1778–1829), Faraday (1791–1867) and Clerk Maxwell (1831–1879).

But there was one aspect of science which troubled the hearts and minds of most thinking men in Early Victorian England. This was the relation of scientific discovery to religious belief. Briefly the point at issue was the historical accuracy of the Bible; and the branches of science from which the challenge came were Geology and Biology. According to the Book of Genesis the world and all it now contains, hills and valleys, rivers and oceans, animals and trees, even the first man and woman, had been created in six days. By a further study of the other books of the Old Testament it was possible to fix the date of this event at 4004 B.C. Yet the re-searches of the great geologist Sir Charles Lyell (1797–1875) rendered this theory utterly untenable. Four thousand years was but a drop compared to the oceans of time revealed by successive geo-logical strata: the age of the world was to be measured in hundreds of thousands of years, perhaps in millions. Nor was this all: embedded in these strata were the fossilized remains of various prehistoric animals, some of them weird and strange, some with a distinct family likeness to the animals of the present day. To people who paid little attention to the discoveries of science this might have mattered little. But the Early Victorians were passionately interested in science. The popular magazines were full of scientific articles, mostly written by experts, and the collection of geological specimens was becoming a favourite hobby among men of education. What were people to think? The scientific evidence was irrefutable; yet the idea that every word, every sentence of the Bible was literally inspired by God was held as certain.

The climax came in 1859 with the publication of *The Origin of Species* by Charles Darwin (1809–1892). The argument of the book was that man and the higher animals had evolved, over millions of years, from the lowest types of living organism and that this had been achieved by a process known as natural selection. Of any given type of animal Nature produces more than can find means of subsistence.

In the struggle for survival it is inevitable that the weakest go to the wall. The fittest in each generation survive and it is from them that the next generation is bred. This process is repeated indefinitely and its result is a gradual improvement in the type itself. Thus the modern racehorse has evolved from a miserable creature not more than a foot high whose remains have been found in the Eocene strata of North America. This theory of evolution was applied by Darwin not only to animals, but to the human race itself. The excitement can well be imagined. Science, it appeared, was launching a frontal attack not only on the historical truth of the Book of Genesis, but on the idea that man was a spiritual as well as an animal being. By the theory of evolution the difference between man and ape was merely a difference of degree, not of kind.

The ensuing battle raged all the more fiercely for the fact that there were few on either side qualified to understand the real meaning of their opponents' position. In the controversy about the truth or falsehood of Darwin's theory the issue was not long in doubt. Darwin was supported from the beginning by the veteran Sir Charles Lyell, by the great biologist T. H. Huxley (1825–1895) and by Alfred Russel Wallace, a scientist who, working in complete independence, had arrived at the same conclusions as Darwin at almost exactly the same moment. The dead weight of public opinion, always suspicious of change, was at first bitterly hostile. But the clergy who attacked evolutionism most virulently were almost entirely ignorant of science and, for the most part, un-instructed in theology. Beaten in argument they had to resort to the weapons of sarcasm and ill-temper. The opponents of Darwinism did at least as much as its advocates to ensure its triumph. But those churchmen who knew something of science, among them R. W. Church, later Dean of St. Paul's, and Frederick Temple, later Archbishop of Canterbury, welcomed *The Origin of Species* as a great contribution to knowledge. "The truth can never be the enemy of truth" is a part of the Church's intellectual tradition which is too seldom remembered. On the whole the clergy and their lay supporters came out of the controversy badly.

But if the evolutionists got the best of the purely scientific argument, their handling of the religious issues involved was somewhat rash. All that the Darwinian theory proved, if it was accepted, was that the account of the Creation in the Book of Genesis was not scientifically or historically true. Whether it was true as an allegorical or poetic explanation of the origin of sin was a matter entirely outside the province of geology or biology to determine. Unhappily the attitude the Church had taken up in the controversy made it only too easy for the hotter heads among the evolutionists to point out that, if Christianity stood or fell by the literal truth of Genesis, then Christianity had fallen. Many of them, indeed, explicitly refused to admit that the theory affected the essential truths of Christianity. Many reluctantly abandoned their religious belief and many, many more were torn with doubt and agitated by difficulties. Sir Edmund Gosse's autobiographical novel *Father and Son* tells in a direct and moving way the story of exactly such a case. It was the tragedy of the Early Victorian period that it opened a rift between Religion and Science which we are only closing today.

## 4. *Early Victorian Literature*

The reading public of Early Victorian England was vast and its appetite for all forms of literature was keen. Sermons, histories, scientific treatises and essays all commanded an enormous sale. Poets and novelists amassed fortunes undreamt of in the eighteenth century. The talent of the period was worthy of its opportunities: the best work of the Early Victorians is among the best English Literature has to offer. This is true of all the branches of writing we have mentioned, but especially of the novel.

Charles Dickens (1812–1870) was considered by Tolstoy to be the greatest of all novelists, and praise from such a quarter is praise indeed. The richness and variety of his character drawing show the highest marks of genius. The very faults of his work, the ungainly, improbable plots, the syrupy emotion and the crude melodrama serve to emphasize the force of his imagination: such material would become unreadable in the hands of any writer who was not a master of his craft, and Dickens is always and everywhere intensely readable. The world in which he is most at home is London as it was before the era of Reform. The dusty city offices, the chop-houses, the debtors' prisons, the rat-infested warehouses, the shoddy tenements and the horror of the slums live for ever in his pages. The effect such descriptions had in awakening public opinion to the need for reform is emphasized in Chapter I. His novels give a panorama of working and lower middle-class life of London in the second quarter of the century.

What Dickens does for the lower strata of society, Thackeray (1811–1863) does for the upper. His work is free from Dickens' faults, but where Dickens had genius Thackeray had only talent— though it was talent of a high order. Witty and satirical, he could achieve a delicacy and lightness of touch that few writers have equalled. *Vanity Fair* is one of the masterpieces of English fiction. Both Dickens and Thackeray are at their best when describing London and its inhabitants. For a picture of provincial society the novels of Anthony Trollope (1815–1882) and George Eliot[1] (1819–1880) are much the best. Trollope, like Thackeray whom he much admired, is more at home in the upper ranks of society. In *Barchester Towers* he portrays with humour and affection the life of a cathedral town. Passionately fond of hunting, he fills his books with the landed gentry he knew so well. Not a satirist like Thackeray or a reformer like Dickens he is content to be a realist, to describe society and its members as he saw them and to leave it at that. George Eliot's characters are drawn largely from the new, rising class of merchants and traders who were gradually becoming the chief power in the country. Perhaps the most intelligent of all the nineteenth-century novelists, she displays an insight and a power of analysis that is never clouded with false sentiment.

Both the novelists and the poets of the Victorian period are more individualistic and independent than their eighteenth-century counterparts. Except for Sterne, the great eighteenth-century novelists worked to a fairly well-defined pattern. It would be possible to imagine Fielding writing the first half of a novel and Smollett the second without the reader feeling a violent transition. But the idea of Trollope completing a novel begun by one of the Brontë sisters is unthinkable. The great novels of the period differ so much that it is impossible to generalize about them. It is the same with the poetry. The Romantics had broken the spell which Pope

[1] The *nom-de-plume* of Mary Ann Evans.

had cast over the poets of his century and their successors made good use of their freedom. It would be hard to find two English poets as unlike each other as Tennyson (1809–1892) and Browning (1812–1889). Richness, variety and originality are the supreme merits of Victorian imaginative literature.

It is fitting that this chapter should close with the names of the two great historians of the day, Macaulay and Carlyle. Macaulay (1800–1859) excels in description and narrative. His clear compelling style and his Whig prejudices engage the interest of the reader in the political controversies of the late seventeenth century. His *History of England* from the time of the Restoration, unfortunately cut short at 1702 by his premature death, remains a masterpiece. The famous third chapter on the state of England in 1685 is the first, and best, piece of social history written by a modern author. Carlyle (1795–1881) lacks the solidity and balance of Macaulay. He was fascinated by strong and ruthless characters like Cromwell or Frederick the Great, and enjoys the dubious honour of having been among Hitler's favourite authors. The violence of his nature expresses itself in his savage handling of the English language and in the sneers and abuse he lavishes on historical characters whom he dislikes. Nevertheless his power to re-create the great scenes of history, to evoke the authentic sights and sounds, places him high in the ranks of historians. In Carlyle, who loathed the age he lived in and deplored its standards, the Early Victorian period had the exact counterpoise to Macaulay, who considered it by far the happiest and most moral age of recorded history.

## CHAPTER III

# ENGLISH POLITICS BETWEEN THE REFORM BILLS, 1832–1867

## 1. *The Significance of the Period*

THE importance of the Reform Bill of 1832 is sufficiently obvious. Its passage made possible the series of political and administrative reforms that laid the foundations of modern Britain. On the other hand, these benefits did not flow automatically from the extension of the franchise. The passing of the Reform Bill did not mean the sudden triumph of the middle class over the aristocracy. For many years yet political and social life was to be dominated by the landed gentry. During the sixties, for example, almost half the enclosed land of England and Wales, some fifteen out of thirty-three millions of acres, was owned by about 2,250 landlords, and in the Palmerston ministry of 1859 only three cabinet ministers were without titles. By 1867 the industrial middle class were beginning to gain the ascendancy over the landed aristocracy, but the process was gradual, and delayed by the conservatism characteristic of the nation. A politician of the old type such as Viscount Palmerston (1784–1865), was much more popular than was a reformer such as John Bright (1811–1889). The Reform Bill did not, therefore, as many had feared, open the floodgate to radical legislation. By 1835 the Whig zeal for reform had petered out and the party drifted from office, under the genial but lax premiership of Viscount Melbourne (1779–1848). Thus the Tories, under Sir Robert Peel (1788–1850), the greatest political figure of the period, found themselves once more on the crest of the wave.

The period was not one of strong administrations. Minority governments held office from 1846 to 1852, 1858 to 1859, 1866 to 1868, and a coalition from 1852 to 1855. Indeed, the progress made from 1832 to 1846 in the extension of political machinery, in the formation of party organizations, the growth of local associations, and the establishment of political clubs in London (such as the

31

Carlton, founded in 1831 by the Tories, and the Reform, founded in 1835 by the Whigs) bore little fruit in the latter half of the period. The reason was a split in the Conservative Party over the repeal of the Corn Laws. The result was a division into Protectionists and "Peelites", who, after the death of their leader in 1850, served to "make Conservatism a little less Tory and Liberalism a little less Whig". The fears aroused by the Reform Bill proved to be unfounded. The Radicals did not gain strength in Parliament, indeed their numbers steadily declined after the election of the first reformed Parliament. The party leaders were still distinguished by their ancestry or by the length of their parliamentary careers. Of the Whigs, Palmerston had entered Parliament in 1807, and seemed a jaunty survivor of Georgian England, adding colour to the Victorian scene, and Lord John Russell, son of the Duke of Bedford, had been elected for the family borough of Tavistock in 1813. Of the Tories, Peel had entered Parliament in 1809, Gladstone in 1832, returned for the Duke of Newcastle's pocket borough of Newark, which had escaped reform, and the leader of the party was the Earl of Derby (1799–1869). Only the manufacturers John Bright and Richard Cobden (1804–1865) were true radicals, owing nothing to the aristocracy and the older Universities. No working man entered the House of Commons till after the passage of the Second Reform Bill (1867). The period does not mark a violent break with the past. Nevertheless, much was accomplished. The economic difficulties of the thirties and forties were overcome, some of the worst effects of the Industrial Revolution were mitigated, and the machinery of government and administration was reformed to meet the changed conditions of Victorian England.

### 2. The Whigs, 1832–1841

The Parliament of 1833 contained a large Whig majority. Party divisions were not yet clear enough for precise figures to be given, but it was estimated that the new Parliament contained 487 reformers (i.e. Whigs, Radicals and Irish members) and 171 Tories. Still the extension of the franchise did not bring an entirely new type of member to the House of Commons. More than half the borough members had held seats in the unreformed Parliament, many who had previously sat for pocket boroughs found their way back into the House through country seats, and 151 members were closely related to members of the House of Lords. Influence and corruption still existed, though on a smaller scale. It was not until 1872 that the secret ballot was instituted, as it was argued that no Englishman should be so cowardly as to refuse to declare his vote openly from the hustings, and votes were bought and sold as before. Landlords still possessed great influence, both in county and borough constituencies; in Westmorland, for example, the traditional Lowther representation continued until 1865, whilst in new factory towns such as Macclesfield and Todmorden, the Brocklehurst and Fielden families established new political dynasties. For a great part of the period it is preferable to speak of Whig and Tory, rather than of Liberal and Conservative.

The noblest act of the reformed House of Commons was the abolition of slavery. The anti-slavery movement, led by William Wilberforce (1759–1833) and Zachary Macaulay (1768–1838), met with a great triumph in 1807. In that year British subjects were forbidden to take part in the slave trade. Not until 1833 was the emancipation of existing slaves achieved. The Act of 1833 provided slave-owners with £20,000,000 compensation, and arranged for the slaves to be set free after a period of apprenticeship. In Althorp's Factory Act (1833) an attempt was made to regulate the employment of children, and to improve the conditions under which they worked. The report of the official inquiry into these conditions stated that "the effects of factory labour on children are immediate and remote: the immediate effects are fatigue, sleepiness and pain; the remote effects, such at least as are usually conceived to result from it, are, deterioration of the physical constitution, deformity, disease, and deficient mental instruction and moral culture". The new legislation, for which the only precedent had been the ineffective Factory Acts of 1802 and 1819, not only extended beyond the cotton industry of Lancashire to all textile factories, except in the silk and lace industries, but set up a body of inspectors to enforce its provisions. In future children under the age of nine were not to be employed at all, under the age of thirteen their hours of work were restricted to eight a day, and from thirteen to eighteen the limit was sixty-nine hours a week. Though the Act of 1833 marked a new departure, it was utterly insufficient: the inspectors numbered only four, yet were expected to cover the British Isles, and in one of the more important of their tasks, that of ensuring that the children received some education, they were handicapped by not having the power to raise a parish rate to pay for schools.

The second measure was the Poor Law Amendment Act (1834).[1] The old method of poor relief, which had remained substantially unaltered from Elizabethan times, was clearly inadequate for the needs of an industrial society. Furthermore, the institution of the Speenhamland system in 1795, which had seemed for a time to soften the hardships of the poor, had proved both costly and inefficient. Based on the principle of subsidizing wages from the local poor rates, it had proved expensive and liable to abuse. In one Buckinghamshire parish, for example, the parish poor rate had risen from £11 in 1801 to £367 in 1832, and many unscrupulous employers deliberately paid low wages, knowing that the poor rate would provide a subsidy. The old workhouses, too, were drastically reformed and centralized under a body of Poor Law Commissioners sitting in London.

The third reform was the Municipal Corporations Act (1835).[2] Many cities which had grown prodigiously in the past century, such as Manchester, Sheffield and Birmingham, lacked even the antiquated machinery of local government of the old boroughs. Other towns, such as Leeds, Liverpool and Leicester, were governed by a close oligarchy. The aim of the Act was to provide elective councils for such towns, in which ratepayers of three years' standing would have the vote.

It was such administrative reforms that the country most urgently required. Although the worst principles in the eighteenth-century system of government had been repudiated by 1832, the new instruments of government which could deal with the problems of an industrial society had yet to be created. The men who did most to tackle these questions were not so much politicians as political

---

[1] See also page 6.                    [2] See also page 7.

*Utilitarian?*

thinkers who had no desire for power or fame. Edwin Chadwick (1800–1890), the secretary to the Poor Law Commission of 1834, was one of the first to see what the Royal Commission, with its powers of investigation and report, could do for reform. It was also the method employed by such men as Southwood Smith (1788–1861), Charles James Blomfield, Bishop of London (1786–1857), Leonard Horner (1785–1864) and Sir James Kay-Shuttleworth (1804–1877). These names are little known, compared with those of the politicians, yet it might well be argued that their contribution to the shaping of modern Britain was considerably greater. Nevertheless they were good Benthamites[1] and would have recoiled in horror from the idea of the Welfare State. The paradox is that their work greatly extended the limits of State interference. To secure "the greatest happiness of the greatest number" they conceived it necessary to sweep away much of the outdated legislation that still encumbered the Statute book. Thus, the Poor Law Amendment Act was not intended to improve the scale of relief to paupers; rather it was designed to force them out of unproductive employment into work which would increase the national wealth. Before long, events made it clear that administrative reform and *laissez-faire* were incompatible, but the Benthamites were slow to recognize this.

By the end of the thirties the Whig cause was sinking fast. There were no leaders left. Earl Grey (1764–1845) retired from politics, Sir James Graham (1792–1861) and Edward Stanley (1799–1869) left the party,[2] while Melbourne had no further policies to put into effect. The constitutional history of the period is largely concerned with the right of the sovereign to select his or her own ministers. This question first arose in 1834 when Melbourne resigned upon William IV's refusal to accept Lord John Russell as leader of the Commons, and again in 1839 when Peel agreed to form a ministry only if he was given the right, as a sign of confidence, to nominate the ladies of the royal household. Both cases raised interesting constitutional issues, but can scarcely be considered of major impor-

---

[1] See pages 21 ff.

[2] Stanley left the Whigs in 1834 and joined the Conservative Party. In 1846, after the split on protection, he became leader of the official Conservative Party. He became Earl of Derby in 1851.

tance. The direct political power of the Crown had been reduced. Victoria, it is true, was able to object successfully to some ministerial appointments, as when in 1851 she exacted a promise that Palmerston would not be appointed Foreign Secretary, and in 1861 the Prince Consort prevented a serious quarrel with the United States by toning down a provocative despatch. But the Queen and the Prince Consort, for all their industry, were advisers rather than instigators of political action. The part played by the Prince Consort in bringing about the Great Exhibition of 1851 exemplified the new, less partisan role of the monarchy.

The decline of the Whigs assisted the recovery of the Tories. The 170 members of 1833 steadily grew, to 250 in 1834, to 300 in 1837, and following the defeat of the Whig ministry in 1841 over the duty on colonial sugar proposed in the budget of that year, the general election brought the Tories once again to power. They were deeply divided within their own ranks, as the events of the next five years were to prove, but their policy of efficiency and economy appeared more attractive than bankrupt Whiggery. However, during the later thirties it was clear that the most significant political activity was taking place outside Parliament, and it is to this activity that we must now turn.

### 3. Industrial Discontent

Chartism was the first political movement to attract the support of working men. Its programme, embodied in the People's Charter, contained six main points: universal manhood suffrage, equal electoral districts, payment of Members, abolition of the property qualification for Members of Parliament, a secret ballot, and annual parliaments. All these, except the last, were subsequently achieved.[1] But Chartism cannot be viewed as an isolated movement, and its origins were not political. Its disappearance after 1848 can only be explained satisfactorily if it is understood that the Chartist question was essentially a question of the condition of the nation—a "knife

[1] There is, however, still some disparity in electoral districts. The following instances are taken from the 1951 election: Stoke Newington, 80,000; Leyton, 79,000; Woodford, 78,000; Gateshead, 39,000; Montgomeryshire, 32,000; Caithness, 27,000.

and fork question" as one of their orators proclaimed. To con-
centrate on the points of the Charter is to give the movement
a unity and political emphasis that it did not possess, for Chartism
was the protest, heartfelt but incoherent, of an industrial population
against low wages, frequent unemployment, intolerable working
conditions, and foul, insanitary dwellings in dreary cities.

Chartism was not the only form these protests took. The years
immediately following the passing of the First Reform Bill saw the
rise and collapse of several ambitious trade union movements, the
most important of which was Robert Owen's (1771–1858) Grand
National Consolidated Trade Union, which attracted much support
in 1834, but collapsed on account of its unwieldy organization, its
lack of financial resources, and its unsuccessful excursions into
co-operative enterprise.[1] More important were the agitations that
accompanied the passing of the Factory Act of 1833, and the fierce
opposition to the enforcement of the new Poor Law. In the first
case, Short Time Committees sprang up throughout the North,
urging the restriction of the hours of work for all under eighteen
to ten hours per day. This demand was not made entirely out of
consideration for the young: its true purpose was to bring about
a general reduction of the hours of labour, by limiting the hours of
work of almost half the factory population. The attempts to put the
Poor Law into effect encountered the most determined resistance.
In the south of England the misery of the agricultural population
was such that the new system of Guardians and Workhouses was
soon installed, but in the north the attempts, made from 1836, to
bring about the change were violently opposed. The resistance was
particularly strong in those areas where modern factory practices
had not been wholly adopted, especially in Yorkshire where hand-
loom weavers still worked in their own homes, and could make
up their pitiful wages by obtaining outdoor relief on the Speenhamland system. They resisted the threat of the hated bastilles[2] with
the strength of despair.

Radicalism is a highly difficult term to define in this period. There
were at least two main varieties. First, the Benthamites who had
enthusiastically supported the New Poor Law; second, the Tory

[1] See Glossary.        [2] The popular nickname for the new workhouses.

37

Radicals who had equally enthusiastically opposed it. In William Cobbett (1762–1835), perhaps the best known opponent of the Poor Law, Radicalism and Toryism were inextricably mixed and neither was of the accepted brand. His ideal was an England of yeoman farmers: he was equally at odds with the Radicals, who were essentially urban, and with the Tories, who represented the interests of the landed gentry. Richard Oastler (1789–1861), Michael Sadler (1780–1835), J. R. Stephens (1805–1879) were all Tories of this type. Oastler's slogan was "The Throne, the Altar and the Cottage", and he poured scorn on those Radicals who had championed the cause of the slaves in the West Indies in 1833 but who cared nothing for the lot, in many ways much worse, of their countrymen in the factories of Yorkshire. Stephens, a former Wesleyan minister, was perhaps the most incendiary speaker against the poor law. Appeals to violence were frequent in his speeches, which contained sentiments such as the hope that "Newcastle should be one blaze of fire, with only one way to put it out, and that with the blood of all who supported this abominable measure". Tory Radicalism had no connection with the growing strength of the parliamentary Tory party. Peel had been born into, and was fully prepared to accept, the new industrial age. Tory Radicalism was a movement of revolt against unbearable social conditions and had no positive political programme. When the Duke of Wellington asked Oastler for a definition of Toryism, the answer he received was, "My Lord Duke, I mean 'a place for everything, and everything in its place'". But in this simple scheme of things there was no place for the factory. The same might be said of Disraeli's programme for "Young England".[1] Disraeli was perhaps the only political figure of prominence to take account of industrial distress and to recognize Chartist disturbance as signs of profound social unrest. However, his remedies, as set forth in his political novels, *Coningsby* (1843) and *Sybil* (1844), hardly appear adequate: gibes at recently ennobled Whigs and despotic factory owners are accom-

[1] The Young England movement was a group of young Tories in the forties who resisted all liberal measures and maintained that the aristocracy should be the friend and protector of the poor. The most persuasive exponent of this romantic idea was Disraeli, who appears to have believed that such a happy relationship between Dives and Lazarus existed in feudal England.

panied by appeals to a vague feudal tradition which would restore the natural alliance between the aristocracy and the people. Disraeli and his friends George Smythe (1818-1857) and Lord John Manners (1818-1906) attracted considerable attention by their parliamentary attacks on Peel for failing to adopt their "policy". Although "Young England" was never a practical movement, *Coningsby* and *Sybil* are still worth reading for their wit and their descriptions of factory life. Nevertheless Disraeli was a new and disconcerting figure among the Tories.

It was from the fury and despair enlisted in movements such as the Factory and the Poor Law agitations that the Chartist movement drew its support. Chartism originated in the severe depression of 1837. The rise and decline of the movement corresponded so closely to the periods of depression and recovery that it is clear that its main impulse was economic rather than political. But the political history of the movement is not to be disregarded, for it reveals the fundamental weakness of Chartism, its lack of unity.

The Chartist movement had three centres, London, Birmingham and Leeds, and the characters of the leaders in each city show the varied aims of the agitation. In 1836 the London Workingmen's Association was founded, a body designed to work for political reform primarily by means of education and peaceful agitation. Its leader, William Lovett (1800-1877), represented the "moral force" group of Chartists. Though imprisoned for his activities, he refused to consider the use of "physical force", the advocates of which established in 1837 the London Democratic Association. The division in the movement over this question of methods was never closed. In Birmingham, the question of currency reform marked the local movement. The Birmingham Political Union, which had been prominent in the agitation for the Reform Bill, was revived, and was at first controlled by a predominantly middle-class group headed by a local banker, Thomas Atwood (1783-1855). Atwood, however, was primarily interested in currency reform, and as the movement grew steadily more radical, he soon lost control. But in Birmingham as in London the essential disunion of Chartism can be observed. The most notorious Chartist was, however, Feargus O'Connor (1794-1855), whose newspaper, the *Northern Star*, published in Leeds, exerted great influence, which was supplemented by his own considerable powers of oratory and display. O'Connor was a true demagogue: contemptuous of the pacific Chartism of men such as Lovett, he was unwilling to commit himself to "physical force" and was determined to gain sole command of the movement for selfish ends. If his personality at first aided the movement, it later helped to shatter its unity. But he did bring colour and life to Chartism, as when he entered Huddersfield,

"preceded by 15 banners and mottoes, then Operatives sixteen abreast

*THE CARRIAGE*

drawn by four greys; postillions, scarlet jackets, black velvet caps and silver tassels; containing the People's Champion
FEARGUS O'CONNOR ESQUIRE."

For a time, many thought that England was trembling on the brink of revolution. The mass meetings by torchlight on northern moors, the rejection by Parliament in July 1839 of the petition for the enactment of the People's Charter, the Bull Ring riots in Birmingham in the same month, a small rising in Newport in November, all seemed to herald revolution. That it did not come about can be traced to several causes. The movement's lack of unity, the failure of the People's Convention, as the central organizing body was called, to agree on a course of action, the prompt steps taken by the government to restore order—the new London constabulary were sent to quell the Birmingham riots—the appointment of Sir Charles Napier (1782–1853), an unconventional soldier, to the Northern command, and the gradual recovery of the country from the economic depression, all played their part. The most dangerous year was undoubtedly 1839. Although Chartism continued to be formidable until 1848 the threat of mass uprisings had passed, and the movement was diverted by O'Connor's attempts to buy up landed estates on which industrial workers might settle. In 1848 the last attempt to revive the Charter proved a miserable failure: for England it was not to be a year of revolution. It is impossible, however, not to admire the moderation and restraint of men such as Lovett who, though they had every reason to bear a grudge against society, consistently rejected the appeal to violence.

## 4. Peel and the Disruption of the Conservative Party, 1841–1846

Peel's triumph at the general election of 1841 was not a sudden reversal of political fortunes. The Whigs had long been waning and the Conservatives had been steadily gaining ground. Too much credit has perhaps been given to Peel for the notable improvement in the machinery of the Tory party: much was due to the labours of the Conservative "political secretary", F. R. Bonham (1785–1863), who organized local branches, selected prospective candidates, and bore most of the burden of administrative detail. But the Conservative victory was not without its problems. Peel belonged to the group of liberal Tories that had, under Huskisson (1770–1830), succeeded in bringing about administrative reforms in the liberal phase of Lord Liverpool's ministry (1822–1827). As Home Secretary he had been responsible for establishing the Metropolitan police—the "peelers" as they were promptly dubbed and "bobbies" as they are still called—and now he set about revising the customs duties, a task which Huskisson had begun but not completed. Many duties yielded less than they cost to collect, and a committee of inquiry set up in 1840 discovered that seventeen articles provided $94\frac{1}{2}$ per cent of the total revenue. The other $5\frac{1}{2}$ per cent was realized from duties on 1,100 separate articles. The result was a tendency towards simplification. Gladstone's budgets in the early sixties virtually abolished all customs duties.

But though administrative reform and the move towards free trade occupied Peel's attention, the same subjects did not fire the enthusiasm of the parliamentary rank and file of the Tory party. Country gentlemen were not interested in such affairs: jealous of the growth of industry, of Parliamentary encroachments on the conduct of local affairs, anxious to maintain the Corn Laws, they accepted Peel as their leader only because there was no other feasible candidate for the position. Peel, for his part, did little to placate them. A cold, reserved man, his conversion to new policies was slow, resolute and solitary. Consequently when in 1846 the complete failure of the potato harvest in Ireland made him determine upon the repeal of the corn laws, the party was already deeply divided. The decision to reduce the protective duties on corn imports to a token sum seemed to many to deal the death-blow to British agriculture, and the protectionist Tories at last had an issue on which to rebel against a leader more feared than loved.

If a point is to be selected from which one can date the ascendancy of industry over agriculture in Britain, 1846 might well be chosen. For seven years past the radical orators Cobden and Bright had organized opposition to protection by means of the Anti-Corn Law League. The League was the first great effort of the industrialists to overthrow the power of the landed aristocracy. Certainly the activities of the League, beginning in 1839, made politics more lively. As one of its members confessed, "speakers at these meetings very often found that *Corn* was a dry subject to talk about, and one that did not easily admit of a popular style of address to an audience". The repealers did not let this cramp their style. Led by John Bright, a Rochdale millowner, and Richard Cobden, a Manchester merchant, they found themselves bidding for popular support against the Chartists, who regarded their activities as diverting attention from the plight of the working man merely to obtain the free entry of cheap foreign corn as a means to lower wages. The one attempt made to combine the two movements, that of Joseph Sturge's Complete Suffrage Union (1842), was unsuccessful. Chartists were unable to accept middle-class leadership, repealers baulked at accepting the People's Charter. But the violence of the attacks launched against landlords and farmers by members of the League shows that the Victorian middle-class Radical was often more extreme than the working man. An opponent of the League has recorded some of the epithets they applied to landlords. They were described variously as "a bread-taxing oligarchy, a handful of swindlers; despicable, base, sordid, detestable, ruthless, unprincipled, beggarly, cruel, brutal, relentless, tyrannous, reckless, merciless, insatiable, voluptuous, unfeeling, haughty, bold, insolent, flesh-mongering, proud, impudent, scoundrel, law-making landlords; parliamentary crew, pocket-picking fraternity, monsters, wretches, demons, knaves, thieves, bread-stealers, heartless band, rapacious harpies, labour plunderers, monsters of impiety, foot-pad aristocracy, power-proud plunderers, putrid and sensual banditti, titled felons, rich robbers, blood-sucking vampires, plunderers of the people". It has been said that the agitation, starting as a business backed by Manchester manufacturers, ended as a crusade supported by those who had come to believe in Repeal as a cure for all economic evils. Probably the movement helped to hasten the decline of Chartism, but it is doubtful if the agitation influenced Peel. At first he would have little to do with the movement: a deputation which he received in 1842, although granted an interview lasting two hours, was not invited to sit down. A speech in the Commons by Cobden in November 1844 is said to have converted Peel, and certainly he was more likely to be won over by intellectual persuasion than by popular agitation. There is, in fact, no evidence that any considerable influence was exerted on Parliament by the League's activities. When, in June 1846, the final vote was taken, Peel's supporters were composed of Whigs, Irish members and his personal following. The country gentlemen stood firmly by the corn laws which were the basis of their ascendancy.

The country members had lacked a spokesman, but during the struggle against Repeal a leader had emerged. Lord George Bentinck (1802–1848), previously known principally for his racing interests, had made a series of savage attacks on Peel's forsaking of Protection. A country gentleman with an astonishing memory for statistics —said to have been developed by his calculations of betting odds— he was really a puppet whose strings were manipulated by Disraeli. The Young England movement had failed to win office for Disraeli, who was now bent on supplanting Peel. The bitterness of the future Tory leader's attacks on his chief lessen the attraction of his character. The split in the party brought the ministry down, the immediate cause being its defeat on an Irish Coercion Bill. As so often in the political history of the century an Irish question turned out a government. After the split the "Peelite" minority commanded most of the political talent of the party. The Whigs, on the other hand, were led by Palmerston and Russell, the one uninterested in domestic affairs, the other contented with minor measures of reform. After the excitement of the period from 1832, the years to 1860 were comparatively uneventful.

## 5. Mid-Victorian Politics

If the middle classes could rejoice at their victory over the landed interests in 1846, the passage of Fielden's Factory Bill in the following year did something to sooth the resentment of the Tories. The restriction of hours of labour to ten a day, or fifty-eight a week, was at last achieved, despite the opposition of radicals such as John Bright. He declared in 1855 when opposing a bill for the fencing of machinery in factories, "we are unpopular, we are envied, we are supposed to be rich, we are radicals, and Whigs and Tories combine to gain popularity by calumniating and robbing us". Rigid divisions cannot be drawn between the landed and industrial interests, for there were great landlords who voted for the repeal of the corn laws, and manufacturers who supported the factory bills. Nevertheless the landowners did not fear, as the manufacturers did, legislation which intervened between employer and worker, and in turn the manufacturer was prepared to support policies which were resisted by the landed classes. From the interplay of landlord and factory owner, of Benthamism and Toryism, Late Victorian England gradually emerged.

A narrative of the political events of the fifties would be tedious and of little value. It was a period of minority or coalition governments,[1] with a third party, the "Peelites", causing confusion amongst the Whigs and Tories. The Tories had been deprived of their most able leaders, and the party of the period was described as consisting of "the Gentlemen of England, with a Player thrown in", the professional being, of course, Disraeli. The nominal leader of the Tory party, the Earl of Derby, appeared to be more interested in his efforts to win the race to which an ancestor had given his name, and

---

[1] A Whig ministry under Russell held office from December 1846 to February 1852, a Conservative ministry under Derby from February to December 1852, a coalition under Aberdeen from December 1852 to February 1855, a Whig ministry under Palmerston from February 1855 to February 1858, a second Conservative ministry under Derby from February 1858 to June 1859, and a Whig ministry under Palmerston from June 1859 to the death of its leader in 1865.

in translating Homer into English verse, than in the prospects of regaining office. The radicals were discredited by the opposition of Cobden and Bright to the Crimean war and could exert little pressure upon the Whigs, whose leader, Palmerston, grew less interested in domestic reform as he grew older. In these circumstances, the choice of the Peelites was difficult. Loyalty to their late chief (he had died in 1850) prevented their return to the Tories: an ingrained dislike of Whiggery, strengthened by the feeling that it had no future, made them hesitate to join their old enemies. Lord Aberdeen (1784–1860) illustrated their dilemma when he wrote "A government of progress is indispensable; none can be too liberal for me provided it does not abandon its conservative character", whilst Gladstone was reported to be leaning to the Liberal side of the Conservative party rather than to the Conservative side of the Liberal party. One thing was sure: an outstanding political talent such as that of William Gladstone could not remain indefinitely in the wilderness. Entering Parliament in 1832 as a Tory, his service under Peel had shown that he was an administrator of genius. In the fifties his conscience shrank from accepting either Palmerston or Disraeli as a colleague, but in 1859 he entered Palmerston's ministry, and served as Chancellor of the Exchequer until 1866. He changed his party because he found himself in sympathy with the government's policy of encouraging Italian nationalism. During this period his skilful handling of the financial affairs of the nation, revealed particularly in his free trade measures, did much to revive economic prosperity.

Simultaneously the condition of the working class improved considerably. Wages increased, and prices fell, so that the purchasing power of the nation grew. Progress was made in the field of public health, and the new industrial towns were improved by the establishment of public parks, libraries and museums. Queen Victoria, when she opened a public park at Salford in 1851 was the first reigning monarch to visit Lancashire for two centuries. A sign that economic conditions had improved was a steady growth of interest in recreations such as football and cricket, whilst political agitations were replaced by less spectacular but more rewarding pursuits: for example, education in the many new Mechanics' Institutes, and membership of the co-operative movement, originated in Rochdale in 1844. By the sixties the "respectable working man" was not an exceptional figure, and was very different from the half-savage inhabitants of the northern towns of a previous generation. Much remained to be done, but that things were better was evident from the arming of the Volunteers during the French invasion scares of the early sixties. Twenty years before, no government would have allowed weapons to pass into the hands of working men.

## 6. The Second Reform Bill, 1867

"Parties are just now in a curious transitional state. The old divisions have disappeared and the new camps have not yet been formed", commented the *Westminster Review* in 1864. In fact, the political struggle had almost ceased. Between 1860 and 1865 the Conservatives were unwilling to enter office, and made no attempt to turn out Palmerston's government. The radical element in the Liberal party was kept in hand by Palmerston, and it was not until after his leader's death that Gladstone could proclaim himself "unmuzzled". The general elections of 1857 and 1865 had been hardly more than plebiscites for or against Palmerston, and there was little economic distress except in the Lancashire cotton industry, where the American Civil War (1861–1865) brought about a cessation of cotton supplies from the Southern States. Why then did the Second Reform Bill come about in 1867? It would seem that both parties were determined to gain the advantage of passing a bill that they felt sure must come about in any case. Disraeli was determined that the Conservatives were not to be branded as a party that always resisted reform. He was not willing, he declared, to allow the party "to be shut up in a cage formed by Whigs and Radicals, confined within a certain magic circle which they were not to step out of at the peril of their lives." The cause of reform was strengthened by Gladstone's conversion to the idea of extending the franchise in 1864, partly as a result of his admiration of the behaviour of the cotton workers in Lancashire. They had steadfastly refused to support the breaking of the Northern blockade of the Southern cotton areas because they believed that the North was for democracy, and the South for a slave-owning aristocracy.

Palmerston's death in 1865 broke up the political log-jam. Proposals of franchise reform had been made intermittently since 1852, but in every case the schemes had been too elaborate to be practicable. "Fancy franchises"—qualifications such as the possession of a savings bank account, a university degree or teaching certificate, had been proposed and rejected. But reform was clearly necessary. In 1865 Dod's *Parliamentary Companion* still noted 51 small boroughs in which family influences were exerted. A redistribution of seats was needed to meet the shift of population to the cities. Knaresborough with 271 voters and Thetford with 223 still returned two members each. It was estimated that the number of voters electing 36 members in large boroughs was sufficient to elect 328 members in small constituencies. These figures would today seem to establish an unanswerable case for the redistribution of seats. But it must be remembered that in this period many considered that the right to representation was based, not on numbers, but on property. "Democracy", or the rule of numbers, was not an ideal, but a fate to be avoided if possible, and Disraeli prefaced his bill with the comment that if he had thought it would tend towards the introduction of democracy, he could not have conscientiously supported it.

The popular agitation that accompanied the bill cannot be compared in extent or violence with that which marked the 1832 measure. Large, orderly meetings were marred only by one small scuffle in Hyde Park, in which the crowd tore up the railings. Though Robert Lowe (1811–1892) and a group of Whigs, nicknamed the "Adullamites",[1] refused to support Gladstone's bill, there was no opposition comparable to that of 1832. Rather, the mood was one of fatalism and a determination to reap what party advantage could be gained from sponsoring a measure that few Whigs or Tories wholeheartedly supported. Neither party could claim full credit for the reform. In 1866 the Adullamites' defection defeated Gladstone's measure, and it was Disraeli's bill that was passed in March 1867. The provisions of the bill virtually provided household suffrage in the boroughs, but did not make such extensive changes in the county constituencies. As a consequence, the electorate in the boroughs

[1] The reference is to David's withdrawal to the cave of Adullam. See I Samuel xxii.

increased from 500,000 to well over a million, whilst in the counties the numbers rose only from 540,000 to 790,000. Moreover, only the most glaring cases of unequal distribution of seats were dealt with, and of 52 seats redistributed only 19 went to the boroughs. Until a complete reform of distribution was attempted, property could still resist the onslaught of numbers.

The politicians who could compare the England of 1867 with her condition in 1832 had a great deal to be proud of. True, the changes were due to the political initiative of individuals, rather than of parties; true, much had been neglected, or left unfinished. Educational reform had foundered on denominational differences, Ireland had received no redress for her basic grievance, the land question. Trade Unions still had no legal standing, the secret ballot had been refused, civil service reform was incomplete. But the accomplishments were great: the country had been covered by a network of railways, the first steps towards industrial reform had been taken, a great part of the population had been relieved from total misery, cities were becoming more than just squalid dormitories for the workers in mills and factories. Between 1850 and 1865 imports almost doubled in value, exports almost trebled, yet a balance was preserved between agriculture and industry. There was room in the land for both aristocrat and manufacturer, there was no great working-class discontent, there was no danger from foreign powers. "Of all decades in our history", G. M. Young declares, "a wise man would choose the eighteen-fifties to be young in". Such a young man would have grown to maturity in the great age of Victorian England.

## CHAPTER IV

# INDUSTRIAL AND AGRICULTURAL CHANGES IN THE NINETEENTH AND TWENTIETH CENTURIES

## 1. *The Development of Communications*

THE Industrial and Agricultural Revolutions may be divided into two main phases which coincide with developments in transport. The years 1700–1840 witnessed the development of the coal and iron industries, the beginning of the factory system, a large number of inventions in the textile industry, the gradual application of steam power to machinery, and the growth of engineering and machine tooling. Industries were still essentially local, they required comparatively small capital, and owing to the fact that Trade Unions had been illegal from 1799 until 1824, labour was still unorganized. Canals and the improved roads were the only means of transport for all but the last decade of this period.[1]

The second phase of the Industrial Revolution not only speeded up the earlier processes, but also itself created new industries and new problems. The construction of railways and the building of steamships effected this transformation. During the nineteenth century Industrialization spread to Germany, Russia, Japan and the United States of America. The vast scale of business and industry after the coming of railways demanded so much capital that it forced the individual employer to give way to the limited liability company, which in its turn tended to develop into trusts and cartels,[2] often international in scope.[3] As the power and extent of capital increased so did that of Trade Unions. As early as 1848 Marx was exhorting the "workers of the world" to "unite". During the Railway Age, old trades were revolutionized by the introduction of machinery (e.g. furniture, clothing and printing), and altogether new trades were developed, for example those concerned with electricity, rubber and oil.

[1] This phase of the Industrial and Agricultural Revolutions is fully discussed in Volume I, Chapter XIV.
[2] For definition of these two terms see Glossary.
[3] This process is discussed more fully on pages 193–4.

Population of more than 100 to the square mile
Towns with more than 10,000 inhabitants
Rivers shown are navigable
Newcastle
Leeds
Hull
WOOLLENS
Liverpool
Manchester
COTTON
Sheffield
CUTLERY
Chester
SALT
POTTERY
Nottingham
STOCKINGS
HARDWARE
WOOLLENS
Norwich
Birmingham
CATTLE
SHEEP
IRON
London
Bristol
WOOLLENS
SHEEP
FRUIT
IRON
CATTLE
TIN
0
50
100
Miles

THE INDUSTRIAL REVOLUTION 1750

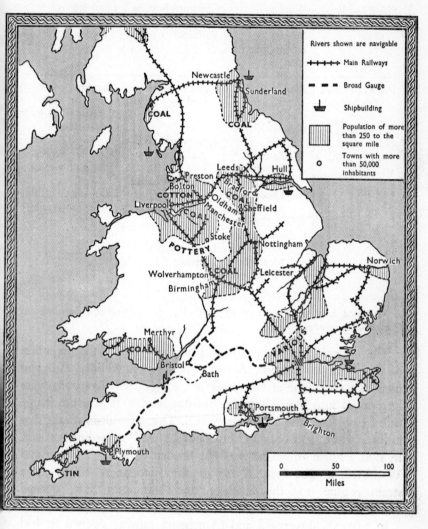

THE INDUSTRIAL REVOLUTION 1850

|  | Trades affected | Organization of capital | Organization of labour |
|---|---|---|---|
| Canal and Road Period, 1700–1840 | Wool<br>Cotton<br>Mining<br>Engineering<br>Iron | One-man business<br>Family firm<br>Partners | Local unions<br>Revolutionary outbreaks |
| Railway Period, 1840 onwards | *Machinery* applied to most trades<br>*Growth of new trades:*<br>Railways<br>Steamships<br>Chemical<br>Electrical<br>Steel, etc.<br>*XXth Century developments:*<br>Aeroplanes<br>Motor-cars<br>Plastics, etc. | Expansion of banking<br><br>Joint stock companies<br><br>Trusts, cartels and amalgamations<br><br><br>International finance | Chartism<br><br>National Unions of one trade<br><br>National Federations of various trades<br>International action and co-operation |

Adapted from a diagram on page 25 of L. C. A. Knowles, *Industrial and Commercial Revolutions.*

The invention of the rail took place long before the invention of the steam locomotive. A truck running on wooden rails was used in a coal mine at Newcastle as early as 1602. Iron rails were introduced into mines in 1767, but not until 1788 was the flange transferred from the rail to the wheel. This, of course, meant that railway trucks and coaches could not be used on ordinary roads. In 1801 a horse drawn railway was opened between Croydon and Wandsworth. The first railway to carry passengers and to use a steam engine was the Stockton and Darlington line, opened in 1825.

In 1830 the Liverpool and Manchester railway opened. It had been built owing to the inadequacy of the canal joining these two towns. In winter the canal froze and in the summer there was often so little water in it that barges could only be half loaded. Moreover, while no alternative means of transport existed capable of carrying heavy loads, the canal company was able to charge exorbitant rates and give exasperatingly bad service. Goods could be sent from Liverpool to New York quicker than from Liverpool to Manchester. Not only was this railway the first directly to challenge canals, but it also proved beyond question the superiority of steam locomotives over horses. The directors of the company offered a £500 prize for the best steam engine submitted to them. As is well known, George Stephenson's "Rocket" won easily. The "Rocket" had a maximum speed of just under thirty miles an hour, but normally averaged about fourteen.

The first long distance line, joining Liverpool, Birmingham, Manchester and London, was opened in 1837. In 1838 the Great Western Railway, founded three years previously, opened their line between London and Bath. The "hungry forties" were the great age of railway building, which helps to account for the prosperous fifties. By 1843, 2,000 miles of railway had been laid; only ten years later there were four times as many.

The cost of building railways in England was higher than almost anywhere else. America built her lines at a quarter of the cost per mile, and Prussia at well under half.[1] The preliminary expense of surveying, obtaining railway acts and legal expenses, has been estimated to have averaged £4,000 per mile. Other countries, of course, had a great advantage in being able to learn from our experience and mistakes, and thus to avoid spending money in unprofitable experiments. A good example of this is the "battle of the gauges". Stephenson's railway lines had a gauge of 4 ft. 8½ ins.; whereas Brunel constructed lines 7 ft. broad. Not until 1892 did the G.W.R. convert all its lines to the narrower gauge. The geography of Britain necessitated steep gradients, tunnels and viaducts, thus the cost of constructing railways in this country was very much greater, distance for distance, than building them across the plains of Russia or Germany. The fact that long hauls work out cheaper per mile than short ones, and that parliament demanded

[1] The United Kingdom built railways at the cost of £64,000 per mile.
England and Wales built railways at the cost of £54,000 per mile.
Prussia built railways at the cost of £21,000 per mile.
The United States built railways at the cost of £13,000 per mile.
The figures given here, and in all following tables, are approximate.

safety precautions unheard of elsewhere, also contributed to the greater cost of English railways.

From the outset, railways met with energetic resistance, and, indeed, much of the expense of building them was incurred in overcoming opposition. The vested interests of other forms of transport were directly and obviously threatened. Shares in the Birmingham Canal Company were over twenty times as valuable in 1825 as in 1770, and those who were fortunate enough to own them were unlikely to look upon railways with favour. Ultimately many canals were bought up by railway companies which were frightened of competition, although they offered a faster and more versatile service. Turn-pike trusts and coaching companies were equally hostile. At the time of Queen Victoria's accession there were three thousand coaches on the road, employing ten times as many men. Moreover, the majority of inns and hotels in the country depended upon coaches for custom. Towns like Northampton and Oxford fought the railways and forced them to keep their distance. The Queen herself persuaded the G.W.R. to build an expensive and circuitous line between Windsor and Slough, in order not to spoil the view from the Castle. Probably the opposition of land-owners was the most formidable of all. Their resistance was partly inspired by the genuine fear that their land would be ruined, and partly by the fact that the harder they fought the higher the compensation they were offered. One landowner extracted £120,000 for land worth £5,000; although the Duke of Bedford was honest enough to return £150,000 compensation when he found, contrary to expectation, that his land was not ruined.

The *Quarterly Review* in 1825 described the steam engine as "visionary" and went on to assert: "We should as soon expect people to be fired off from rockets as trust themselves to the mercy of such a machine." An extraordinary assortment of objections were raised. Tunnels were supposed to be dangerous to health, crops, it was predicted, would wither wherever trains passed; horses, foxes, and pheasants would die out, cows would cease to yield milk, and everything would catch fire, including the trains. Others thought that travelling at 20 miles per hour would mean certain death, that canals were cheaper, that private property was being attacked, and even that engines would be too heavy to move. But the pioneers persisted, and proved in practice how ungrounded were most of these fears.

Railways in England were built entirely by private capital and enterprise on no uniform plan; whereas abroad they were financed and often worked by the Government. *Laissez-faire* in this country was far too strongly entrenched to favour parliamentary control, although the unique status of railways made some degree of collectivism inevitable. Once railways were established, the amount of capital they absorbed and the essential public service they performed, put them on an entirely different footing from other undertakings. Arguments for some measure of governmental control over what was unquestionably a national concern were put forward by Gladstone as early as 1844, and he was not the man to advocate state interference lightly. In that year the "Parliamentary train"[1] was forced on the railway companies, and later several acts were passed insisting on safety precautions.

Very soon attempts were made to overcome some of the drawbacks inherent in the piecemeal construction and planning of English railways. Between 1845 and 1847, Hudson, "the railway king", began the amalgamation of small railway companies in the interest of greater economy and efficiency. Although the railway mania he inspired received a serious blow when he was convicted of fraud, a network of lines had been established by 1850, controlled by fewer and much larger companies. The G.W.R., for example, grew out of the gradual merging of 115 smaller lines.[2] Such amalgamations not only increased the need for state control, but stimulated all railway workers except the footplate men to combine their separate unions into the National Union of Railwaymen (1913), so as to keep their organization on the same scale as that of their employers. By 1921 only four main companies were left, which were nationalized in 1948.

The development of railways affected practically every sphere of life. In America they introduced agricultural prosperity, thereby

---

[1] Every line had to run one train a day for third class passengers at a penny a mile.
[2] The development of the G.W.R. provides a good illustration of the way in which competition led to monopoly. See pages 193–4.

indirectly ruining farming in England. They made the growth of huge towns possible, they employed hundreds of thousands of men, and they put members of parliament on a new footing with their constituents. After their invention football teams from opposite ends of the country were able to play against each other, annual holidays by the sea became common and houses were built of cheap and easily transportable brick rather than of local material. Even poetry was affected: Tennyson's line "Let the great world spin for ever down the ringing grooves of change" is clearly inspired by the railway, although the metaphor is inexact. Tennyson, not so acute an observer of mechanical wonders as he was of nature, thought that steam engines ran along grooves in the ground. Everywhere, railways transformed industry and commerce. On the Continent railway building became a feature of national and strategic policy (e.g. the Trans-Siberian and Berlin–Bagdad Railways). Few previous inventions, except perhaps printing and gunpowder, so changed the world.

Vast improvements in communications in the nineteenth century were not confined to railways. The construction of metal ships, driven by steam, revolutionized sea-borne transport. In 1787 Wilkinson built an iron canal barge, thereby proving to sceptics that it was not "against nature" for metal to float. After 1818 iron vessels were built in increasing numbers, although most early steamships were still made of wood. Steel began to replace iron after 1880.

The first successful attempt to construct a steam-driven ship was made in 1802. She was called the *Charlotte Dundas* and was used on the Clyde Canal. By 1838, a steamer had crossed the Atlantic in under sixteen days. The invention of the compound engine (1863), reduced coal consumption by half and enabled the space thus saved to be used for additional freight. The Triple-expansion Engine (1881) greatly increased the speed of steamers. In 1884 the *Umbria* crossed the Atlantic in less than six days. The opening of the Suez Canal struck one more blow at sailing ships, as only steamers were able to use it, thereby saving 4,500 miles on the voyage from London to Bombay.

Britain, partly on account of her abundance of iron and coal, partly because of her ancient maritime traditions, was the pioneer, and by far the greatest builder, of steamships. Nevertheless, even by 1860, she had only 447 steamers, compared with nearly 7,000 sailing ships.[1] The troops dispatched to suppress the Indian Mutiny (1857) were all sent out under sail.

Between 1830 and 1860 American clippers strongly challenged Britain's merchant shipping; but the Civil War (1861–1865) ended the rivalry. After 1865, America was too concerned with reconstruction and railway building to bother much about ships. From 1860 to 1914 Britain's mercantile marine was easily the largest in the world. Just before the beginning of the Great War, Britain carried over fifty per cent of the world's seaborne trade; she had four times as many merchant ships as her nearest rival, Germany, and she possessed just under half of the world's steam tonnage. Between 1914 and 1918 Britain lost nearly 4,000,000 tons of shipping, and her loss of trade, particularly in the Far East, was almost as serious. After the war, Japan and the United States were firmly planted in Britain's world markets, and challenged the supremacy of her merchant navy.

Unlike railways, shipping hardly raised the question of parliamentary control, except for laws concerning the safety of ships (e.g. the Act of 1875 making it illegal to load a ship beyond the "Plimsoll line"). Many of the restrictions imposed by the State on railway companies were simply the conditions on which Parliament was prepared to authorize the compulsory purchase of land. As the sea is free, shipping companies never gave the government the same sort of opportunities. Besides, foreign competition made it impossible for a British firm to monopolize a particular route, and it

[1] *A Table Showing How Sail Gradually Gave Way to Steam*

| Year | Sailing Ships | Steamers |
|------|---------------|----------|
| 1870 | 4,580,000 tons | 901,000 tons |
| 1875 | 4,200,000 tons | 1,900,000 tons |
| 1881 | 3,690,000 tons | 3,005,000 tons |
| 1885 | 3,400,000 tons | 4,000,000 tons |

(See R. C. K. Ensor, *England 1870–1914*, page 108.)

was mainly to avoid the evils of monopoly that the Government had departed from rigid *laissez-faire* in the case of the railways.

Steamers, faster and more reliable than sailing ships, were one of the greatest technical triumphs of Victorian England. William Morris described them as the cathedrals of the industrial age. They share with railways the responsibility for the decline of British agriculture, they made the growth of a widespread Empire feasible, and they enabled the workshop of the world to sell its produce in every corner of the earth.

Towards the end of the nineteenth century and during the early years of the twentieth century, two entirely new forms of transport were invented. In 1886 Daimler, a German, patented his internal combustion engine, and eight years later, Levassor, a Frenchman, constructed a motor-car called the Panhard, recognizable as such even today. Because of its lightness the petrol engine made flight possible. In 1903, the Americans, Wilbur and Orville Wright constructed and flew a primitive form of aeroplane, and in 1909 the Frenchman Blériot crossed the Channel. Motor-cars were at first regarded with the gravest suspicion, or at the best as a harmless eccentricity. Not until 1896 were they permitted to travel without being preceded by a man with a red flag, or to go at over 4 miles per hour. The use of motors and aeroplanes in the Great War developed both design and technique of production, so that they became a common sight in the early twenties. The internal combustion engine, like railways, revolutionized war, producing no less than three new weapons: the aeroplane, the tank and the submarine.

Every form of transport mentioned above did something to hasten the spread of news and ideas. But in 1837 a new type of communication was invented—the electric telegraph. In 1866 both sides of the Atlantic were linked by a cable. Ten years later the telephone made it possible to transmit speech as well as Morse. Exactly twenty years after that, Marconi constructed the first wireless. These wonderful inventions reacted upon news, commerce and transport. The railways soon had a telegraph signalling system, and ships used wireless to send out distress signals or receive instructions while at sea. Also, of course, they influenced military and naval strategy. It is now possible, for example, for a modern warship or bomber to locate and attack an invisible target. Man's attempts to conquer space have progressed far more rapidly during the last century and a half, than in all the thousands of years of his previous history.

## 2. *The Agricultural Revolution*

The building of railways and the speed, reliability and cheapness of steamers, made it possible for foreign competitors to sell their farm produce at prices which eventually ruined English agriculture. Even before English farming was ruined by foreign competition (1870–1890), the nation only produced two-thirds of the food it required. The demands of industry forced people to live in towns so that in 1900 only 23 per cent of the inhabitants of England lived in the country. The incessant flow of workers from the country to the towns and the ever growing population[1] to be fed, made England dependent upon imported food. The increased efficiency of all forms of transport, and new methods of preserving food (e.g. canning, refrigeration, etc.), made it possible to import it from all over the world.

By the middle of the nineteenth century the change from the open field system to modern farming was more or less complete. The small yeoman farmer was either driven off the land, or reduced to a labourer. The Government gave every encouragement to enclosing because large farms had proved the most productive. The yeoman farmer, however socially valuable he might be, was unable to produce cheap and abundant food for the new industrial towns. He could only have been saved by Government help and in an age of *laissez-faire* that was not forthcoming.

In the nineteenth century, science and invention did much to improve agriculture. The Royal Agricultural Society was founded in 1838 to encourage scientific farming. Between 1840 and 1850 great advances were made by English chemists in producing artificial manures. Steam engines were soon harnessed to agricultural

[1] The population increased owing to a rising birth-rate and a falling death-rate, made possible by great progress in medicine. In 1820 the population of Great Britain was just over 20,000,000. Between 1820 and 1870, 1870 and 1900, and 1900 and 1950, it went up by roughly 10,000,000.

machinery; for instance, a steam driven thresher was invented in 1850. All the same, English agriculture in the period 1870–1914 was far less mechanized than agriculture in the United States. Since then the widespread use of tractors in this country has evened the balance and has also done much to remedy the shortage of farm labourers.

The years 1850–1870 were prosperous ones for English farming. Despite the repeal of the corn laws in 1846, foreign competition was insignificant. America fighting a civil war, Germany pursuing her policy of "blood and iron", and Russia recovering from her defeat in the Crimea, were too preoccupied to build up an extensive export trade. Not until after 1870 were communications sufficiently cheap and easy for foreigners to undersell home grown produce; unless, of course, the harvest was a bad one.

The great depression in English farming came between 1870 and 1890. This was largely owing to American competition. By 1870 America had recovered from the Civil War. Her railways were three times as extensive in 1880 as they had been twenty years before.[1] The fertile interior of the United States was opened up at the very moment when sea transport was becoming much quicker and cheaper. Nearly every European country protected its agriculture from the blast of American competition with high tariff walls, but Britain refused to abandon Free Trade. Frozen meat from Australia and corn from Canada completed the ruin of English farming. The seed sown in 1846 was now reaped with a vengeance. It is a revealing commentary on Disraeli's opposition to Peel that, when he became Prime Minister in 1874, he never raised the issue of protection. He realized then, as perhaps he had realized all along, that power in the House of Commons was passing from the land-owners to the manufacturers who wanted cheap foreign food imported, because it kept down their wages bill.

It would be difficult to paint in too dark colours the agricultural depression of the last quarter of the nineteenth century. Alarming numbers of farmers became bankrupt, landlords were often forced to remit up to half their rent, the wages of farm labourers went down at a time when everybody else's wages were going up, and

[1] In 1860 America had approximately 30,000 miles of railway. In 1880 she had 94,000 miles.

land was allowed to go to waste. Even in 1850 the land employed about half the working class and was a very important part of the national life, but after 1870 a great exodus took place into the towns and to Australia, South Africa and Canada. Between 1870 and 1880 nearly a million people emigrated from Britain, and between 1870 and 1900, over 350,000 labourers left the land. Farming had lost its social supremacy, and Britain had staked her future on remaining the workshop of the world.

In the present century farming began to recover. Despite its cost, there was a demand for quality home-bred meat. Dairy and fruit farming were not so vulnerable to foreign competition, nor was market gardening. English farmers consequently abandoned the idea of growing much wheat, and turned to a more specialized form of agriculture. Parliament, having already swallowed collectivism in other spheres, was prepared to give some help to farmers. In 1889 the Board of Agriculture was established, and in 1908 a Small Holdings Act was passed attempting to prevent workers drifting from the land. The Great War revived farming, particularly as submarine warfare in 1917 reduced our food reserves to a fortnight's supply. During the 1939–1945 war our food imports were halved as the result of the "Dig for Victory" campaign. Because of the great importance of farming in wartime, and because State control and State subsidies are now the order of the day, English agriculture has been buttressed by Government subsidies, and the post-war period has been one of reasonable prosperity.

### 3. The Workshop of the World

From the Great Exhibition of 1851 until the Franco-Prussian War, Britain was not only the world's workshop, but also its banker, its carrier, its clearing house and its ship-builder. While other countries were struggling to destroy internal tariffs and create a national economy, Britain's trade was worldwide. "A chandler's shop in the dirtiest, darkest thoroughfare of London cannot exist without supplies from every quarter of the globe."

Britain's supremacy owed much to the fact that she began the Industrial Revolution, and bred a race of inventors and skilled workmen unrivalled elsewhere. Such was the prestige of British manufactures that unscrupulous competitors sometimes stamped their products: "Made in England." Our banking and commercial traditions and markets, our merchant navy, and our Empire, all combined to make us pre-eminent. But the most important single reason for Britain's industrial and commercial success was the accessibility and abundance of her coal. It was excellent coking coal for smelting iron, it could be mined cheaply and thus kept the cost of steamers and railways down, it was a convenient outward freight for cargo vessels, and coalfields were situated near ports and sources of iron ore. Until 1870 Britain produced over half the world's coal, and not until 1900 was her output surpassed by the United States.

*Increase in Britain's Output of Coal, 1700–1913*

| | |
|---|---|
| 1700 | 2,000,000 tons of coal produced |
| 1750 | 4,800,000 tons of coal produced |
| 1795 | 10,000,000 tons of coal produced |
| 1854 | 64,700,000 tons of coal produced |
| 1870 | 110,000,000 tons of coal produced |
| 1913 | 287,400,000 tons of coal produced |

*British Coal Output Compared with that of Other Countries*[1]

| Year | Britain | America | Germany | France |
|---|---|---|---|---|
| | tons | tons | tons | tons |
| 1855 | 66,000,000 | 12,400,000 | No extensive coal industry | 7,500,000 |
| 1865 | 103,000,000 | 26,700,000 | 23,500,000 | 12,400,000 |
| 1875 | 133,300,000 | 52,200,000 | 38,400,000 | 16,300,000 |
| 1885 | 165,200,000 | 115,300,000 | 60,900,000 | 20,700,000 |
| 1895 | 201,900,000 | 189,100,000 | 89,300,000 | 29,600,000 |
| 1905 | 254,100,000 | 382,200,000 | 135,300,000 | 34,000,000 |

The coal production figures given above are the average production for the five years including and following the date, e.g. the figure 66,000,000 opposite the year 1855 is the average coal output for the years 1855, 1856, 1857, 1858, 1859.

The prosperity produced by industrial progress both increased the purchasing power of the pound and the wages of the working

[1] L. C. A. Knowles, op. cit., page 165 (adapted).

classes. Between 1830 and 1914, continually rising wages, collectivist legislation, and the development of trade unions[1] combined to increase the security, health and happiness of the majority of the nation. Towards the end of the nineteenth century, Joseph Chamberlain began to apply collectivist theories to the Empire. Railways were subsidized in the Sudan, and cotton growing financed in Uganda. The Empire not only provided excellent markets for British manufactures, but Canadian wheat, Australian wool, and West African cocoa became the staple of English consumption.

Just as foreign imports ruined English farming after 1870, so also English manufactures were exposed to the full blast of American and German competition; some of the effects of this are shown in the following table.

*The Decline of Britain's Industrial Supremacy, 1880–1900*

| | Britain | America | Germany | France | Year |
|---|---|---|---|---|---|
| Population .. | 35,000,000 | 52,500,000 | 45,000,000 | 38,000,000 | |
| Total exports | £234,000,000 | £165,000,000 | £153,000,000 | £138,000,000 | |
| Total imports | £344,000,000 | £140,000,000 | £152,000,000 | £191,000,000 | |
| Tonnage of ocean going ships .. | 7,000,000 tons | 1,300,000 tons | 1,200,000 tons | 970,000 tons | 1880 |
| Cotton manufactures exported .. | £76,000,000 | £2,600,000 | £5,000,000 | £3,700,000 | |
| Wool manufactures exported .. | £18,500,000 | £70,000 | £11,300,000 | £14,700,000 | |
| Population .. | 42,000,000 | 79,000,000 | 58,000,000 | 39,000,000 | |
| Total exports | £283,000,000 | £292,000,000 | £235,000,000 | £169,000,000 | |
| Total imports | £466,000,000 | £186,000,000 | £287,000,000 | £182,000,000 | |
| Tonnage of ocean going ships .. | 10,000,000 tons | 900,000 tons | 2,200,000 tons | 1,200,000 tons | 1900 |
| Cotton manufactures exported .. | £75,000,000 | £5,000,000 | £15,000,000 | £7,500,000 | |
| Wool manufactures exported .. | £15,800,000 | £130,000 | £11,500,000 | £8,700,000 | |

Like the table on page 62, all figures shown here are based on five year averages. Although it might appear from this table that Britain spent more than she earned, no account is taken of her invisible exports (e.g. insurance, income from foreign investments, etc.).

[1] See Chapter I for a discussion of the condition of the working classes. See page 194 for an account of the growth of collectivist legislation. The index should be used to find references to the development of Trade Unionism.

Despite the fact that by 1900, Germany and America were producing more steel than Britain, our total foreign trade was still higher than that of both countries put together.[1]

*Britain's Foreign Trade Compared with that of Other Countries*

| Year | Britain | America | Germany | France |
|------|---------|---------|---------|--------|
|      | £       | £       | £       | £      |
| 1870 | 547,000,000 | 165,000,000 | 212,000,000 | 227,000,000 |
| 1880 | 698,000,000 | 308,000,000 | 294,000,000 | 339,000,000 |
| 1890 | 740,000,000 | 320,000,000 | 367,000,000 | 311,000,000 |

What gave ground for alarm was the very rapid pace at which German and American industry advanced. If they maintained their rate of progress and Britain failed to increase hers, her lead could not remain unchallenged for long.[1]

By the end of the nineteenth century steel rather than iron had become the basic metal of industry. At first the processes of manufacturing steel, the Bessemer converter and the Siemens–Martin open-hearth, required non-phosphoric iron ore. This Britain obtained from Sweden and Spain; and because her shipping was cheap and plentiful and because her coalfields were near her ports (e.g. Middlesbrough and Barrow-in-Furness), she was able to produce steel economically. But the Germans, whose iron was also unsuitable, had such a long overland haul from the ports to their coalfields in the Ruhr that steel production was prohibitively expensive. When in 1879 Sidney Thomas, an Englishman, discovered how to make steel from phosphoric iron, Germany soon became a large-scale producer. At about this time a railway was built joining the iron deposits of Lake Superior to the coalfields of Pittsburg, and America began to produce such quantities of steel that its price fell more than fifty per cent.

[1] Between 1893 and 1913 British coal production increased by 75 per cent, German by 159 per cent, and American by 210 per cent. British steel output increased by 136 per cent, German by 522 per cent, and American by 715 per cent. British exports of manufactures rose by 121 per cent, German by 239 per cent, and American by 563 per cent.

*British Steel Production Compared with that of Other Countries*

| Year | Britain | America | Germany | France |
|------|---------|---------|---------|--------|
| | tons | tons | tons | tons |
| 1884 | 1,800,000 | 1,600,000 | 800,000 | 400,000 |
| 1890 | 3,579,000 | 4,275,000 | 2,195,000 | 670,000 |
| 1896 | 4,133,000 | 5,282,000 | 4,745,000 | 1,160,000 |
| 1900 | 4,901,000 | 10,188,000 | 6,260,000 | 1,540,000 |

At the beginning of the new century Britain's iron and steel industry had been surpassed by that of America and Germany, her coal output had been exceeded by America, foreign competitors were building their own ships, often helped by State subsidies, and the countries that used to buy our goods were now producing their own. There are several reasons for this decline in Britain's position. German technical education was superior, English industrialists were becoming conservative, America offered more of a career open to talents, the export of machinery enabled other countries to dispense with our manufactures, and high tariffs closed many of our markets. In addition to all these drawbacks, many workers mistakenly believed that the less work they did themselves, the more work there would be for others, that reduced productivity meant reduced unemployment. Unfortunately the Trade Unions tended to support this doctrine. Workmen opposed the introduction of labour-saving machinery. Consequently when other countries were rapidly increasing their output, British productivity fell. Between 1898 and 1906 the English miners' output of coal fell from an average of 301 tons a year to 289. In the same period in America it rose from 497 tons to 555. Of course other factors enter in, but it is no accident that the growth of Trade Unionism coincided with a general decline in the rate of production.

At present we live in the third stage of the Industrial Revolution. It differs from the canal stage or the railway stage in two important respects: Britain no longer leads the world, and the motive power and material of industry are different. Atomic energy, electricity, and internal combustion engines replace steam; while aluminium, steel, concrete and plastics are the prevailing materials. During the past two hundred years man's way of life has changed more radically than in all the previous centuries of his existence. It is too early to judge how far these changes have been for the better. Perhaps a century from now historians will date the origin of the "new Jerusalem" from the middle of the twentieth century; or possibly by that time the overgrown ruins of a few great cities will be man's only memorial.

In the twentieth century completely new problems have arisen in the place of old ones solved. Despite discoveries which have greatly increased the amount of food the world produces, the earth's resources are not limitless. The prosperity and happiness of mankind is bound to be affected by the size and growth of population. In some countries the birth-rate has increased enormously, while at the same time modern medicine has greatly reduced illness and epidemics. More children are born, people live longer, and there are more mouths to feed than food to go round. Consequently poverty and starvation afflict two-thirds of the globe. If the world's population were proportioned to its resources a mass of misery could be averted and the benefits of science enjoyed.

## CHAPTER V

# FOREIGN POLICY, 1830–1870

## 1. *The Nature of British Diplomacy*

FOREIGN policy ultimately depends for its success upon the power behind it. A bank note is of little value unless the credit and resources of the bank are sound: in foreign affairs the same principle applies. However skilful the approach and however subtle the method, no foreign minister can be successful in the end without the certainty of material strength to support his policy. In the years from 1830 to 1870 Great Britain was vastly superior to any other nation in prosperity and power, and it would therefore be strange if her record in foreign policy did not contain some notable triumphs. Britain's power rested upon the coal dug from her mines, the iron smelted in her furnaces and the cotton spun in her mills. Her ships carried trade to every ocean, her capital poured into foreign and colonial investments and an invincible navy protected her far-flung interests. She had no rivals until the last decade of the period and they only became serious after it had ended. In Europe, France was hemmed in by the provisions of the peace settlement of 1815 and she had undergone four revolutions by 1870; Germany and Italy were divided and only achieved their national unity after long and fierce struggles. Russia was not yet formidable. Across the Atlantic the United States grappled with the problem which finally resulted in the Civil War of 1861–1865. In none of these states was industry developed beyond its early stages and agriculture remained their major occupation. Moreover, in Europe no state possessed the political stability which England secured by the Reform Act of 1832 and buttressed by her material wealth. Europe was governed by autocratic monarchs who retained their position only by stamping out the first sparks of revolt and discontent: 1830 and 1848—the years of revolution—were outbursts of a deep resentment. British power was pre-eminent; sometimes it was used for unworthy objects and offensive assertions of strength, sometimes to help oppressed peoples, whether continental refugees or African slaves. After the Act of 1832 statesmen had to pay more attention to middle-class opinion on foreign affairs.

## 2. Palmerston's Foreign Policy, 1830–1865

Free trade, commercial expansion, the support of liberalism abroad, and the maintenance of national prestige were the main objects of British diplomacy under Lord Palmerston, who held the Foreign Office from 1830 to 1851, except during the Tory ministry of Peel from 1841 to 1846. He became a cabinet minister again in 1852, and was Prime Minister from 1855 till his death ten years later, with a brief interruption during the shortlived ministry of Lord Derby in 1858–1859. In Peel's ministry Lord Aberdeen (1784–1860) was a passive rather than active Foreign Secretary. Lord Malmesbury (1807–1889) in the other Tory ministries unashamedly took advice from Palmerston. At a time therefore when the outlines of political parties were becoming blurred, Palmerston stood out in sharp relief. Buoyant, resourceful and aggressive, physically vigorous and well built, he was the personification of Britain at the peak of her power.

Palmerston remains a controversial figure in history as he was in life. He infuriated the Queen and horrified pacific idealists like Cobden, Bright and Gladstone. He was often indiscreet and tactless. His unauthorized message congratulating Louis Napoleon of France on his *coup d'état* in 1851 was merely the last of a series of incidents which drove Queen Victoria to insist that Palmerston should never hold the Foreign Office again. Lord John Russell (1792–1878) as Prime Minister had his own ideas on foreign policy but he was never able to control his colleague. In 1859 he became Foreign Secretary in Palmerston's ministry and the two men found their views almost identical. Their differences were largely of method and temper. Palmerston constantly irritated foreign diplomats by his manner in conversation, and often in dispatches adopted a hectoring, impatient tone.

The most famous incident in which Palmerston asserted national prestige was that of Don Pacifico, a Portuguese moneylender who claimed British citizenship because he was born in Gibraltar. In 1850 Pacifico's house in Athens had been damaged in a riot and the Greek Government refused to pay the compensation he claimed, a fact which is not surprising as the claim was evidently fraudulent, if not entirely baseless. Palmerston at once ordered a blockade of Greece, a country with which we had always enjoyed the most friendly relations. In Parliament he defended his policy in a famous speech which was widely acclaimed throughout England. Ten years before, Macaulay (1800–1859), talking of the English merchants in Canton and their reaction to the arrival of a naval squadron had said, "It was natural that they should look with confidence on the victorious flag which was hoisted over them, which reminded them that they belonged to a country unaccustomed to defeat, to submission or shame—it reminded them that they belonged to a country which had made the farthest ends of the earth ring with the fame of her exploits in redressing the wrongs of her children". The nineteenth century was pre-eminently the time of self-assertive nationalism; from the Tagus to the plains of Cracow men were seeking national unity, and Palmerston and Macaulay in England had both the strength and weakness of their age. British foreign policy was often arrogant and aggressive but it was to some extent redeemed by the endless negotiation to end the African slave trade,[1] and the support of continental liberalism.

Though Palmerston's diplomacy had no consistent plan, certain tendencies are evident. He inherited Canning's distrust of the Holy Alliance powers (Austria, Prussia and Russia) and he disliked the principles of their governments. In a Europe disturbed by national movements and claims for self-government, he declared that "the independence of constitutional states never can be a matter of indifference to the British Parliament". His diplomacy, which was unpopular abroad, aimed at securing "the creation of satisfied, peaceably inclined states, under intelligent rule throughout the world". While sympathizing with liberal movements he was realist enough to respect the strength of the great powers. In much of his

---

[1] Palmerston waged a long crusade, against opposition both at home and abroad, to secure the co-operation of foreign nations to suppress the slave trade. He made over fifty separate treaties for this purpose.

thought Palmerston was a Conservative. He wished to retain the European settlement of 1815, and he saw that Britain could preserve the balance of power through her naval and commercial strength. The greatest threats to European peace came from France and Russia. Europe feared the revival of French militarism; and the deliberate resurrection of the titles "Empire" and "Napoleon" in 1852 seemed ominous. The fear of Russian expansion was more recent and developed with the growth of British interests in the Far East. Russian pressure on Turkey and her attempts to reach the Mediterranean threatened the British route to India, and alarmed France. Farther east, Russian intrigues on the boundaries of northern India led England into acquiring more territory so as to be able to hold her in check. Palmerston was anxious that the great powers should act in concert and he wished London to become the centre for discussions of European conflicts. This was his ideal but he was often forced to work with the power whose independent action was most to be feared.

### 3. The Belgian Revolt, 1830

Palmerston's methods were well illustrated in his handling of the Belgian crisis of 1830–1831. By the peace settlement of 1815 Belgium and Holland had been united under the Dutch king as the kingdom of the Netherlands. The two peoples were divided by culture, language and religion, and the Dutch had shown little consideration for Belgian susceptibilities. In August 1830 the people of Brussels rose in revolt and when the Dutch used force, the rising spread. The situation was a tense one for Europe; the Belgians were likely to appeal to France for aid and the presence of the French in the Low Countries was a threat which Britain had fought many wars to prevent. France herself had just had a revolution, in which Louis Philippe had replaced Charles X, and it might well be that the new king would seek an easy popularity by assisting the Belgians. Austria, Prussia and the German states sympathized with the Dutch and their reactionary governments were glad of an opportunity to crush a rebellion. There were in fact the makings of a general war. Palmerston on becoming Foreign Secretary in November found that his predecessor had arranged that a conference of the great powers should be held in London that month. He and Lord Grey, the Prime Minister, together devised a policy of acting in partnership with France, thereby restraining French ambitions and providing a counterpoise to the Holy Alliance. In this they were helped by the good sense of Louis Philippe, who was supported by the conservative and propertied classes of France, and wished to prove that he was no Jacobin king. By the end of 1832 the danger was over; a French army and a Franco-British naval squadron coerced the recalcitrant Dutch, the concert of great powers, faced by this Franco-British alliance, gave way; Leopold of Saxe-Coburg[1] became King of the Belgians and in 1839, when the frontiers of Belgium were defined, the powers signed a guarantee of her neutrality. Thus the peace of Europe was preserved and the object of the Treaty of Vienna maintained. The guaranteed neutrality of Belgium was as sure a safeguard against French expansion as the union of Belgium and Holland under one crown. It was the German violation of this guarantee that brought Great Britain into the war in 1914.

## 4. Entente with France, 1834–1846

Palmerston shares the credit for the Belgian settlement with Grey. Their efforts had been assisted by the moderation of the French and the fortunate outbreak of a revolt in Poland which prevented any chance of Russian intervention. France and Britain continued to work together in the crises caused by the Spanish and Portuguese revolutions (1833–1834). This *entente* with England was welcomed by the government of Louis Philippe. With English support the revolutionary July monarchy became respectable. On the other hand French public opinion did not welcome this dependence on England, and Louis Philippe was torn between retaining English friendship and satisfying French national ambitions. His failure to resolve this dilemma in the end cost him his throne. Palmerston, although he made use of the *entente* when it suited him, was determined to maintain British predominance in the partnership, which meant that he was unwilling to make any concession to French

[1] Queen Victoria's uncle.

public opinion. A wise consideration towards France would have encouraged Louis Philippe to curb the aggressive tendencies of his subjects. Instead Palmerston took every opportunity to emphasize French subordination; he made her play a secondary part in the Spanish affair, humiliated her as will be seen over Mehemet Ali in 1840, and prevented legitimate French expansion in Algeria. Diplomatic pinpricks did not improve the situation. Although from 1841–1846 the *entente* flourished under the Tory government of Peel and visits were exchanged by the two monarchs, on Palmerston's return to office accumulated resentment drove France into a rash policy. In 1846, in spite of a promise previously made to Britain, Louis Philippe consented to his son's betrothal to the Queen of Spain.

This action on the part of Louis Philippe ended the negotiations with England and caused intense ill-feeling. Whatever the provocation, it was a foolish policy since neither Britain nor the other great powers would ever allow the dynastic union of France and Spain. The English public knew nothing of Palmerston's rebuffs to France in the past; all they knew was that the King of France had gone back on his word. It was the end of the *entente*, and an empty triumph for Louis Philippe. Within two years he was an exile in England, thrown out by a revolution which heralded risings throughout Europe. After three years of unsteady government, a new ruler of France, Louis Napoleon, nephew of the great Emperor, made his power absolute in 1851. He could never be the natural ally of England and although there were moments of friendship and co-operation on major issues, the distrust remained. Napoleon III, as he proclaimed himself in 1852, seemed to Englishmen to be a trouble maker in Europe and consequently in 1870, when Napoleon was forced by Prussia into a war he did not want, England sympathized with the Prussians.

### 5. *The Eastern Question, 1830–1870*

The Eastern Question plagued Europe throughout the nineteenth century and in the end was a prime cause of the 1914 war. The problem can best be understood by looking at the historical origins of the Turkish Empire. In 1453 Constantinople, the last stronghold of the ancient Byzantine Empire, fell to the assaults of the Turks. After its fall the advance continued into the Balkans; in 1523 Hungary collapsed and Europe made a desperate effort to hold back the tide. The highwater mark was reached at the siege of Vienna in 1683. The Turkish hosts invested the city, which appealed to all Europe for assistance. This came in the form of a cosmopolitan army led by a Pole, Jan Sobieski, and the Turks were decisively defeated. From that time the Turkish empire decayed. The Turks had never done more than govern as military conquerors peoples of alien culture and religion. They had lived by plunder, and for centuries their ships had terrorized the Mediterranean. The problem of resisting Turkish conquest was replaced by the problem of what was to happen to the territories which the Turks could no longer control. In the nineteenth century public opinion made it difficult to overlook the brutal misgovernment of the Turks in the provinces still left to them.

All the powers of Europe were concerned. Russia and Austria had the most to gain in the Balkans; Britain and France feared Russian expansion to the Mediterranean and were themselves interested in the fate of Egypt, Syria and Greece. From 1821–1830 Greece had fought for her independence, and the great powers had interested themselves in her struggle. Britain under Canning had tried to co-operate with Russia, thereby preventing her from interfering in Turkey. Throughout the period Russia always had an excellent excuse to interfere since a treaty with the Sultan in 1774 (Kuchuk Kainardji) had granted her certain ill-defined rights to protect his Christian subjects. The Turkish answer to the Greek revolt had been to enlist the aid of Mehemet Ali, the Viceroy of Egypt. His troops were in the process of crushing the rebellion when Britain, France and Russia decided to intervene. The Turkish fleet was destroyed at Navarino Bay (October 1827), Russia invaded the Danubian provinces of Turkey, and the independence of Greece was guaranteed by the three powers in 1830.

Although Britain had been willing to assist the Greeks, British policy had not changed fundamentally. This policy was to maintain the integrity of the Turkish Empire proper, while encouraging the

Sultan to make reforms. The main threat came from Russia, but apparently by our working in partnership with her, her ambition could be checked. Actually the reason for Russian moderation was a change in her policy towards Turkey. In 1829 Russia realized that a break-up of the Empire would not at this stage serve her interests. France, Austria and Britain would all demand their share, Constantinople would become a free port, the Black Sea would be open to foreign fleets, and Russia would have strong neighbours instead of a weak Turkey. It would be better therefore to keep Turkey alive and extend Russian influence in the guise of protection, or as Palmerston put it later, better "to take the place by sap than by storm". The pursuit of this policy made Russia willing to co-operate with Britain in the next major crisis in the Near East. This occurred in 1839 when Mehemet Ali the Viceroy of Egypt reopened the whole problem by routing the Turkish armies at the battle of Nezib.

Mehemet Ali was a romantic figure. Born in Albania, he had been a merchant until service with an Albanian contingent in the Turkish army brought him to Egypt at the end of the eighteenth century. In 1805 he had been chosen Pasha, or Viceroy of Egypt, and within twenty years had made himself master of the country, though nominally he was a vassal of the Sultan. In return for the Sultan's promise to extend his dominions, he had sent troops to Greece in 1825. The interference of the great powers had resulted in the independence of Greece and the destruction of his fleet. Mehemet therefore felt that he had a claim to some reward but the Sultan did not keep his word. In 1831 Mehemet resorted to arms and Turkey was only saved by the protection of Russia, acting from motives of self-interest. Mehemet's ambition was to secure Syria, which would round off his dominions in the North, and he made another attempt in 1839. Among the great powers only France was sympathetic; Mehemet seemed a kind of Eastern Napoleon, and the French Government wanted to assert its prestige by helping him. In the event they were rudely shaken; Palmerston regarded Mehemet as "an ignorant barbarian" and was suspicious of French support of him. An agreement between Russia, Austria, Prussia and Britain resulted in an ultimatum; Acre was bombarded and Mehemet gave way. He was guaranteed hereditary possession of Egypt on payment of an annual tribute to the Sultan, and in July 1841 the powers, in apparent harmony, agreed that the Black Sea should be closed to the warships of all nations.

For the next ten years there was outward calm and Britain hoped that Turkey might make a determined effort to reform herself. But not even the majestic personality of the British ambassador, Stratford Canning (1786–1880), could stir the Turkish officials to end the corruption and incompetence which were undermining the Empire. Meanwhile Russia was reconsidering her policy. She had not been successful in obtaining a decisive hold over the Turkish Government, since the British Ambassador, Stratford Canning, had the ear of the Sultan. Would it not be more profitable to extend her co-operation with Britain and persuade the British Government to take part in a combined partition of the Turkish Empire? This was the plan proposed by the Czar Nicolas in 1844 on a visit to London. Turkey was a "sick bear"; if she should collapse there was the possibility of French intervention and therefore the most intelligent course would be for Austria, Britain and Russia to come to some arrangement. Lord Aberdeen, the Tory Foreign Secretary, was non-committal, and it is evident that Russia did not understand Britain's rooted objection to her expansion. Past collaboration had been intended to check Russian ambition, not to encourage her with ideas of a joint partition. Moreover English public opinion was becoming openly anti-Russian and the *entente* with France was still in existence.

In 1852 Louis Napoleon, anxious to secure his position within France by winning the Catholic vote, claimed a share in the Holy Places of Palestine which included the Church of the Holy Sepulchre in Jerusalem and the Church of the Nativity at Bethlehem. In the past the French had had rights within these churches but they had been supplanted by the Greek Orthodox Church. In February 1852 the Sultan granted the French claims by allowing them the keys of the Bethlehem church and the right to place a star emblazoned with the arms of France in the Holy Grotto. At the same time he assured Russia, the home of the Orthodox Church, that her rights within the Holy Places were not thereby infringed. But Russia was not to be satisfied; the occasion was too good to miss and it offered a chance to assert Russian influence in Turkey. Early in 1853 an embassy was dispatched to Constantinople to demand a guarantee of Russia's right to protect all Christians within the Turkish Empire. The Russians, encouraged by the apparent passivity of Britain and France, increased their demands, and in May withdrew their ambassador from Constantinople. On June 2nd the British fleet was sent to the Dardanelles as the Cabinet were suspicious of Russian intentions. On July 3rd Russian troops invaded Moldavia. Even now war was by no means inevitable and at a meeting in Vienna the ambassadors of the great powers drew up a note for the Sultan's acceptance. The Turks, prompted by the British ambassador, refused to accept such a compromise. On October 4th the Sultan declared war on Russia. Not until March 1854 did France and Britain become allies of Turkey and the interval was spent in ineffective attempts to prevent hostilities. Russia would gladly have backed out, but the Czar could not afford to lose prestige on the one question over which Russian public opinion supported him. In England, Aberdeen refused to make a decision and believed that he could still achieve peace at the same time as he was ordering British warships into the Black Sea to stop the Russian fleet moving from its base at Sebastopol. The public demand for intervention, which had been insistent ever since the Russian naval victory over the Turks at Sinope in November 1853, was at last decisive.

The actual operations of the Crimean war were not on a large scale. A naval expedition to the Baltic accomplished little, and the main effort was directed against the great fortress of Sebastopol in the Crimea which was the centre of the Russian threat to Turkey. The French and British both sent armies to the Crimea in September 1854. The French Commander-in-chief refused to advance at once on Sebastopol, after an initial victory over the Russians. There followed a long winter siege in which the generals showed their incapacity and the men their grit. Not till a year later was the fortress captured. The year 1855 revealed yet more plainly the military incompetence and the hopeless administration of the British army. It was an army which had not fought since the Napoleonic wars and the conditions of life for the private soldier were appalling.

Not that they were anything new. What was new was the attitude of the public. For the first time newspapers and photographs having a wide circulation emphasized the horrors of war, and in the liberal, humanitarian England of the mid-nineteenth century there was an explosion of wrath against the officials who allowed such conditions to exist. This reaction brought Palmerston to the premiership in January 1855 and won recognition for the work of Florence Nightingale (1820–1910) in the Crimean hospitals. These hospitals were no more than evil-smelling Turkish barracks without any form of sanitation, and matters were not improved by a lack of hospital stores, drugs and blankets. The medical service was swathed in red tape and brought up to believe that the soldier must not be spoiled. The result was calamitous; cholera took a far heavier toll than Russian bullets, and when the wounded arrived from the Crimea, after a nightmare crossing in ill-equipped ships to the Turkish base of Scutari, they entered a death-house. It is impossible to describe adequately here the work of Miss Nightingale. Regarded by many as an eccentric, for nurses were generally women of easy virtue, she was met by obstinate discourtesy from the regular medical officers, who disliked this interference by an amateur. The terrible winter gave her her chance. Boatloads of sick and wounded arrived daily at the verminous and overcrowded barracks of Scutari. The only drugs and equipment available belonged to Miss Nightingale. With superhuman energy she rose to the occasion and created a legend in which, for once, there was little exaggeration. It has been well said "Two figures emerged from the Crimea as heroic, the soldier and the nurse. In each case a transformation in public estimation took place, and in each case the transformation was due to Miss Nightingale."

The British public, realizing the squalor and misery of war, lost their taste for home-front heroics. During the siege of Sebastopol peace negotiations were opened. Austrian interests in the Balkans were extensive and Vienna became the scene of successive con- ferences. In the end it was Napoleon III who insisted on compromise; France had nearly four times the number of British troops in the Crimea and the inconclusiveness of the campaign made French opinion restive. Only Palmerston wished to continue the war after the fall of Sebastopol, but he was compelled to give way and on the 30th of March, 1856, the Treaty of Paris was signed. The Black Sea was closed to warships of all nations, Russia evacuated Turkish territory, and the Danubian principalities were to be granted constitutions though remaining under Turkish sovereignty. Turkish independence was guaranteed by the signatories and the Sultan promised to make reforms. Russian claims to an exclusive protection of Turkish Christians were abandoned. Obviously these measures provided no permanent solution of the Eastern question. Reforms were not made in Turkey and in 1870 Russia had recovered sufficiently to denounce the Black Sea clauses. Thereafter the situation remained tense until the general explosion of 1914. In fact France and Piedmont were the only two nations to gain anything from the Treaty of Paris; Napoleon III triumphed as the arbiter of Europe, and acted as host to the implacable foes of his uncle. Piedmont achieved international standing by sending a contingent of troops to fight for the allies, and her leading minister, Cavour, made clear at the Paris peace conference his ambitions for Italian unity.

## 6. The Unification of Italy, 1830–1860

Since 1815 when the Italian states were restored to their legitimate rulers it had been the aim of the Italian people to achieve national unity. Language and geography were on their side, but the great obstacle was the power of Austria. Occupying the provinces of Lombardy and Venetia, and having dynastic relations with many small Italian duchies, she intervened at the first sign of rebellion. In 1830 and 1848 the hated "white coats" crushed the movements for unity. Cavour (1810–1861), the Prime Minister of Piedmont, the only independent and constitutional state, realized that unless Austria was expelled from Italy there was no chance of unification. Alliance with Napoleon III seemed the easiest way to get rid of the Austrians. Napoleon III came to an agreement with Cavour in July 1858 and in April 1859 they declared war on Austria.

Englishmen had sympathized with the Italians for many years. Italian refugees had been fêted on visits to England and there were close ties between the scholars of both peoples. The middle-class

Victorian Liberal naturally disliked the tyrannical and corrupt governments of the Italian states, although the Queen and the Conservatives inclined to the Austrian side. During the revolutions of 1848 Palmerston had shown that his desire to preserve peace in Europe was tempered by a dislike for autocratic régimes. He and Lord John Russell were out of office in 1858, but they returned in June 1859. Their sympathy for the Italians was lessened by their distrust of Napoleon III and their concern, in the interests of the balance of power, that Austria should not be crushed. Quarrels between the Queen and Palmerston broke out once more, but this time Russell supported Palmerston. The two men attempted to use English influence to assist Italian ambitions without upsetting the peace of Europe. Napoleon withdrew from the war, and the struggle for Italian unity took a new turn in May 1860 when Garibaldi and his thousand volunteers landed in Sicily and expelled the Neapolitan government. The British Government made it clear that they would not use the Royal Navy to prevent him from landing on the mainland, and on October 27th Russell sent a dispatch which proclaimed that Britain viewed with satisfaction "the gratifying prospect of a people building up the edifice of their liberties and consolidating the work of their independence". This dispatch was unexpectedly well timed; it heartened the Italians and made it clear that Austria would be well advised to accept the situation. British influence throughout was indirect, but Italians have testified how timely was the sympathy of the nation which, if she had been hostile, could have prevented Italian unity.

## 7. Anglo-American Relations, 1840–1872

The story of Anglo-American relations in the early nineteenth century was largely one of bickering and recrimination over boundary disputes. There was a legacy of bitterness over the two wars fought in 1776 and 1812, but a sense of mutual respect and common interest was developing. Both nations possessed great territories with ample room for expansion without conflict, and in 1842 the dispute over the north-eastern boundary between Canada and the United States was settled by the Webster–Ashburton Treaty. The other controversy over the Oregon boundary aroused much more feeling. Earlier negotiations had failed, but by 1840 increasing American immigration into the area north of the Columbia River made an agreement necessary. Strong language was heard from both sides, and not till 1846 was a settlement finally reached. Britain's desire to retain the disputed area had diminished with the decline of the fur trade, and the United States conceded the British claim to Vancouver Island in return for the extension of the boundary along the 49th parallel to the Pacific. This did much to improve Anglo-American relations. It was fortunate that Peel's government was in power, for Palmerston might have reacted violently to the original American demand of "54°40' or fight", the slogan by which the most extensive claims were made.

The Civil War of 1861–1865 caused the most dangerous tension in our relations with America. Public opinion in this country did not approve of slavery but many of the upper class thought that the Southern states had a perfect right to secede from the Union. The Government at once proclaimed British neutrality and prohibited British subjects from helping either side. The Southern states for their part hoped that their control of the greater part of the world's cotton supply would force Britain to intervene on their behalf. One-fifth of the British people depended on the cotton trade for their livelihood and great distress was caused in Lancashire by the interruption of supplies. Southern hopes were, however, disappointed owing to the accumulation in England of the bumper crop of 1860 and the steady increase in cotton imports from Egypt and the East. The North at the beginning of the war imposed a blockade on the South and it is remarkable how calmly Great Britain accepted this maritime restriction. Britain appears to have viewed the dissolution of the American Union with equanimity.[1] The Cabinet toyed with Napoleon III's suggestion for joint mediation, but finally rejected it.

The blockade caused two famous disputes. The South decided to send two envoys to Britain. Eluding the blockade they took passage

[1] For example in 1842 Britain recognized the independence of Texas and in 1862 sympathized with Napoleon III's establishment of an empire in Mexico. Canada, however, was a perpetual hostage for any active designs against the integrity of the United States.

from Havana on an English ship, the *Trent*. This ship was stopped by an American man-of-war, and the two Southerners were removed. When the news arrived in England there was great indignation at this violation of maritime rights, a violation, let it be said, which England had often practised against America in the past. The Cabinet drew up a dispatch demanding the return of the two envoys within seven days. Prince Albert, as the last official act before his death, was responsible for softening the asperity of the note. The American Government showed sense, the men were allowed to proceed on their way and the incident ended. The other issue was over the building of warships in England with which the South hoped to break the Northern blockade. One ship ordered in October 1861 sailed in March 1862 from Liverpool. Another, the *Alabama*, was fitting out and protests were made by the American minister. There is no doubt that Russell was dilatory over the matter but chance increased the delay. The American case had been sent to the Queen's Advocate, the senior law officer of the Government, who suddenly went mad. This held matters up for two days, and not until the afternoon of July 29th was it decided that the *Alabama* should be detained. It was by then too late; the *Alabama* had sailed that morning on a voyage which did much damage to northern commerce. Thereafter the Government was more alert, and although there was one occasion on which the American minister had instructions to break off diplomatic relations if necessary, no other Southern warship was allowed to fit out in English ports. The *Alabama* case had the most important consequences in the history of international arbitration. After the war the British Government agreed to submit the claims made by the Americans, in respect of the damage done by the *Alabama*, to an impartial international tribunal. The award, considered favourable to America, was nevertheless honoured by the British Government.

## 8. *The Chinese Opium Wars, 1839 and 1858*

Ever since 1715 the East India Company had been established at Canton where it was allowed to trade under strict regulations imposed by the Chinese Government. This Government regarded all foreigners as barbarians, and permission to trade was given with the sole purpose of squeezing as much money as possible out of the merchants. Foreigners were allowed to live in an isolated part of Canton closed in by a wall; their ships were to come no further than a port thirteen miles away, and all business had to be conducted through an exclusive body known as the Hong merchants. Business under such conditions could not be very profitable and the East India Company soon found that it had an adverse balance on its trade with China. This unsatisfactory situation was remedied by an illegal trade in opium which was grown in the company's Indian territories. The annual produce was sold by auction in Calcutta in the knowledge that it was to be smuggled into China against the wishes of the Chinese authorities. The company recognized that their conduct was disreputable in every way, but they could not prohibit the sale of opium without losing the revenue they needed to govern India. The only way to end the opium traffic was for China to open all its ports to legitimate trade. On two occasions, in 1795 and 1816, the British Government had sent embassies to the Chinese Emperor seeking a commercial treaty, but both were humiliated by being treated as the envoys of barbarians, bearing tribute to the Lord of the World.

An aggressive commercial power could not long tolerate such behaviour. The turning point came in 1833 when the East India Company's monopoly in the Far Eastern Trade was abolished. The firms which had hitherto been confined to smuggling could now compete in the legal trade and they pressed the English Government to force the Chinese to remove all restrictions. Two Scotsmen, William Jardine and James Mathieson were the leading opium traders and they realized the great possibilities of proper trade in China. They provided Palmerston with facts, figures and a policy. Another embassy was sent from England, arriving at a time when the Chinese Government was making an attempt to destroy the opium trade. The ambassador found himself committed to maintaining British prestige which involved protection of the opium ships. In the autumn of 1839 war broke out, Canton was bombarded and the Chinese agreed in a treaty of 1842 to open Shanghai and three other ports to trade, to cede the island of Hong Kong and to pay compensation for opium and other goods destroyed. This could not be a permanent settlement for the door once opened must be opened fully. The Chinese Government had granted their concessions under pressure and naturally wished to limit them. Tension increased and in 1858 war broke out again; a joint Franco-British expedition reached Pekin and burnt the Summer Palace. In 1860 a treaty was signed opening still more ports and giving official sanction to the opium trade which the Chinese were powerless to suppress. Furthermore they abandoned their traditional attitude to the barbarians by accepting diplomatic representatives at Pekin. On moral grounds there is no excuse for Britain's conduct; China did not wish to have any contact with the West and should have been left in peace. The English Government was not prepared, however, to sacrifice material interests for a principle. Necessity was held to justify her actions.

### 9. The End of an Age

The last ten years of the period saw a waning of British predominance, which Palmerston and his contemporaries failed to recognize. On the Continent Prussia under Bismarck was becoming the most formidable military power. Bismarck's avowed intention was to create a united Germany by force and to this end he fought three wars, against Denmark, Austria and France. Britain's role was that of a spectator and her one attempt at intervention resulted in a bitter humiliation. An alliance with France might have checked the advance of Prussia, but the traditional fear of French aggression continued unabated in England and poisoned relations with Napoleon. Britain's diplomatic defeat occurred when Austria and Prussia went to war against Denmark in February 1864. The dispute centred on the two duchies of Schleswig and Holstein which were ruled by the King of Denmark. Holstein in particular had a predominantly German-speaking population and Bismarck was anxious to incorporate both duchies in Prussia. The dispute was complicated, and Britain sympathized with the Danes.[1] Palmerston encouraged their hopes by stating in Parliament that "if any violent attempt were

[1] In 1863 the Prince of Wales had married Princess Alexandra of Denmark.

made to overthrow the rights and to interfere with the independence of Denmark, those who made the attempt would find in the result that it would not be Denmark alone with which they would have to contend". When war came and the Danes appealed for help, none was forthcoming. Without allies Palmerston and Russell could do nothing.

It was a sad epilogue to Palmerston's career. He died in 1865 and his successors stood aside as Prussia conducted two further victorious wars.[1] British public opinion and policy were still coloured by the fears of 1815, and a Welsh parson merely voiced the feelings of the nation when he declared that he sided with the Prussians against France "in the wickedest, most unjust, most unreasonable war that ever was entered into to gratify the ambition of one man". The wheel had come full circle; Napoleon III, a sick and listless man in 1870, was thus condemned on the record of his great ancestor. Energetic and blustering at the beginning of the period, British foreign policy was bankrupt at the end.

[1] Against Austria (1866) and France (1870–1871).

## CHAPTER VI

# ENGLISH POLITICS, 1868–1885

## 1. Gladstone's First Ministry, 1868–1874

WHEN Disraeli committed the Conservative party to supporting a Reform Bill, he was indeed taking a "leap in the dark" for the electorate to whom he had given votes, contrary to his expectations, failed to return him with a majority at the following election. The part he had played in 1867 was uncommonly like Peel's role in 1846: both had "dished the Whigs", both had been accused of political betrayal, and both were defeated in the ensuing election. In February 1868 Derby resigned, and Disraeli who had already been directing Conservative policy, became Prime Minister in name as well as in fact. "I have climbed", he said, "to the top of the greasy pole", and in an age when politics still tended to be exclusive and aristocratic, such pre-eminence was no mean achievement for this son of a Spanish Jew. At about the same time Gladstone succeeded Lord John Russell as leader of the Liberal party,[1] and the stage was set for one of the most sustained and dramatic of rivalries which have enlivened our political history.

In the autumn of 1868 Disraeli decided upon a general election, and was somewhat surprised to learn that the Liberals had been returned with a majority of 112. This result seems to indicate that the working classes regarded his Reform Bill as a political manœuvre, rather than as a sign of a change of heart in the Conservative party. During the election campaign Gladstone advocated the disestablishment of the Irish Church and consequently regarded his victory as a mandate for Irish reform. "My mission", he said, when he heard that he was to become Prime Minister, "is to pacify Ireland".

The period which begins with Gladstone's first ministry and ends with the declaration of war in 1914, was one of far-reaching change. It saw the transfer of European supremacy from France to Germany and it witnessed the slow conversion of English government towards

[1] See Glossary.

full democracy. The Reform Bill of 1867 (see page 46), the 1872 Ballot Act (see page 90), the extension of the franchise to country people in 1884 (see page 97), the Trade Union Acts of 1871, 1875, 1906 (see pages 90, 92 and 175), and the 1888, 1894, 1899 local government reforms (see Chapter XII) all tended to broaden the basis of effective political power. As the franchise was extended so it became necessary to educate the new electorate; hence the Acts of 1870, 1880, 1891 and 1902 (see pages 154-5). During this period, Britain's export trade was seriously threatened by foreign competition, particularly from Germany; and English agriculture was nearly ruined. Moreover, our dependence upon food brought from overseas, together with the necessity of finding new markets for our exports, led to an immense extension of the Empire.

All these great events involved changes in the methods and objects of diplomacy and politics. It is perhaps not without significance that, except for Disraeli, Gladstone was the first nineteenth-century Prime Minister to have been born after 1800. Palmerston's death (1865) and the victory of the North in the American Civil War (1861-1865) heralded a period of reform, rather like that following on the fall of Wellington's ministry in 1830. Certainly Palmerston's prophecy that when Gladstone "gets my place we shall have strange doings" was swiftly fulfilled.

## 2. Gladstone and the Irish Question

Ever since Tudor times English statesmen had been unable either to coerce or to conciliate Ireland. Again and again Irish affairs had forced themselves to the front of English politics, and even threatened the safety of the whole kingdom. William of Orange, for example, had been forced to defend his title by fighting James II on the banks of the Boyne, and so late as 1798 an Irish rebellion looked for a time as if it might force England to come to terms with France. In 1845 famine in Ireland converted Peel to free trade in corn, thus dividing his own party. For three centuries Ireland had been a thundercloud over English politics and it is hardly surprising that one of the main results of Gladstone's attempts at pacification was a storm which took half a century to die down.

The so-called "Irish problem" was simple enough. Irishmen

would not willingly accept the political dominion of the alien English and Scots. The impoverished Roman Catholic population were forced by their Protestant masters to contribute to the Established Church of Ireland. This caused bitter resentment.[1] Moreover, between 1815 and 1845 the population of Ireland doubled, and the country was consequently threatened with starvation. Racial pride, resentment at their subjection, religious antagonism, and poverty made the Irish reckless in their despair and relentless in their hatred of tyranny.

Nevertheless, Englishmen might have continued to avert their eyes from the horrors in Ireland which they preferred not to see, had it not been for the Fenian outrages. The Fenians were a society founded in America in 1858, which planned to support rebellion with money and men. In Ireland itself they only became formidable at the end of the American Civil War (1865), since in that year large numbers of Irish Americans were released from the Federal Army. These troops, accustomed to the excitement of war, supplied with American dollars, and inspired by the example of the Italian Nationalists, determined to set up an independent Irish Republic. Their activities forced the English Government to take severe counter measures, including the arrest of the Fenian leader, Stephens, and the suspension of the Habeas Corpus Act in Ireland. In 1867 the Fenians committed a number of violent outrages in England. An attempt was made to seize Chester and the arms stored in the castle. It was only frustrated by the prompt action of the Mayor, who telegraphed to London asking for a battalion of Guards to be sent to the city by train. Other Fenians were involved in clashes with the police and in an attempt to blow up Clerkenwell jail.

Gladstone, like many other Englishmen, was disturbed by these events. Fenianism led him to believe that any delay in Irish reform might prove dangerous, while on the other hand the fact that the movement had not been vigorously supported in Ireland, suggested that timely conciliation might still be successful. Accordingly he disestablished the Protestant Church of Ireland in 1869. He was fully supported in this measure by his Nonconformist electors; but

[1] Cf. A. H. Clough: "Thou shalt have one God only: who
Would be at the expense of two?"

the Conservatives, the party of "Church and King", agreed with Disraeli that "we have legalized confiscation, we have consecrated sacrilege, we have condoned treason."

In 1870 Gladstone attempted to remedy another serious grievance. Arable farming had become so unprofitable in Ireland that many landlords evicted their tenants, without compensation, in order to turn their land to cattle-grazing. The Irish peasant consequently had no security of tenure and knew that however much he improved his land by his own efforts, such improvement would not be taken into account if the landlord demanded it back. The Land Act of 1870 arranged for tenants to be helped to buy their holdings with loans of public money, limited the landlords' power of arbitrary eviction, and established the principle of compensation for improvements. Nevertheless its provisions could be evaded since it did nothing to control eviction by exorbitant rent-raising. Despite these measures, Ireland was not satisfied. The time was not far off when many politicians, including Gladstone himself, decided that Irish grievances could only be redressed by repealing the Act of Union.[1]

## 3. Gladstone's English Reforms, 1868–1874

The theory of eighteenth-century government was that "the best governed country is the least governed country". Consequently in the age of Walpole and Chatham, Ministers felt that the preservation of public order, the conduct of foreign policy and the control of the purse, were the natural limits of political action. The Victorians, while loudly proclaiming this doctrine of *laissez-faire* in the economic and political sphere, did not necessarily fit their practice to their principles. In fact the nineteenth century saw the gradual extension of governmental control.[2] This movement is particularly well reflected in the history of educational reform. Before 1832 there is not a single debate on record or a single Act of Parliament concerned with the education of the country; by the beginning of the twentieth century education had become a department of state.

When Gladstone became Prime Minister in 1868, well over half the children of England were completely untaught, and unable even

See Glossary.         [2] For a fuller discussion of this trend see Chapter XII.

to write their own names. Such education as there was, was carried on partly by the Church and partly by a variety of private, grammar, and so called "public" schools, many of which were utterly inadequate. Moreover the Reform Bill of 1867 made it increasingly necessary to educate the new electorate; while the successes of Germany against Austria in 1866, and France in 1870, provided an advertisement for schooling difficult to ignore, particularly as the victors themselves attributed the efficiency of their armies mainly to their system of compulsory education.

W. E. Forster's Education Act (1870)[1] lost the Ministry some support. Anglicans, already alienated by Irish disestablishment, felt that rate-aid gave Board schools an unfair advantage; while on the other hand many Nonconformists strongly objected to the increased grants given to Church schools. Gladstone's reforming zeal led him to disregard the electoral consequences of the measures he advocated. Disraeli's victory in 1874 was the bitter fruit of this disdain.

Not only did Gladstone reform general education but he also took steps to improve higher education. In 1870, except for the Foreign Office, the Civil Service was opened to competitive examination. This stimulated the Universities to improve their teaching. If the victory of the Germans in the Franco-Prussian war had encouraged England to reform education, it had a more direct and powerful influence in stimulating Army reform. Many Army traditions shocked the Liberals both because they were inefficient and because they were undemocratic. The "career open to talent" was unknown in the British Army, where commissions were bought and sold. Moreover Gladstone's ministry, which disliked spending public money, regarded the Army as unduly expensive. The Secretary for War, Cardwell (1813–1886) soon took the matter in hand. In 1868 he abolished peacetime flogging in the army, making a soldier's career more attractive to a better class of recruit. In 1871 the practice of buying commissions was abolished by royal warrant.

By the Army Enlistment Act of 1870, it became possible for soldiers to sign on for short service. Instead of joining up for twenty-one years, they could now serve six years in the army and six years on the reserve. The size of the army was increased by 20,000 men,

[1] See page 154.

and infantry battalions were divided into county regiments. Despite all these great changes, including the formation of twenty-five new battalions, the army estimates were reduced, partly owing to the policy of leaving colonial defence to be paid for by the colonies themselves.

The nation's debt to Cardwell was enormous. Nevertheless neither the country nor the Army supported him whole-heartedly in his reforms, which were carried out in face of the continuous opposition of the Commander-in-Chief, the Duke of Cambridge.[1] Wellington had regarded his soldiers as "the scum of the earth". Lord Roberts, at the close of the century, remarked that his men "bore themselves like heroes on the battlefield and like gentlemen on all other occasions".

Two other reforms of Gladstone's first ministry helped to lay the foundation of modern England. The legal existence of Trade Unions was recognized for the first time in 1871. Hitherto[2] Unions had been thought undesirable, because they were set up "in restraint of trade". This recognition of the rights of working men against their employers gave them an influence in industry still denied to most of them in Parliament. The Ballot Act of 1872 put an end to voting in public, which had only too often involved violence and riots. Electors could now vote in secret, unintimidated and uninfluenced by their landlord or employer. In Ireland the Bill had revolutionary consequences, since the small-holders freed from the threats of their landlords, could vote for whomever they pleased. Charles Parnell (1846–1891) was not slow to realize that a secret ballot made possible the formation of an all-Irish party.

In 1872 the Government passed a Licensing Act which lost it a great deal of support in the country. The measure gave magistrates the right to grant or withhold licences for public houses, the right to analyse the contents of drinks sold, and to regulate opening and closing hours. Publicans complained that the Act robbed the poor man of his beer, and the temperance party grumbled that the Ministry had not introduced prohibition (i.e. making the sale

---

[1] Labouchere once described the Duke of Cambridge as "standing at the head of the troops, his drawn salary in his hand".

[2] For the earlier history of the Unions see Vol. I, page 262.

of alcoholic drinks illegal). Until this Licensing Act publicans and brewers had on the whole supported the Liberals; but after 1872, suspecting ·Gladstone of plotting to destroy their industry, they supported Disraeli, contributed handsomely to Tory funds and used nearly every public house in the country as a platform for Conservatism. Gladstone had once again alienated a formidable number of his own supporters and indeed he attributed his defeat in 1874 to this ill-judged Act. "We have been borne down", he said, "in a torrent of Gin and Beer."

The Government did not in fact resign until February 1874. They had suffered their first serious defeat in the previous year, when Gladstone's proposal to found a Roman Catholic College in Ireland was rejected by 287 votes to 284. The Prime Minister consequently resigned, but Disraeli, unlike Salisbury twelve years later (see page 99) refused to form a minority ministry, thus forcing the Liberals to resume office. The Government, however, had threatened too many interests by its reforms. Since 1872, according to Disraeli, its Ministers were "a row of exhausted volcanoes", and their policy one of "blundering and plundering" which "harassed every trade, worried every profession and menaced every class, institution and property in the country". The Liberals finally resigned when Cardwell objected to Gladstone's proposal to reduce army expenditure. Although Queen Victoria disapproved of Gladstone, regarding him as dangerously radical, most historians, whatever their party, agree that this ministry was one of the most successful of her reign.

## 4. Disraeli's Social Reforms, 1874–1880

At the general election of 1874 Disraeli was returned to power with a majority of 50. His position was very strong since he had been elected with no particular mandate: his most formidable opponent, Gladstone, had resigned the leadership of the Liberal party; the Queen was his personal friend; and many of the middle class had been won over to Conservatism, because they suspected Gladstone of pandering to the working class. On the other hand Disraeli was 70 when he came into office and suffered acutely from asthma and gout. It would have been difficult for his ministry to embark on an extensive policy of reform, since the Conservatives had never ceased to attack the Liberals for menacing every interest in the country. Nevertheless they did amend the Licensing Act of 1872 in the interest of the liquor industry, and they did pass a number of Acts designed to regulate and improve social conditions. Disraeli had already shown in his novels that he was something of a radical. Now as Prime Minister he had the opportunity to put his theories into practice.

Disraeli believed that it was the duty of the State to pass laws to safeguard the interests of working men; a theory which many Liberals objected to on the grounds that it was bad economics, and an unwarrantable interference with the liberty of the individual. It is one of the curious paradoxes of history that Disraeli's Conservative Ministry took the first steps in Socialism. In 1875 the Public Health Act was passed, incorporating features from over 100 separate Acts, many of which had hitherto merely been local regulations. Until 1937 this measure provided the basis of our sanitary laws and rendered a great service to the country by controlling the dispersal of sewage and the cleaning of streets, and thus did much to check the spread of disease. In the same year the Artisans' Dwelling Act was passed, which made a start on the problem of slums, and also an Act which protected the public from impurities in the drugs and food they consumed. The Conservative programme of reform was completed by a Trade Union Act, 1875, which improved the act of 1871 by allowing peaceful picketing, and an Education Act, 1876, providing that poor parents should be assisted from the rates if they could prove to a local board of guardians that they were unable to pay their children's school fees. The most spectacular feature of Disraeli's policy was undoubtedly his imperialism (see page 245). But his abandonment of the Liberal principle of *laissez-faire*, and the encouragement he gave to local government (e.g. by legislation which made education, drainage and housing their special concern, and by the "grants in aid" given to municipalities by the Exchequer) were equally important. It was not inappropriate that the Queen should have asked Disraeli what the word "bureaucracy"[1] meant.

[1] If the reader feels inclined to ask the same question, he may answer it by turning to the Glossary.

## 5. *The Home Rule Agitation*

At the general election of 1874, partly owing to the Ballot Act (1872), a new party was returned to the House of Commons. It was led by Isaac Butt (1813–1879), the inventor of the term "Home Rule", and it supported the repeal of the Union and the independence of Ireland. Every year the 58 members of Butt's party voted for Home Rule, and every year their motion was defeated by a vast majority, until it became one of the standing jokes of the House of Commons. Nevertheless the failure of the party to achieve its object by parliamentary debate soon had most serious consequences. It lent force to Charles Parnell's argument that it was hopeless to expect concessions from England unless she were compelled to yield them.

Butt eventually lost his influence over the Irish party, and Parnell became Ireland's "uncrowned king". In the House of Commons he followed a policy of obstruction. In 1877, for example, he forced members to divide 17 times, and kept the House sitting 26 hours before it could pass an Army Reserve Force Bill. Meanwhile in Ireland he helped Michael Davitt to found the Land League for the relief of Irish tenants. In the last years of the seventies both England and Ireland were hit by a trade depression, and agriculture throughout Europe suffered bitterly from its effects. Disraeli, who 30 years before had attacked Peel for favouring Free Trade (see page 43), now in his turn failed to protect the British farmer, and Ireland in particular was affected by the slump. Agrarian discontent and general economic distress provoked ferocious support of the Land League, whose members agreed with Davitt that "Rent is an immoral tax upon the industry of a people". Faced with the Zulu and Afghan Wars, with sullen obstruction in England and continual outrages in Ireland, the Liberal opposition broke out in a frenzy of criticism, culminating in the Midlothian campaign (1880). Gladstone, who had been provoked out of his temporary retirement, travelled up and down the kingdom from Liverpool to Edinburgh, condemning Disraeli's imperialism and the whole policy of the Government. The Queen was horrified by such tactics. Previously it had been unheard of for a Minister to address a series of meetings outside his own constituency, and now the dangerous and radical

Mr. Gladstone was attacking dear Lord Beaconsfield (Disraeli took this title in 1876) from platforms all over the country. But neither royal disapproval, nor Gladstone's considerable age (he was over 70) abated his energy. At the general election of 1880 the Liberals were returned to power with a majority of 137 over the Conservatives. The Irish Nationalists, led by Parnell, won 65 seats and consequently became a formidable third party in the State. This great Liberal victory was due partly to Gladstone's immense energy and eloquence, partly to discontent amongst the electorate engendered by economic distress, partly to the fact that the Liberals had decided to extend the franchise to the agricultural labourer, and partly because their own internal quarrels (e.g. the Nonconformist resentment over the religious compromise in the 1870 Education Act) were forgotten in their opposition to Disraeli. Harmony had been restored by a common hatred.

### 6. Political Personalities in 1880

The Queen, exercising her prerogative to choose the Prime Minister from the party which had obtained a majority at the election, sent for Lord Hartington, who had succeeded Gladstone in 1874 as leader of the Liberal party. By inviting him to form a ministry, the Queen hoped to escape Gladstone, whom she feared and disliked. The manœuvre, however, proved fruitless, since Gladstone told Hartington that he would accept no office other than that of Prime Minister, and it was inconceivable that a Liberal ministry could be formed without him. In the Midlothian campaign Gladstone had appealed directly to the electorate. It would have been folly on the Queen's part to persist in frustrating their clearly expressed will. Resigning herself to the inevitable, she asked him to form a ministry.

The Liberals, who had united to overthrow Disraeli, found themselves divided on nearly every other issue. Some of them were becoming impatient with Gladstone, criticizing his love of mystery, and his tendency to be "radical in the open and whiggish behind the scenes". Others thought that in forming his ministry he had not given sufficient weight to the radical wing of his party; indeed Joseph Chamberlain (1836–1914) was its only representative in the

Cabinet. Nevertheless if one man could make do for many, Chamberlain was certainly the man. He had already organized the party on modern political lines, setting up Liberal associations for the first time in most of the great manufacturing towns of the North, and had thereby largely contributed to the recent victory. He strongly supported Trade Unionism, direct taxation, disestablishment, free education, payment of members of parliament, and manhood suffrage, and attacked the power of the House of Lords. The fact that the Cabinet did not fairly represent all shades of Liberal opinion helps to explain why, despite its enormous majority, it achieved so little.

With the exception of the Prime Minister, already the Grand Old Man of English politics, the great parliamentary figures of the previous decade were giving place to younger men. In April 1881 Disraeli died. Perhaps more than any other Conservative of the nineteenth century, he had proved to the electorate that the old Toryism of the Duke of Wellington, who had resisted nearly every reform as dangerous or unnecessary, was a thing of the past. In truth it must be admitted that Disraeli was more of a Radical than most of his bewildered, if trusting, disciples; none the less the Reform Bill of 1867 and the social policy of the Conservative ministry between 1874 and 1880, provided a guarantee that this "superlative Hebrew conjurer" had educated his party, and that if his magic was not permanent it had at any rate been potent while it lasted. Disraeli's deep and genuine love for the Queen and the confidence she reposed in him had, among many happy results, led to her return to public life. Her retirement after the death of the Prince Consort in 1861, for a time made her unpopular. When she emerged again, now not only a Queen but an Empress,[1] she soon regained her subjects' loyal and enduring affection.

Disraeli's political heirs were Lord Randolph Churchill (1849–1895) and, to a lesser extent, Arthur Balfour (1848–1930). Both opposed the "old gang" of Tory back benchers and both emphasized the necessity of establishing a Tory democracy embracing the interests of the working man. This section of the Conservative party was in some way analogous to the radical wing of the Liberals, and was certainly equally embarrassing to older statesmen.

[1] See page 244.

## 7. *Gladstone's Irish Policy*

In June 1880 Gladstone announced that he intended to rule Ireland without coercion. Such a bold stroke was feasible only if followed by immediate reform, since distress was driving Irishmen to desperation. The measure of relief proposed, however, was carried by a small majority in the House of Commons. Seventy Liberals abstained or voted against it. As the Bill had been concerned with compensation for evicted tenants, a controversial issue at the best of times that would lead inevitably to similar demands in England, the Lords threw the Bill out by a majority of over 5 to 1. Increasing misery in Ireland, and the lack either of reform or martial law, brought the country to the verge of revolution. Houses were burnt, landlords were assaulted and sometimes murdered, and anybody who took over a farm which had belonged to an evicted tenant was treated "as if he were a leper". Captain Boycott was the first victim of this policy, which bears his name.

The utter lawlessness of Ireland, where "Captain Moonlight" was said to reign, forced Gladstone to return to coercion, and this reversal of his policy was carried out in face of continuous obstruction from the Parnellites. Habeas Corpus was suspended and Irish magistrates were given the power of preventive arrest. In 1881 Parnell was arrested and kept in Kilmainham jail for six months, but even the imprisonment of their leader did little to discourage the violence of his followers. Agrarian outrages increased alarmingly during 1880 and 1881.

Recognizing that force alone was no solution of Ireland's problems, Gladstone passed a second Land Act in 1881. This gave Irish tenants the three F's: fixity of tenure, fair rents and free sale. The Act was admirable because it accepted drastic reform as the only remedy for long-standing abuses, but as had happened too often in the past, the Ministry appeared to concede "to violence and crime what it had denied to reason and justice". At about the same time, mainly due to the efforts of Chamberlain, the Government came to an agreement with Parnell. An informal treaty was concluded in 1881, sometimes known as the "Kilmainham treaty". Parnell was to be set free, and an Act was to be passed admitting about 100,000

Irish tenants to the advantages of the Land Act, from which they had been excluded, because they were in arrears with their rent. In return for these considerable concessions Parnell promised to exert all his tremendous influence in attempting to pacify Ireland.

Unfortunately the attempt to replace coercion by co-operation met a violent end. Lord Frederick Cavendish, a son of the Duke of Devonshire, and thus a member of one of the greatest of the Whig families, was appointed to Ireland as Chief Secretary. Shortly after his arrival (1882) he was murdered by members of a rebel society known as the "Invincibles". In fact his assassins had intended to kill only the Under-Secretary, Burke, with whom he was walking in Phoenix Park. This crime naturally embittered English opinion against Ireland. Lord Frederick Cavendish was a charming young man of great promise, whose murder was committed in circumstances of singular atrocity—he was hacked to pieces with surgical knives. Parnell himself was appalled by this outrage, which he regarded as a "stab in the back".

## 8. Reform and Defeat

As early as 1881 the whole of the Liberal party, including the Whig section, had recognized in principle the desirability of extending the franchise to agricultural labourers, but Gladstone had been too fully occupied to do much about it. In 1884 the Third Reform Bill became law and the electorate was increased from 2,600,000 to 4,400,000. As in 1832 so again in 1884: the Bill was rejected by the Lords. Such was the agitation against the Upper House that even moderate men thought that the only solution was to "mend them or end them". The Queen induced Gladstone and the leader of the Opposition, Lord Salisbury, to come to terms, and the Bill was ultimately passed. Her intervention on this occasion provides a striking example of the important part the Crown has played in resolving constitutional deadlocks. The 1884 Reform Bill, like the Ballot Act twelve years before, had a profound effect in Ireland, for the extension of the franchise involved an extension of Parnell's power.

By 1885 Gladstone's Ministry was divided and discredited:

divided because Chamberlain and his fellow Radicals felt that the Prime Minister favoured the Whigs rather than themselves,[1] because Gladstone and Lord Rosebery disagreed on imperial issues, because Lord Hartington and the Whigs were disgusted with the Irish land settlement, and because many Liberals including Forster (the Irish Secretary whom Cavendish succeeded) still favoured a policy of coercion. In addition to all these troubles, Gordon's death at Khartoum was laid by many, including the Queen, at Gladstone's door. While divisions were growing in the Liberal ranks, Randolph Churchill managed to come to an agreement with Parnell. The Irish leader promised to support the Conservatives in overthrowing Gladstone, if they in their turn undertook to withdraw his coercive measures. In June 1885 this uneasy coalition of Irish and Conservative members defeated Gladstone's budget and Lord Salisbury became Prime Minister.

[1] For example in sending Cavendish rather than Chamberlain as Irish Secretary in 1882.

## CHAPTER VII

# ENGLISH POLITICS, 1885–1902

## 1. Salisbury's First Ministry, 1885–1886

WHEN Gladstone resigned on the defeat of his budget, Lord Salisbury could have refused to form a ministry, leaving the Liberals with the choice of an immediate election, or of carrying on the government in spite of their defeat, as Disraeli had forced them to do in 1873. In accepting office the Conservatives failed to realize the advantage they would undoubtedly have secured, either by prolonging Gladstone's discredited administration and thus increasing the electorate's hostility towards him, or by going to the country at a moment when the reaction against Liberalism had reached its climax. As it was, they attracted to themselves the criticism which they could so easily have directed at their opponents.

The Conservatives had only come into power because Lord Randolph Churchill had secured Parnell's support. Consequently Salisbury had to fulfil his part of the bargain and end the policy of coercion in Ireland, at the very moment when it was beginning to show signs of success. This reversal of policy convinced Gladstone that there could be no lasting settlement of Irish problems while the fate of that country was at the mercy of English party politics. Only if Ireland were granted Home Rule would its real interests ever be served. In short Gladstone had come to accept Parnell's view that the Irish party had "a platform with only one plank, and that one plank national independence".

At the general election of December 1885 the Liberals obtained a majority of 86 over the Conservatives. Gladstone wanted Home Rule. But it seemed to him that it would be easier to obtain if the Conservatives initiated the measure. Moreover the unity of his party would not be put to so severe a test. As he said nothing about his changed views during the election campaign, Parnell naturally instructed his followers to support Salisbury. The Liberal victory over the Conservatives was partly the result of the gratitude of the new electors enfranchized in 1884; and partly the outcome of Chamberlain's "unauthorized programme", which consisted of speeches delivered all over the country, explaining his personal schemes of social and agrarian reform. Parnell's party exactly held the balance between Gladstone and Salisbury, since it consisted of 86 members. This third party, "the 86 of '86", now had a power altogether out of proportion to its weight in the country. Although it had been returned to Westminster by a tiny proportion of the total electorate, it was nevertheless the arbiter of Parliament.

For a short time after the election Salisbury remained Prime Minister; Parnell and the Conservatives exactly balancing the Liberal forces in the Commons. The situation immediately changed when Herbert Gladstone indiscreetly told the newspapers of his father's conversion to Home Rule. Much against Gladstone's will, Parnell transferred his allegiance to the Liberals, who consequently outvoted the government in February 1886 and forced Lord Salisbury to resign.

## 2. The First Home Rule Bill, 1886

When Gladstone was forced to admit his conversion to Home Rule, he opened a fissure that ran right through the Liberal party. Hartington, one of the old-fashioned Whigs, refused to join a ministry committed to give Ireland her freedom, and the Radical-Imperialist Chamberlain resigned from the Cabinet rather than support Home Rule.

The Home Rule Bill proposed to set up an Irish Parliament at Dublin, which was to be free to legislate for Ireland, as long as it did not trespass on certain "reserved subjects". Questions relating to the Crown, to foreign policy and to major constitutional issues, were still to be decided at Westminster, although Ireland was no longer to be represented in the English House of Commons. Irish judges were to be appointed and paid for by the Irish, but the Privy Council in England was to be the ultimate court of appeal.

One feature of the Bill which pleased many Englishmen was that there would be no Irish members at Westminster to confuse and complicate English party politics and to obstruct the proceedings of

Parliament. Yet just as the American colonies in the preceding century had declared their independence of Britain on the grounds of "no taxation without representation", so the Home Rule Bill could only be regarded as a half-way house on the road to full independence. It was not likely that Ireland would contentedly hand over 40 per cent of her revenue to a country which she hated, and to a Parliament in which she was no longer to be represented. The terms of the Bill involved an unworkable compromise between giving Ireland her independence and at the same time retaining some control over her policy. This endeavour to reconcile incompatibles and please everybody in fact pleased nobody; and there was much force in the argument of the opponents of the Bill when they said that it would in the end lead to the complete independence of Ireland.

Despite Gladstone's eloquence in defence of Home Rule, the measure was defeated in the Commons by 343 votes to 313, 93 Liberals voting against the Bill. Hartington and Chamberlain spoke against it, John Bright condemned it in a letter to the Press, and Conservatives, Whigs and Radicals combined to vote it down. Gladstone then decided to fight an election on the issue of Home Rule, expecting to gain some additional support in the country since Parnell could now instruct his supporters in England to vote Liberal rather than Conservative. The electorate, however, proved more bitterly opposed to the principle than the Prime Minister anticipated and they returned 316 Conservatives, 191 Liberals, committed to Home Rule, 85 Parnellites and 78 "Unionist" Liberals. Salisbury's majority was now so great that it no longer mattered to the Conservatives which way the Irish voted; thus the immediate consequence of Gladstone's support of Home Rule was the restoration of the two party system, and the permanent alliance of the Liberal and Irish vote.

### 3. Salisbury's Second Ministry, 1886–1892

Although Salisbury himself represented the right wing of his party, he had the good sense to make Lord Randolph Churchill, who was only 37, Chancellor of the Exchequer and Leader of the House of Commons. The new Chancellor's budget, introduced in the first year of his office, would have continued, had it been accepted by all his colleagues, the Disraelian policy of Tory Radicalism. Local government grants were to be reduced, every sort of economy was to be imposed, and death duties were to be increased, thus enabling Churchill to lower income tax, reduce the duties on tea and tobacco, and still leave a surplus of over half a million. W. H. Smith, the War Minister, opposed the budget because he refused to cut army expenditure, with the result that the Chancellor resigned. Doubtless he hoped that the Prime Minister would be unable to replace him and consequently that he would be reinstated with increased authority. The loss of Churchill was indeed a serious blow for his party, which without his Radical energies pursued a more placid course. Goschen, a Liberal Unionist, who was appointed to succeed him, was in many ways a great asset, as his acceptance of office cemented the Unionist-Conservative alliance. Moreover he was a great financier and a brilliant debater, though, unlike Churchill, his influence was steadying rather than stirring.

### 4. Conservative Policy Towards Ireland

Despite the temporary reversal of 1885, dictated by Churchill's alliance with Parnell, the traditional Conservative attitude towards Ireland was one of coercion. Owing to Salisbury's alliance with the Liberal Unionists, particularly with Chamberlain, it became necessary for a time to modify this policy and to be rather more conciliatory. The "plan of campaign" of 1886 was devised by John Dillon and William O'Brien, and never really won Parnell's enthusiastic support. The idea was to organize Irish tenants on Trade Union lines, to offer landlords a reasonable rent and, if this was refused, to pay the proffered sum into a campaign fund. The movement spread with alarming rapidity, and the evictions it provoked led to serious discontent. This persuaded the Unionists that Ireland could only be governed by martial law. By the end of the year Salisbury declared the plan to be illegal and early in 1887 passed the Criminal Law Amendment Act giving the Lord Lieutenant of Ireland power to proscribe such societies and to enable crimes committed in Ireland to be tried, if necessary, in England, so as to avoid the protection offered to trouble-makers by the partiality of Irish juries.

Irish disorder soon involved bloodshed. The police opened fire on a crowd at Mitchelstown and three people were killed. In October 1887 O'Brien was sent to jail and forced to wear prison dress, whereas previously political offenders had been treated more leniently than common criminals. "Remember Mitchelstown" and "O'Brien's breeches" became the slogans of the Home Rule party. In London, despite police prohibition, a meeting took place in Trafalgar Square to protest against O'Brien's treatment (November 13th, 1887, "Bloody Sunday"). After an ineffectual baton charge, the crowd had to be dispersed by the Life Guards, and over one hundred people were injured in the process.

By the end of 1887 six Irish M.P.'s were in prison. Gradually, however, a strict enforcement of the law restored order, and A. J. Balfour, the Irish Secretary, was deservedly praised for his handling of the situation. The Criminal Law Amendment Act of 1887, which involved a return to coercion, was helped through the House of Commons by a new procedure. The Irish Nationalists in Parliament had come very near to putting an end to all parliamentary proceedings by continuing to debate motions day after day, thus preventing a division. Accordingly the "guillotine" was introduced, which enabled a motion to be put to a vote, provided the Speaker and at least two hundred members were in favour of doing so.

A series of articles entitled "Parnellism and Crime", published in *The Times*, also did much to encourage the belief that coercion was the only possible policy towards Ireland. One letter in particular, allegedly written by Parnell, contained the phrase "Burke[1] got no more than his deserts". This inflamed public opinion against him, but when in 1890 a Parliamentary Commission reported that the letter was a forgery, Parnell became the hero of the hour.

Unfortunately for the Home Rule party this reaction in favour of Parnell did not last long. Shortly after the revelation of the forgery the Government lost a series of by-elections. But in November 1890 Parnell was cited as co-respondent in an action brought by Captain

[1] Burke was murdered with Cavendish in Phoenix Park, 1882 (see page 97).

O'Shea for divorce from his wife. Public opinion, and particularly that of Gladstone's Nonconformist supporters, was deeply shocked to learn that the great Irish leader had been living with Mrs. O'Shea for over nine years. Quarrels soon broke out in the Irish party itself, which was confronted with a cruel dilemma, well stated by R. C. K. Ensor in *England 1870–1914*: "Should they, at English bidding, depose their brilliant National leader or should they, by retaining him, sacrifice all chance of home rule? By their inability to agree on embracing either loss, they eventually incurred both." The decisive factor proved to be the intervention of the Irish clergy on behalf of Justin McCarthy, who was elected leader of the Irish party in Parnell's place. Only 26 of the 70 Irish members in the House of Commons remained loyal to Parnell.

In October 1891 Parnell died. The feuds he had created by refusing to resign his leadership divided the Irish party, so that at the election of 1892 there was little hope of a considerable Home Rule majority. Parnell was not only a great parliamentary tactician, but as Gladstone said of him, he did for Home Rule what Cobden did for Free Trade, "he set the argument on its legs".

Partly owing to the break up of the Irish party, and partly because of the success of a sustained policy of coercion, Balfour in 1890 was able to mitigate the Criminal Law Amendment Act of 1887. In 1891 he introduced a Land Purchase Bill which was designed to assist the Irish tenant in buying the land he rented by advancing him long-term loans. Balfour's policy of firmness followed by concessions made his own reputation as a statesman and was the greatest achievement of Salisbury's ministry.

### 5. *Conservative Reforms, 1886–1892*

The reforms of Lord Salisbury's second ministry were almost as extensive as those of Disraeli between 1874 and 1880. What the party had lost in the radical influence of Churchill, who died at the age of 45 in 1895, was soon supplied by the Liberal Unionists. It was partly because the Government were anxious to win closer support from these Liberal opponents of Home Rule that their policy was one of widespread reform. Conservative reform, however, proceeded on collectivist rather than *laissez-faire* principles.

The 1884 Reform Bill, like the 1832 Reform Bill,[1] was soon followed by a Local Government Act (1888). It was obviously impolitic to deny a newly enfranchised electorate the right to vote in local elections. The 1888 Act, which set up County Councils elected by ratepayers, constituted another step towards full democracy. The County Councils were to have their own paid officials and to be responsible for public health, roads and, eventually, poor relief and education. A great deal of subsequent legislation extended the authority and activities of the councils. The Act, moreover, rationalized a century or more of piecemeal legislation which had made local government chaotic. In 1888 for example there were more than 27,000 local authorities. The Local Government Act replaced them by 62 County Councils.

In 1890 a Housing Act was passed providing for the "clearing of insanitary areas, the removal of unhealthy or obstructive buildings, the rehousing of persons displaced, and the erection of dwellings for persons of the working classes". A Factory Act (1891) empowering local authorities to insist upon sanitary conditions in factories, and a Shop Hours Act (1892) forbidding employers to work people under 18 more than 78 hours a week, were measures which forty years before would have been attacked as intolerable interference on the part of the Government. The 1891 Education Act was perhaps the greatest reform of the ministry. By the Acts of 1870 and 1880 (see page 154), education had been made compulsory and universal; in 1891 it was made free.

Despite the social reforms of the Government there were more than 500 strikes in 1888. In 1889 the London Dock strike won a great victory for the Trade Unions. The strike was started by Ben Tillett, supported by Tom Mann and John Burns.[2] The dockers struck for a standard wage of sixpence an hour. Partly because the

[1] The 1832 Reform Act was followed in 1835 by the Municipal Reform Act (see page 7).

[2] Tillett was a Bristol street arab, who after a period at sea and in the tea trade, started organizing dock strikes (1888). In 1889 he became secretary of the Dockers' Union. He was a Labour M.P., 1917–1924 and 1929–1931. Mann was a miner's son, who went down the pits at the age of nine. In 1893 he became the first secretary of the Independent Labour Party. Burns, after a career as a Trade Union leader, became a Liberal-Labour M.P. in 1892, and President of the Local Government Board, 1905–1914.

strike paralysed the trades and industries dependent upon the Port of London, and partly because public opinion was on the side of the dockers, the employers, after a month's struggle, were forced to concede the "docker's tanner". Thereafter Trade Unions preached political as well as industrial action.

In 1892 Salisbury advised the Queen to dissolve Parliament, and at the subsequent election Gladstone was returned with a majority of 40 pledged to Home Rule. Before Gladstone took up Home Rule there had been no real social difference between the parties. But in 1886 a great majority of the Whig peerage and gentry left Gladstone; and London society, following the example of the Queen, ostracized the supporters of Home Rule. The Liberal party was increasingly forced to depend upon the "Celtic fringe" (i.e. Scotland, Wales and Ireland). In 1891 the Liberals put forward the Newcastle programme, which embodied the radical demands of the various minorities which Gladstone hoped to unite into a majority. It promised Home Rule to please the Irish. It promised Disestablishment in Scotland and Wales to please dissenters. It promised reform of the land laws to please the rural voter. It promised to introduce a bill establishing employers' liability for accidents in factories to please the Trade Unionists, and it promised to restrict the sale of drink to please the advocates of temperance.

The Newcastle programme alienated many interests which might otherwise have voted Liberal, and burdened the party for years with promises it could not hope to fulfil, and yet could not in honesty disown. It did, however, help Gladstone to win the general election of 1892, even if in the long run, like Home Rule, the Newcastle programme proved to be a step towards the downfall of the Liberal party.

## 6. The Second Home Rule Bill, 1893

When Gladstone became Prime Minister for the fourth time, his majority in the House of Commons was smaller than it had ever previously been. Chamberlain and the Unionists had announced before the election that there was no longer any hope of Liberal reunion. When the second Home Rule Bill was introduced in 1893 Gladstone realized it could only be passed by a small majority. The tragedy was that the bitterest and most effective opposition to the measure came from Gladstone's former colleagues: Chamberlain[1] in the Commons, and the Duke of Devonshire (Hartington) in the Lords. The energy which Gladstone displayed in piloting the Bill through the Commons was amazing, particularly as he was 83 at the time. He might be "an old man in a hurry" as Randolph Churchill described him, but few men fifty years younger could have rivalled his eloquence and resource.

The second Home Rule Bill of 1893 differed from the first in that Irish members were to be returned to the House of Commons, although they were only to be entitled to vote on Irish measures. After long debates the Bill passed the House of Commons by 34 votes, and was thrown out by the Lords. 419 peers voted against the measure and only 41 for it. Gladstone was anxious to go to the country on the issue of reforming the House of Lords, but the rest of the Cabinet were so opposed to the idea that he was forced to accept defeat. In March 1894 he resigned his office, partly because of failing sight and hearing, partly because his colleagues' decision against dissolution meant that he personally could never have another chance to deal with Ireland, and partly because he disagreed with the policy of naval expansion, which he regarded as violating the Liberal principles of "Peace and Retrenchment".

Gladstone died in 1898 at the age of 89. Whereas most people grow more conservative as they grow older, Gladstone began his career as a Tory and ended it a Radical. He, more than any other man, translated the theory of Liberalism into political fact. No statesman of the nineteenth century was his equal either as a parliamentarian or a financier. "He raised in the public estimation", said Balfour, his political opponent, "the whole level of our proceedings". Certainly at no time in our history has the attention of the whole country been so riveted upon political events as it was in the age of Gladstone and Disraeli. As Sir John Marriott wrote of him:

[1] "He never spoke like this for us", commented Gladstone during a speech of Chamberlain's attacking Home Rule.

"Here was a man cast in an heroic mould, and whether right on a given question or wrong, in nothing was he less than great."

## 7. Rosebery and the Lords

When Gladstone resigned in 1894, Queen Victoria did not consult him about his successor, as was customary, but on her own initiative appointed Lord Rosebery to take his place. Throughout Rosebery's ministry (1894–1895) the Lords conduct was thoroughly partisan. They had never touched a single measure presented to them by Salisbury, but between 1892 and 1895 they threw out the Home Rule Bill, and three measures promised in the Newcastle programme: an employers' liability bill, a bill to establish a local veto on the sale of drink where a majority of a County Council voted for it, and a bill for the disestablishment of the Welsh Church. Public opinion apparently was on the side of the Lords, particularly in their rejection of Home Rule and the local veto, as the election of 1895 conclusively showed. Nevertheless the precedent they had set was a very dangerous one to follow and when from 1906 onwards the peers played the same game with another Liberal Government, they brought on themselves the Parliament Act (1911) which drastically reduced their powers.

When the Government was defeated in 1895 by a snap vote they took the opportunity to resign. The Liberals had in any case been reduced to impotence since none of their measures could pass the Lords. At the general election in July, 340 Conservatives, 71 Liberal Unionists, 177 Liberals and 82 Home Rulers were returned, giving the Government a majority of 152. The Gladstone–Rosebery Liberal Ministry (1892–1895) did not achieve much if we judge its success only by the impression it left on the Statute Book. It was in fact a useful interlude in what would otherwise have been nineteen years of Conservative government, an interlude which gave young Liberals like Asquith and Campbell-Bannerman ministerial experience.

## 8. Salisbury's Third Ministry, 1895–1902

In 1895 Salisbury persuaded five Liberal Unionists to join his new cabinet. Thereafter the two parties may be regarded as one in the House of Commons, although the Unionists for some time retained their separate party organization in the constituencies. The Unionists in the Cabinet were Devonshire, Chamberlain, Goschen, Halsbury and Lansdowne. Although strong in talent, they roused the jealousy of many Conservatives, who thought that the Unionists, who had come in at the eleventh hour, were being rewarded at the expense of those who had borne the burden and heat of the day. Salisbury combined the offices of Prime Minister and Foreign Secretary, Balfour was First Lord of the Treasury[1] and Leader of the House of Commons, while Chamberlain emphasized his interest in imperial affairs by refusing the Exchequer and taking the Colonial Office.

Salisbury's third ministry was more active in the imperial than social sphere (see page 253). However, the Workmen's Compensation Act (1897), the Education Acts (1897 and 1899) and the Committees on Old Age Pensions (1896–1899) suggest that the Government was not blind to the need for reform. The bill to establish employers' liability, which was thrown out by the Lords in 1894, was largely inspired by Chamberlain. Since Chamberlain was almost as powerful as the Prime Minister he was able to persuade Salisbury to introduce a bill making employers liable for accidents in industry. The 1897 Education Act empowered the Government to give financial grants to needy voluntary schools, and the 1899 Act set up the Board of Education to co-ordinate the work of primary and secondary schools and to standardize elementary education. Chamberlain was also responsible for the Committee on Old Age Pensions, which suggested that the deserving poor, over 65 years old, should be given five shillings a week. The expense of the South African War was made an excuse for not carrying this out till 1909.

The Boer War, which had forced old age pensions to be put on the shelf, used up all the Government's energy. In 1900 the Conser-

---

[1] This was one of the rare occasions when the First Lord of the Treasury was not Prime Minister.

vatives held an election at a time when it appeared that the war was won. This "khaki" election successfully made capital of British victories, so that Lord Salisbury was returned to power with a majority of 128. Soon after the election Salisbury resigned and his nephew, Balfour, became Prime Minister. The death of the Queen early in 1901 and the resignation of Salisbury in 1902, mark the end of an era in British politics. The political problems of the twentieth century, although many of them have their roots in Victorian times, are utterly different from the problems which confronted Disraeli and Gladstone.

## CHAPTER VIII

# LITERATURE AND THOUGHT IN THE LATE VICTORIAN AND EDWARDIAN AGES

## *1. New Creeds*

THE self-awareness of the Early Victorian Age is equally evident in its successor. The best criticism of the ideas of the period has been made by writers who belonged to it. The intellectual fashions of the day were made fun of in the still popular comic operas of Gilbert (1836–1911) and Sullivan (1842–1900) and depicted with incomparable wit in the essays, parodies and drawings of Sir Max Beerbohm. Perhaps the most penetrating and brilliant analysis of them is to be found in *The New Republic* by W. H. Mallock, published in 1877. The variety and profusion of ideas which makes the Early Victorian Age so confusing, so exciting and so rich grows ever wider in the half-century before the first world war. The stream of thought, which in the eighteenth century had flowed between narrow, unyielding banks, was in the nineteenth century for ever branching out and branching out again, so that it becomes harder and harder to say which is the parent river and which its offshoots. The old unity is gone. We are approaching the earthquakes and overturnings of the war of 1914.

To draw the character of the Late Victorian Age in clean, bold lines is unfortunately impossible. The transition from the Early Victorian period was gradual and many of the Early Victorian giants survived till almost the end of the century. Carlyle died in 1881, Darwin in 1882, Browning in 1889, Tennyson in 1892, Huxley in 1895, Ruskin not till 1900. Yet the change from the atmosphere of the fifties to that of the eighties is unmistakable. The eager seriousness, the boundless confidence, the Elizabethan energy of the earlier period has almost vanished and in its place there is a faintheartedness which sometimes expresses itself in frivolity and irresponsibility and sometimes in depression and self-pity. There are fewer prophets and visionaries; more wits and men of the world. The decadence of the Edwardian Age is just beginning.

The conflict between religion and science discussed in Chapter II had weakened or destroyed the beliefs of a great many people. But the habits of belief are not easily discarded. If, as it then appeared, Christianity in its traditional form would not do, then Christianity must be modified or some other creed would have to be found to take its place. The alternative of agnosticism was, of course, always possible but it was difficult for those who had had a religious up-bringing to find peace of mind in so negative a position. The firm, uncompromising agnostic was a rare bird. Most people preferred a temporary refuge such as that offered by Jowett (1817–1893), the great Master of Balliol, who emphasized the moral and ethical sides of Christianity without committing himself too deeply in matters which involved the supernatural. Others found comfort in con-tinuing to use the language of religion while occupying a position which was essentially agnostic, such as Matthew Arnold (1822–1888), the poet and critic, who described religion as "morality touched with emotion". But such makeshift creeds offered no real resting place. Those to whom a position of suspended judgment was distasteful had either to retrace their steps to some form of orthodox Christianity or else find some new cause to serve or some new ideal to adore. By this means they could satisfy their need for an object of worship without the embarrassment of a God whom their reason told them could not exist. The search for a substitute for God recalls Dryden's couplet of two centuries earlier:

> Gods they had try'd of every shape and size
> That God-smiths cou'd produce, or Priests devise.

Social Justice, the Idea of Beauty, Imperialism and many other causes and ideals received the devotion and the desire for service which had been diverted from their traditional channels.

Perhaps the most important of the new secular religions was Social Justice or, as it is sometimes loosely called, Socialism.[1] The connection with Christianity is a very obvious one and many of the

[1] Socialism is so often redefined that, like Toryism and Whiggism before it, it is coming to stand more for an emotional attitude than a system of ideas. Probably the most important of all socialist thinkers were Karl Marx (1818–1883) and Friedrich Engels (1820–1895). Though both men lived and worked in England their influence in this country was never as great here as it was on the Continent.

great social reformers of the nineteenth century, from Lord Shaftesbury (1801–1885) to Charles Kingsley (1819–1875) and Cardinal Manning (1808–1892) were devout Christians, were, indeed, concerned with social justice just because they were Christians. But to those who were without any belief in God, the cause itself became a religion. In Late Victorian England there were two main sects of this faith. One, headed by William Morris (1834–1896), a writer, artist and craftsman of astonishing versatility, was generally known as Guild Socialism. Its inspiration was derived from the individual craftsmanship of the medieval workman. Ruskin had been the first to insist on the importance of enabling a man to express himself in his work and to maintain that the routine labour of the factory hand was morally and physically degrading. The dignity of work was the first concern of the Guild Socialists and to achieve it they were prepared to throw over the machine and the greater material prosperity it had brought. Morris himself, not content with writing and painting, designed and produced furniture, textiles, wallpaper and glassware. He was also a scribe, illuminator and typographer of great distinction. If Guild Socialism was too high-minded a creed to win wide support, it nevertheless did much, through the work of Morris and his friends, to raise the standards of design and workmanship in the products of industry.

The other sect of Socialists, still with us today, was the Fabians. The Fabian Society, founded in 1883, took its name from the Roman general whose success against Hannibal had been achieved by his cautious and gradual tactics. The Fabians accepted by and large the Marxian analysis of society but, unlike Marx, they thought that a step-by-step advance towards Socialism was both more desirable and more practicable than a violent revolution. The policy of gradualism which they advocated has played an important part in the shaping of the present Labour Party. Like the Philosophic Radicals before them they went into battle well armed with statistics and reports. But although their approach to the problems of society seems somewhat dry, scientific and inhuman, they were animated by a real and generous faith. Among the distinguished men and women who founded the Fabian Society, Beatrice Webb and George Bernard Shaw lived to see the great Labour victory of 1945.

The worship of Beauty, otherwise known as the Aesthetic Movement, was perhaps the most brilliant and striking of the new religions. The high priest of the cult was Walter Pater (1840–1894) who developed a highly-coloured, sensuous prose style appropriate to his faith. Aesthetic experience—that is, the apprehension of beauty—was for him the chief, the only good. This view is put with force and eloquence at the end of his essay on Leonardo da Vinci in *The Renaissance:*

"Every moment some form grows perfect in hand or face; some tone on the hills or the sea is choicer than the rest; some mood or passion or insight or intellectual excitement is irresistibly real and attractive for us—for that moment only. Not the fruit of experience, but experience itself, is the end. A counted number of pulses only is given to us of a variegated dramatic life. How may we see in them all that is to be seen in them by the finest senses? How shall we pass most swiftly from point to point and be present always at the focus where the greatest number of vital forces unite in their purest energy? To burn always with this hard gemlike flame, to maintain this ecstasy is success in life."

Pater, who was a don at Oxford, exerted great influence over the undergraduates of the day and notably over Oscar Wilde, who was largely responsible for transplanting this exotic growth to the drawing-rooms of London society. In Gilbert and Sullivan's comic opera *Patience* the ridicule is directed against Wilde and his friends. The prose of Pater, the epigrams of Wilde and the humorous verse of Gilbert are the memorials of the movement. At its worst there was something namby-pamby and precious about it, a point that Gilbert hits off neatly in the lines:

> If you walk down Piccadilly
>> With a poppy or a lily
> In your medieval hand,
>> Then everyone will say
> As you walk your mystic way,
>> "If he's content with a vegetable love,
>> Which would certainly not suit me,
> Why, what a most particularly pure young man
>> This pure young man must be."

At its best it was a passionate protest against the materialism, the grossness and the strident vulgarity of the age.

These last qualities were at times only too evident in the Imperialism of the Late Victorian period. The belief that Britain had been destined by Providence to be the mistress of the coloured peoples of the world may seem extravagant, but it did inspire colonial administrators with a sense of mission and the politicians at home with a sense of responsibility. Of course it often led to a mere arrogant jingoism—a patronising assumption that the British race was by nature superior to any other and would, if necessary, demonstrate this by force. Certainly in a man like Cecil Rhodes (1853–1902) Imperialism amounted to a religion. The best and worst sides of it are to be found in the stories and verses of Rudyard Kipling (1865–1936) and Sir Henry Newbolt (1862–1938).

Social Justice, Aestheticism and Imperialism were the most important of the new beliefs that the Late Victorian Age had to offer. But there is another note struck in these years that we do not hear in the earlier period—a note of deep and overwhelming pessimism. In the novels of Thomas Hardy (1840–1928) it is stoical and resigned, like the slow movement of a great symphony; in the poems of A. E. Housman (1859–1936) it is querulous and haunting.

To sum up this brief description of the ideas prevalent in Late Victorian and Edwardian times, it must be emphasized that the influence of the Early Victorians remained powerful right up to the eighties and nineties. Where the later period differed from the earlier it was in loss of balance and steadiness. The Late Victorians are less serious, less confident; more inclined both to melancholy and to light-heartedness, and, as the turn of the century is reached, more shallow and superficial. The reasons for this change are complex, but by far the most important single cause was the unsettling of traditional religious belief by the geological and biological discoveries discussed on pages 26–28.

## 2. Late Victorian and Edwardian Literature

The literature of this time, if not equal in range and genius to the earlier age, is nevertheless rich and varied. The chief poets of the day were Swinburne, Matthew Arnold, Clough, Meredith, Hardy and towards the end of the period, A. E. Housman, Bridges, and Rupert Brooke. Of the earlier poets Swinburne and Matthew Arnold were outstanding. Swinburne (1837–1909) possessed a sense of rhythm that no other English poet has ever surpassed. The obscurity, even, some would say, the lack of meaning of some passages does not check the exhilarating sweep of his verse. Who could be bothered to stop and burrow about for meaning when the magic and beauty of the sound are of themselves entrancing and irresistible? Such was evidently the opinion of the Cambridge undergraduates who swung down King's Parade with linked arms, chanting the famous chorus from *Atalanta in Calydon.*

> When the hounds of spring are on winter's traces.

Matthew Arnold's poetry, though less spectacular, is no less accomplished. *The Scholar Gipsy* and *Thyrsis* are two of the most perfect poems of the nineteenth century. No poet except perhaps Tennyson can evoke the atmosphere, the sights and sounds of a particular landscape with a touch so masterly and so economical.

Among the poets of the Edwardian Age Rupert Brooke (1887–1915) enjoyed a reputation that has not worn well. A. E. Housman, the great classical scholar, won fame as a poet with the staccato despondency of *A Shropshire Lad*, a book still widely read. Robert Bridges (1844–1930), later Poet Laureate, displayed a lyrical talent of a high order. A good example of his work is the sonnet, which can be found in most anthologies, beginning

> Whither, O splendid ship, thy white sails crowding
> Leaning across the bosom of the urgent West.

But the greatest poet then writing in English was not an Englishman. W. B. Yeats (1865–1939) was one of the leaders of that flowering of Irish genius which centred on the Abbey Theatre in Dublin. The best of Yeats' poetry was written after the close of the Edwardian Age, but his earliest writings proclaim his quality.

The dramatists of the Irish Revival made the fullest use of the inherited riches of Irish peasant speech. The comedies of J. M. Synge (1871–1909), and notably *The Playboy of the Western World*, are still as fresh and colourful as at their first performance. The lilting rhythms and unexpected turns of phrase have an attraction that is timeless.

It was to Ireland that the English theatre owed the greatest of her comic writers. Oscar Wilde (1865–1900) is the outstanding playwright of the Late Victorian Age. His wit never turns flat. *The Importance of Being Earnest* is perhaps the most popular comedy in the language and is certainly one of the best. Hardly less amusing are *Lady Windermere's Fan* and *An Ideal Husband*. The Celtic fantasy of Wilde's humour playing over the solid Anglo-Saxon aristocracy of the Late Victorian Age is an endless delight. In his own peculiar field Wilde could have neither rival nor successor. The farces of Sir Arthur Pinero (1855–1934) held pride of place in the period between Wilde's last play and the outbreak of the first world war. Their deft construction and finished workmanship have stood the test of revival. Pinero also won a considerable reputation as a serious dramatist dealing with moral and social problems. The most famous of his plays, *The Second Mrs. Tanqueray*, is of this sort.

The treatment of specific problems of contemporary life on the English stage derives from Ibsen, whose plays were translated and performed in London from the end of the seventies. Pinero was deeply influenced by Ibsen but an even more enthusiastic disciple was George Bernard Shaw (1856–1950). Plain speaking in public on unpleasant subjects was not relished: Ibsen's *Ghosts* and Shaw's *Mrs. Warren's Profession* were long banned from the English stage. As Ibsen angrily pointed out in *An Enemy of the People* the reaction of society towards those who tried to cure its ills was to attack the doctor for saying there was anything wrong. Shaw did not reach the height of his popularity until after the Great War but much of his best work belongs to this period.

The Late Victorian stage was wider in range and richer in talent than it had been in the first half of the reign. But with the Late Victorian novel it is the other way round. Kipling's charming fantasies and clear, absorbing narratives of army life in India seem sure of immortality; so does the easy, pleasant humour of Somerville and Ross's *Experiences of an Irish R.M.*; so, too, the robust early novels of H. G. Wells (1866–1946) like *Kipps* and *The History of Mr*

*Polly*. None of these, however, can take rank with the Titans of Early Victorian fiction. Alone among their contemporaries Robert Louis Stevenson (1850–1894) and Thomas Hardy (1840–1928) achieved greatness. Of Stevenson's stories *Treasure Island* is deservedly the best known. He is the most exact stylist of all the nineteenth-century novelists: there are no slack phrases, no words which are not pulling their weight. Like his fellow Scot, John Buchan, he seems to have been a born story-teller. His stature as a novelist is, however, surpassed by Thomas Hardy. Hardy did for the countryside of South-West England what Scott had done for the Border country. His pages embalm the villages and country towns of Dorset and the surrounding counties as they were in the nineteenth century. A whole way of life is chronicled with a minuteness that never becomes boring and with an affection that never obscures the sharpness of the vision. As a creator of character Hardy is supreme: Gabriel Oak in *Far From the Madding Crowd* and Michael Henchard in *The Mayor of Casterbridge* have the depth and intensity of a portrait by Rembrandt.

Two of the greatest critics and essayists of this age have already been mentioned in this chapter—Pater and Matthew Arnold. As critics and as stylists they are the reverse of each other. Pater in an intricate, carefully modulated prose pleaded passionately for the cause of art as an end in itself. Matthew Arnold in straightforward, vigorous English maintained the view that art—and especially poetry—should serve as "a criticism of life". By this he meant that it should explain man to himself. The merits of this controversy cannot be examined here; but the merit of the essays in which these opinions are expressed is very great. The Edwardian Age produced two fine essayists in Hilaire Belloc and G. K. Chesterton, whose work is distinguished by its pungency and gusto. With the coming of the twentieth century the amplitude of the Victorian essay begins to contract. The eighteenth-century virtues of pithiness, succinctness and point become fashionable once again. The wit and grace of Sir Max Beerbohm's essays would have delighted the Augustans.

The period is flooded with Memoirs and Biographies. As in our own day anyone of any eminence who did not take the precaution of writing his own life was sure to have it done for him. And at what length! Bishops were usually good for a fat volume, politicians for two or even three. The climax was reached with Sir Theodore Martin's life of the Prince Consort which extends over two thousand five hundred pages. As Lady Bracknell remarks in *The Importance of Being Earnest* "A life crowded with incident". By the end of the nineteenth century the production of the standard biography of the Distinguished Man had become an established industry. To select among such a mass of material is almost impossible, but Lord Morley's *Life of Cobden* (1881) and *Life of Gladstone* (1903) are perhaps worth mentioning, as is Winston Churchill's *Life of Lord Randolph Churchill* (1906).

The Autobiographies of the time include those of three outstanding Early Victorians. Those of Trollope (1883) and John Stuart Mill (1873), which were published posthumously, are among the most interesting in our literature. But the third one, Cardinal Newman's *Apologia pro vita sua* (1864) is a masterpiece of an unusual kind. Provoked by a blundering and stupid attack on his good faith, Newman replied by giving a complete and candid history of his religious opinions from his childhood to his old age. It is one of the most sensitive and exact records that we have of the movements of a single human mind, expressed in language of rare lucidity and grace. What it must have cost a man of his haughty and reserved temper to lay open the secrets of his heart can only be imagined. But it is the consciousness of this inward struggle, in which the deepest convictions will be content with no half-truths, no glossing over painful memories, that makes the book great. To read it is to see and feel the collision of the ideas of the age from inside the age itself.

Of all the fields of Late Victorian literature perhaps the richest was history. The great names grow thick: Stubbs and Maitland, Acton and Bury, Lecky and Gardiner, Froude and J. R. Green. Between them they changed the whole study of history. Lecky, Froude and Green followed the trail blazed by Macaulay. That is to say they wrote detailed and vivid narratives of English history, based on wide reading and coloured by fashionable Whig prejudice. Froude (1818–1894) concentrated on the sixteenth and Lecky (1838–1903) on the eighteenth century while J. R. Green produced in 1874 his *Short History of the English People* intended primarily for the educated working man. All three wrote excellent, clear, readable English and their works show every sign of surviving, although subsequent research has thrown a different light on many of their conclusions and has uncovered a great deal that they did not know.

Acton (1834–1902) and Bury (1861–1927) were the prophets of a new scientific school of history of which the German historian Ranke was the founder. "History", proclaimed Bury in his inaugural lecture as Professor at Cambridge, "is a science, no less and no more." Much ink has since been spilt on the question whether history is a science or an art, and the controversy seems to have died away in a general agreement that it is both. But what Acton and Bury were pleading for was an impartial approach by the historian. Let him unearth the facts and then let the facts speak for themselves. This doctrine is not as simple as it looks. In many cases it is not at all clear what the facts are. If the historian accepts one version and rejects another—as in practice he must—he has compromised his impartiality. Again even supposing the facts to be well established the conclusion that the reader will draw from them depends to a great extent on their selection and arrangement—in fine, on the historian's presentation of them. But, whether or not scientific history is a goal that is humanly attainable, there can be no doubt that modern historical scholarship has benefited enormously from the insistence of the scientific historian on documents as opposed to memoirs, pamphlets, hearsay and the like.

The greatest of the nineteenth-century historians was William Stubbs (1825–1901), Bishop of Oxford. As one of his contemporaries pointed out, what was even more remarkable than his vast learning was the way in which he could bring it all to bear on a single point. As the historian of the English Constitution he is without a rival and without fear of one. It was he who explored that undiscovered country and the maps he made are still the most reliable. Stubbs is perhaps as good an example as any of the astonishing energy of the Victorians. Not only was he the first historian of the day but also an exemplary bishop who never shirked the tedious routine work of running a diocese. Besides this, tradition has it that he was an avid reader of novels. In an age when such time-saving expedients as the telephone and the short-hand typist were unknown it is all the more marvellous.

If Stubbs was the greatest, Maitland (1850–1906) was unquestionably the most brilliant historian working in this period. The sort of
questions he asked—"What was the Domesday Survey meant to
do? What did people mean when they said a piece of land belonged
to a town?"—opened a new and fascinating approach to the dusty
problems of legal history. His large, humorous, sensible mind makes
what appeared abstruse and technical at once interesting and alive.
Although he wrote about subjects which, in so far as they were
known at all, were the closed preserve of the expert, he is never dull,
never obscure, never pedantic. Of all the figures of this golden
age of English historical writing he is the model most worthy of
imitation.

## CHAPTER IX

# FOREIGN POLICY, 1870–1918

## 1. The Age of Bismarck, 1870–1890

THE year 1870 is a most significant one in the history of British foreign policy, for it witnessed France's defeat by Germany and the beginning of a new balance of power on the Continent. "Europe", said Lord Morley, "has lost a mistress and found a master." After the Congress of Vienna (1815) Germany consisted of a considerable number of independent states. Like Italy it longed to become a united nation; but whereas the Italians achieved unity by their own effort, the Germans achieved it by the sword of Prussia. The King of Prussia, William I, was persuaded by his Chancellor Bismarck that the unification of Germany could only be accomplished by means of "blood and iron". In pursuit of this policy the Prussians in 1864 seized the Duchies of Schleswig and Holstein from Denmark. Two years later Austria was invaded and rapidly defeated. At the ensuing Peace of Prague a confederation of North German States was established under Prussian leadership, and Austria was excluded from further participation in German affairs. The final step towards the creation of a united German Empire was taken after the collapse of France in 1871. In the Hall of Mirrors at Versailles, the princes who had not already joined the North German Confederation acclaimed the King of Prussia as Emperor of Germany.

The struggle between France and Prussia which broke out in 1870 was really fought to decide which power was to be supreme in Europe; although the immediate cause of the war was a disputed succession to the Spanish throne. Contrary to nearly everybody's expectations the Prussians won the war after a series of swift, overwhelming victories. Napoleon III was taken prisoner, Paris capitulated after a desperate siege, and despite heroic attempts to rally their forces in the provinces, the French were compelled to make peace. On May 10th, 1871, they signed the Treaty of Frankfort, which forced France to pay an enormous indemnity to the victor and to hand over the frontier provinces of Alsace and Lorraine. "It was over two centuries since France had arisen on the ruins of Spain and of the Holy Roman Empire as the strongest power in Europe. Only six months before that position was still apparently unshaken. But on January 18th, 1871, the German Empire had been proclaimed in that Palace of Versailles, built by the great king whose proud motto had been *nec pluribus impar*—'not unequal to several'. That France was dead beyond hope of resurrection."[1]

Having defeated France and united Germany, Bismarck declared that his country was a "sated power" whose only desire was to live in peace with her neighbours. France, he realized, was unlikely to regard her defeat with complacency. "What we have gained by arms in six months", he said, "we shall have to defend by arms for fifty years." In order to prevent France from seeking revenge, Bismarck directed all his energies to keeping her diplomatically isolated. "We have to prevent France finding an ally. As long as France has no allies she is not dangerous to Germany." By 1873 Bismarck had managed to combine Austria and Russia in the *Dreikaiserbund*, or League of Three Emperors. This pact guaranteed Russian and Austrian neutrality should France, or any other power, attack Germany. It thus freed the Germans from the fear of having to fight a war on two fronts. In negotiating the treaty Bismarck emphasized that the Third Republic, established in France after the capture of Napoleon III, encouraged revolution and anarchy, and constituted a dangerous threat to monarchy. In many ways the *Dreikaiserbund* was a very delicate mechanism, particularly as Austria and Russia had conflicting ambitions in the Balkans. It often required all Bismarck's skill to prevent his two partners from falling out. Such harmony as he managed to secure was achieved by playing on European fears of France. In the end Russia withdrew from the League because of her rivalry with Austria. Even then she preferred for some time to remain in dangerous isolation, rather than make an alliance with republican France.

When the Franco-Prussian War broke out English sympathy was on the Prussian side; partly because France was regarded as the aggressor and partly because the Prussians were Protestants. But

[1] D. W. Brogan: *The Development of Modern France 1870–1939.*

when Paris was being besieged and the French armies had been defeated at Sedan and Metz, most people began to regard the Germans as conquerors and to sympathize with the French. Gladstone and his colleagues remained strictly neutral, although soon after the war broke out, the Government, after making it perfectly clear that violation of Belgian neutrality by either side would bring Britain into the war against the aggressor, managed to persuade the combatants to reaffirm the guarantee of Belgian neutrality which both had given in 1839.[1]

Apart from Britain's intervention on behalf of Belgium there was one other repercussion of the Franco-Prussian War which forced the Foreign Secretary, Lord Granville, to take decisive action. In order to keep both England and Russia distracted and thus reduce the danger of their interfering in the war, Bismarck in 1870 suggested to Prince Gortchakov, the Russian Chancellor, that the time had come to repudiate the clauses of the Treaty of Paris (1856) in which Russia had promised not to use warships in the Black Sea, a concession for which Palmerston had continued the Crimean war six months. When Prussian victories made it evident that France was not in a position to help Britain enforce the clauses, Gortchakov renounced them. The Government had then to decide whether to fight Russia single-handed in order to maintain a treaty already partly unobserved (for example, the Sultan of Turkey had made extraordinarily little effort to give his Christian subjects in the Balkans equal rights with his Moslem subjects) or whether to submit to the principle that treaty obligations lasted only so long as it was convenient to observe them. In the end a conference was held in London (January 1871) and a protocol was signed which asserted that no single power could free itself from any of the stipulations of a treaty, unless it had obtained the previous consent of other powers concerned. However, Britain had to give her consent to the repeal of the Black Sea clauses, and so a negotiation was concluded which saved Britain's face and gave the Russians what they wanted.

It is very difficult to see what else Gladstone and Granville could have done. Yet many Englishmen grumbled that Palmerston in

[1] See page 71.

similar circumstances would never have been frightened by Russian threats. Undoubtedly one of Gladstone's merits was that he accepted so literally the Liberal slogan "Peace, Retrenchment and Reform". Nevertheless the Peace that he unfailingly pursued was not always popular, for example when he refused to send an expedition to relieve General Gordon.[1] What Englishmen really desired was to play a conspicuous part in the councils of Europe, without risking the war which such a policy might easily bring about, and without paying for the army which alone could win them a hearing. Much of the popularity of Disraeli was derived from the dexterity with which he contrived to satisfy these apparently irreconcilable desires.

After the general election of 1874, Disraeli succeeded Gladstone as Prime Minister, and Derby succeeded Granville as Foreign Secretary. In 1875, Disraeli bought £4,000,000 worth of Suez Canal shares. This purchase gave England a new interest in Egypt and soon became an important factor in our foreign policy. The Suez Canal had been constructed by a French engineer, Ferdinand de Lesseps, and the venture had been originated, financed and organized by a French company. The ruler of Egypt, the Khedive Ismail, owned almost half its shares. But owing to his oriental extravagance, which included commissioning Verdi to write the opera Aïda to celebrate the opening of the Canal, he decided to sell out. Parliament at the time was not in session. Consequently Disraeli, on the advice of a journalist called Frederick Greenwood and contrary to the advice of several members of the Cabinet, borrowed the sum from his friends the Rothschilds and purchased the shares. Not only was this a brilliant financial investment, the original capital sum being repaid seven times over in interest within fifty years, but it was also a masterly piece of strategy which greatly extended our control of the Mediterranean and eventually Egypt. Most important of all it secured our lines of communication with our eastern possessions.

As was shown by the purchase of the Suez Canal shares, Disraeli fully appreciated the importance of our sea route to India. When in 1878 the Russians appeared at the gates of Constantinople, he felt

---

[1] See page 250.

that the time for decisive action had arrived. After all, the Crimean War had been fought in order to frustrate Russia's traditional ambition to capture Constantinople, to dominate the Straits, and thus to penetrate into the Mediterranean.

The trouble began in 1875 when the Bosnians revolted against Turkey. In the following year their example was followed by Serbia and Bulgaria. The Sultan of Turkey, Abdul Hamid II, confronted with widespread rebellion, suppressed the Bulgar revolt with the utmost ferocity. The Bashi-Bazouks, a regiment of savage, irregular cavalry, were let loose on the population. Soon stories of massacres, pillage and torture reached Britain. Relying on misinformation received from Sir Henry Elliott, the British Ambassador at Constantinople, Disraeli tried to discredit these atrocity stories. Unfortunately for himself, as they happened to be only too true, he described them as "coffee-house babble" and "to a large extent inventions".

Gladstone, highly incensed by the way in which the Government had sided with the Turks, emerged from retirement. In a famous pamphlet entitled "The Bulgarian Horrors and the Question of the East" he demanded that the Turks should "clear bag and baggage from the provinces they have desolated and profaned". Within a week 40,000 copies of this pamphlet had been sold. Then, in a series of speeches delivered all over the country, he denounced the Turks and the sympathy which Disraeli had shown towards them. The indignation which he provoked did greater credit to the public's morals than to its intelligence. If we had stood wholeheartedly behind Turkey the Russians probably would not have intervened. As it was, they marched into the Balkans in April 1877 to "liberate" the subjects of Abdul Hamid from the intolerable tyranny or Turkish misrule. Disraeli, not without some justification, blamed Gladstone for what had happened, since he had given the Russians such a perfect excuse, under the guise of philanthropy, to fulfil their ancient ambition to capture Constantinople. Moreover Gladstone had worked up English public opinion to such a frenzy that any attempt to protect the Turks from the Russians had become unthinkable. Nobody, of course, realized this better than the Russians.

THE BALKANS

The Czar had hesitated to go to war with Turkey, but since Serbia, Bosnia and Bulgaria had been encouraged in their nationalist revolt by Russian promises, he felt obliged to assist them, particularly when they appeared to be on the verge of collapse. The Turks, after a gallant defence at Plevna, were defeated by sheer weight of numbers. The Treaty of San Stefano, signed in March 1878, imposed terms so severe to Turkey and so advantageous to Russia, that they proved to be utterly unacceptable both to Britain and to Austria.

The valour with which the Turks resisted attack and the manifest aim of Russia to become a Mediterranean power, produced a change in the popular attitude towards Turkey, and the Bulgarian atrocities were almost forgotten. A British fleet was sent to the Sea of Marmora and Indian troops were sent to Malta. The Queen bristled with imperious indignation. She told Disraeli that "if England is to kiss Russia's feet, the Queen will lay down her crown. Oh, if the Queen were a Man she would like to go and give those Russians such a beating"! From every music-hall the Czar was reminded:

> We don't want to fight;
> But by Jingo, if we do,
> We've got the men, we've got the ships,
> We've got the money too.

Fortunately there was to be no occasion to employ these resources.

Lord Derby, who was more pacific than his sovereign, regarded the Prime Minister's measures as too warlike and in April 1878 he resigned. Lord Salisbury, who succeeded him at the Foreign Office, immediately suggested that a conference should meet to revise the Treaty of San Stefano. The fact that this meeting took place in Berlin, where Bismarck described himself as "an honest broker" showed the extent to which France had been eclipsed by Germany. In fact, most of the decisions attributed to the Congress of Berlin were reached by previous secret agreements. Nevertheless Disraeli, who attended the Congress in person, had to order a special train and threaten to leave Berlin, before he got all that he wanted.

The Congress completely undid the Russian settlement of San Stefano. Austria was allowed to occupy Bosnia–Herzegovina, and

Russian power in the Balkans was reduced by the partition of Bulgaria, which otherwise seemed likely to become a Russian dependency. Great Britain was given Cyprus as a naval base from which her ships could steam to the protection of Constantinople and the Straits.

When Disraeli returned to London he told the crowds waiting outside Charing Cross Station that he had brought them "Peace with honour". The dangerous crisis had passed and the European peace which he had helped to establish lasted over thirty-five years. Yet if the flames had been extinguished, the fire still smouldered. Balkan nationalism remained eruptive, and Russian rivalry with Austria gradually led the Czar to reject the *Dreikaiserbund* and to ally himself with France, thus dividing the world into two armed camps. In 1879 Germany and Austria signed a secret treaty, later known as the Dual Alliance, agreeing to remain benevolently neutral if either were attacked by a third power, for example, France. If, however, Russia were the aggressor, then the power which had not been attacked promised to come to the other's assistance, with its whole war strength. Bismarck suggested this alliance because he feared that Russia would eventually withdraw from the *Dreikaiserbund*. This fear was not unreasonable since the Czar had openly stated that he regarded the Congress of Berlin as a "European coalition against Russia under the leadership of Prince Bismarck". Moreover what Bismarck anticipated actually occurred. In 1882 Italy joined the German-Austrian alliance. This group of powers remained known as the Triple Alliance despite the fact that Rumania soon became a member. Two years later, although the Czar must have been partly aware of what had been going on behind his back, the league of Three Emperors was renewed, as it turned out for the last time. Bismarck's extremely intricate alliances were intended to promote German security. Because Austria and Russia were allied to Germany, France was kept isolated; and because Russia and Austria were such quarrelsome associates, Germany was insured against all emergencies by the secret triple alliance.

In order to entice Italy into the German system of alliances, Bismarck encouraged France to occupy Tunis. Its seizure in 1881 infuriated Italy, who had regarded Tunis for some time with hungry eyes. Moreover when Bizerta became a French port she was encircled by French naval bases (e.g. Toulon and Corsica). On joining the Triple Alliance, Italy insisted that the Treaty should include a clause stating that the alliance was in no way aimed at England. From the first her allegiance to Austria and Germany was conditioned by her respect for English sea-power, and when war between England and Germany eventually broke out Italy's defection to the allied side was not altogether unexpected. A little later Bismarck encouraged the British occupation of Egypt, which, as he desired, led to twenty years of strained relations between France and England.

In 1887 both the League of Three Emperors and the Triple Alliance were due for renewal. Both alliances were threatening to disintegrate. But the Triple Alliance was held together because Bismarck persuaded Lord Salisbury to sign a naval agreement with Italy. This agreement made Italy a much more desirable partner for Austria, particularly as Britain's well-known fear of Russian expansion might eventually lead her to support Austria's Balkan schemes. Bismarck first proposed an Anglo-Italian treaty in a conversation with the British Ambassador in Berlin. He told the Ambassador that "if England persists in withdrawing from all participation in European politics we shall have no further reason to withhold our approval of French desires in Egypt, or those of Russia in the Far East however far they go". Salisbury thought that Bismarck had proposed "a desirable grouping of the powers", and agreements with Italy were signed in 1887 and 1888, promising "in general and to the extent that circumstances shall permit, mutual support in the Mediterranean in every difference which may rise between one of the signatories and a third power".

Although the Triple Alliance had been renewed with Lord Salisbury's assistance, Bismarck could do nothing to persuade Russia to renew the *Dreikaiserbund*. The Czar's relations with Austria had steadily deteriorated, and a Bulgarian crisis in 1886 had nearly involved the two countries in war. Russia, however, did sign a separate "Reinsurance" Treaty with Germany in 1887. This Treaty, like the Dual Alliance of 1879, was to be kept a profound secret. Bismarck in fact had violated the secrecy of the Dual Alliance by revealing its provisions to Russia in order to show the Czar how completely isolated he was and how desirable it was for him to come to terms with Germany. The Reinsurance Treaty guaranteed the *status quo* in the Balkans, and provided that if Russia were attacked by Austria, Germany would remain neutral and if Germany were attacked by France, Russia would remain neutral.

The Kaiser died in 1888, and after the short reign of Frederick III, was succeeded by William II. The new Emperor soon quarrelled with Bismarck, who consequently resigned in 1890. Having "dropped the pilot" William II embarked upon a policy all his own. Even had he wished to continue Bismarck's policy he would probably have been unable to do so, for it needed a man of the Chancellor's genius and prestige to maintain his precarious balance of alliances. By leaving France humiliated and alone Bismarck kept her desire for revenge at white heat, and by trying to combine incompatible elements in his alliances, he attempted the impossible. Nevertheless he shares with Frederick the Great the distinction of having created modern Germany.

Before Bismarck fell from power he approached Salisbury in 1889 about an Anglo-German alliance. The Prime Minister, anxious as always to avoid European commitments, replied that it was impossible to bind future Parliaments by a definite treaty. So, apart from the Mediterranean agreement, Britain had no European alliances. This policy of isolation lasted until the signing of the Anglo-Japanese Treaty in 1902. But our position in the Mediterranean, our policy towards Turkey, imperial rivalry in Africa, India and the Far East and above all German naval competition, made it more and more difficult for us to remain aloof.

## 2. The Growth of Rival Alliances, 1890–1908

Twenty years after the humiliation of 1871, French resentment remained unabated. The German Empire had offered France nothing but insults and threats, but so long as she remained isolated she was powerless to protest effectively. After the Congress of Berlin, Russia began to realize that partnership with Bismarck involved submission to Germany. Obviously the solution to the problems of

France and Russia lay in an alliance. For a time the Czar was reluctant to face this conclusion as he regarded the Third Republic as atheistic and revolutionary, but in the end it was forced upon him, mainly by German policy.

In 1890 William II refused to renew the Reinsurance Treaty, thus leaving Russia without an ally. Moreover large increases in the German army in 1888 had been justified to the Reichstag (the German parliament) on the grounds that "the Russian tradition demanded an advance to the Straits and Constantinople, even if the road were through Berlin. We cannot sacrifice Austria to gain temporary concessions from Russia. In these circumstances we must be prepared for a war on two fronts". The "new course" on which the Kaiser told the world he proposed to sail drove a reluctant Russia into a French alliance.

Russian finances, always insecure and mismanaged, had been buttressed for years by German loans. In 1890 these stopped abruptly, and Paris bankers rushed to the rescue. The French army manœuvres of the same year greatly impressed foreign observers and the Russians were not slow to notice how fully the French had recovered. In 1892 the French fleet visited Kronstadt, and Alexander III stood bareheaded while a Russian band played the Marseillaise. Two years later, soon after Alexander's death, his son, Nicholas II, visited the French President. While he was staying in Paris, one newspaper rapturously declared that the French army's message to him was *"Quand vous voudrez!"*

The Franco-Russian Treaty of 1894 which was the permanent expression of all this cordiality, provided for mutual defence in case of attack, that the terms of the Treaty should be kept a close secret, and that it should last as long as the Triple Alliance. Except for England, the great powers had now ranged themselves into the two camps, the Dual and Triple Alliances, which were to come into conflict in 1914.

Englishmen regarded the Franco-Russian Alliance with some misgivings. Both powers were traditional enemies and the precedent of such an alliance, the Treaty of Tilsit 1807, was not one to inspire confidence. Wherever the interests of France and England clashed, as they did particularly in Morocco, Egypt and Siam, the French pursued a policy of pin-pricks. Two incidents may be taken as typical. In July 1893 a French naval squadron ordered British gunboats to withdraw from Siam. For forty-eight hours it seemed probable that this action would lead to war, which was only avoided by a timely apology and explanation. Again in 1893 the arrival of a French expedition at Fashoda in the Sudan,[1] despite previous British warnings that such an expedition "would be an unfriendly act and would be so viewed by England", led to a serious crisis.

The Liberal party was sharply divided on Foreign and Colonial policy, a cleavage which widened during the Boer war. The Conservative victory at the khaki election (1900) was partly the result of this division. Lord Rosebery, Asquith and Sir Edward Grey were "liberal imperialists", who favoured a policy of expansion and self-assertion. On the other hand "little Englanders", like Sir William Harcourt and Morley, were virtually pacifists. Rosebery believed in continuity of foreign policy despite party changes, whereas Morley wished to reverse the policy pursued since the Congress of Berlin by both parties, and to renounce the Palmerston tradition in foreign affairs.

Although the Conservative party was not divided on foreign policy, it had begun to wonder whether isolation was not becoming dangerous. Nearly every great power had bitterly resented our alleged oppression of the Boers, but owing to our overwhelming supremacy at sea none of them dared intervene. However when the Germans began to build a fleet, and when our interests in the Far East were challenged by Russian expansion in Manchuria, it became clear that we might not be strong enough to deal with these new threats single-handed.

As has already been noted, the Anglo-Japanese Alliance (1902) marked an important revolution in Britain's foreign policy. From the early seventeenth century until 1858, Japan had refused to have any contact with the European world. Then in 1858 she was forced to open her ports to foreign trade by an American squadron under Commodore Perry. During the last quarter of the nineteenth century a unique transformation took place. Japan changed from a medieval

[1] See page 254.

Asiatic power into a modern, westernized state. A Parliament was established, universities were built and an up-to-date army and navy were organized with the help of Germany and England. Just as industrial demands for raw materials and markets had led European powers to open up Africa, so Japanese manufacturers determined to exploit the vast resources and opportunities of the mainland opposite. This naturally brought Japan into conflict with China and Russia. The Kaiser encouraged the Czar to look eastwards, because, as he explained to the Emperor of Austria, "if we can keep Russia tied down in Eastern Asia, Germany will not have to fear an attack by France, nor Austria a revolt in the Balkans". Russia, frustrated in her attempts to get a warm water port in the near and Middle East,[1] was ready to accept the Kaiser's suggestion and began to build the Trans-Siberian Railway.

In 1894 the Japanese drove the Chinese out of Korea, destroyed their navy, crossed into Manchuria and seized Port Arthur. Russia, Germany and France, thinking themselves threatened by the completeness of this victory, compelled Japan to return part of her conquests. China, like Turkey, was a declining empire, unable to defend herself effectively, and therefore all the more tempting to unscrupulous neighbours. Despite the apparent regard of the European powers for the integrity of Chinese soil, it soon transpired that their consciences were sensitive only when Japan was the aggressor. Soon a scramble for China took place. By the end of 1898 Russia had occupied Port Arthur and Manchuria, while Germany seized the port of Kiao Chow. Britain, who had carried on an important trade with China for a considerable time, determined not to be outdone. Consequently she leased Wei-hai-wei as a naval base (1898) and began to consider an alliance with Japan, who was equally eager to halt Russian expansion.

The Anglo-Japanese Treaty was signed on January 30, 1902. Japan turned to England as the old enemy of Russia, as the greatest sea power, and as the chief nation who had not conspired in 1896 to deprive her of the spoils of victory. When the Czar demanded the ending of Japanese influence in Korea, Count Hayashi hurried to

[1] e.g. By the Congress of Berlin 1878 and the Penjdeh Settlement (1885) by which Britain prevented Russian infiltration into Afghanistan.

London and negotiated the Treaty with Lord Lansdowne, the Foreign Secretary. This upheld the *status quo* in China and Korea and provided for protection of British and Japanese interests in the Far East. It was also agreed that if either power should go to war to protect these interests, the other should remain neutral, but if a third power should join the struggle, then both partners of the Treaty would resist the attack (e.g. if Russia attacked Japan, Britain would remain neutral, but if France came to the Czar's assistance, then Britain would be obliged to support Japan). The Treaty emphasized Japan's position as a civilized power, while it relieved the strain on British naval resources in the Pacific and helped to maintain the "open door" to commerce with China.

In 1904 Japan suddenly occupied North Korea and destroyed a Russian fleet in Korean waters before its commander realized that the war had begun. In 1905 Port Arthur was captured, Manchuria invaded, and the Russians routed at the battle of Mukden. When the Russian Baltic Fleet at last arrived on the scene (having already created a serious incident on the way by firing at the Lowestoft fishing fleet, which it mistook for Japanese gun-boats) it was sunk by Admiral Togo within half an hour. This battle of Tsushima finished the war. By the Treaty of Portsmouth (1905) Russia surrendered her lease of Port Arthur to Japan, evacuated Manchuria, and recognized Korea as a Japanese sphere of interest. (Korea was formally annexed by Japan in 1910.)

The Japanese victory over Russia amazed the rest of the world. It is doubtful if Japan would have embarked on the war without the security of her alliance with Britain. The effects of the victory were world wide. In Asiatic countries, particularly India, it was represented as a victory of the East over the West; it turned Russia's attention from the Far East back to the Near East; it reduced the value of the Russian alliance in the eyes of France and encouraged her to seek a closer understanding with Britain.

Although the Anglo-Japanese Treaty (1902) removed many of the dangers of British isolation in the Far East, it did not dispense with her need for allies in the West. Many British ministers, foremost among them Joseph Chamberlain, advocated an alliance with Germany. Between 1898 and 1901 several overtures were made to the Kaiser but with little success. "John Bull", he said, "wants some-one to help him out of his fix."

The Anglo-German negotiations broke down for a variety of reasons. The Kaiser's attitude towards the Boers, as manifested in the Kruger telegram,[1] was hardly likely to create good feelings between Britain and Germany. The German naval schemes of 1898 and 1900 whereby Tirpitz, the Navy Minister, planned to build a great fleet, was regarded as a direct threat to our supremacy at sea. The diplomatic methods of Baron Holstein, the permanent Secretary of the German Foreign Office, were calculated to destroy the most promising negotiations. Moreover it had become only too clear that the "new course" was a departure from Bismarck's conception of Germany as a "sated" power. For example, Bismarck had de-clared that the Balkans were not worth "the bones of a single Pomeranian soldier", but William II projected a Berlin–Bagdad Railway, and entered into friendly relations with Turkey. Bismarck, who recognized far more clearly than Tirpitz or Hol-stein, the limits of Germany's power, told Tirpitz that it was folly to irritate Britain by naval competition, unless Russia was Ger-many's ally. Otherwise Britain would be driven into the Dual Alliance, Italy would detach herself from the Triple Alliance, and Germany and Austria would be confronted with the overwhelming might of France, Italy, Russia and Britain. Bismarck's advice was ignored and his prophecy fulfilled.

There were a great many difficulties to be cleared away before any understanding could be reached between Britain and France. However, Germany's rejection of Chamberlain's advances con-fronted Britain with the choice of isolation or settlement. France was our traditional enemy, she had opposed us in extending our Empire and she had sympathized with the Boers. In 1893 in Siam and in 1898 at Fashoda, we had been on the brink of war. Disputes over fishing rights in Newfoundland, rivalry in Indo-China and the fact that France was allied to Russia, were all stumbling blocks. But when the French saw the friction created between Germany and England by the building of a German fleet, they seized the oppor-tunity to negotiate a treaty. In 1903 Edward VII's visit to Paris

[1] See page 254.

was a diplomatic triumph. Everywhere his charm and bearing won the hearts of Frenchmen; and when in the same year President Loubet repaid the visit, the first phase of a diplomatic revolution was completed.

After many delicate negotiations it was agreed in 1904 that France and Britain would guarantee each other diplomatic support on Moroccan and Egyptian problems and a number of old grievances were cleared up. Since no precise obligations were contracted the arrangement was known as an "*entente*", rather than as a "treaty" or "alliance"; but as far as Germany was concerned, we had become a partner of the 1894 Dual Alliance. The British public thoroughly approved of the negotiations, and the signing of the *entente* was regarded as a Conservative triumph.

Early in 1905 the Germans decided to break up the *entente* by challenging the French in Morocco. Since Russia had just been defeated by Japan, the Germans no longer feared a war on two fronts, and consequently were prepared to take considerable risks. In March the Kaiser visited Tangier in his yacht, encouraged the Sultan to protest against the French occupation of his kingdom, and demanded a conference of all the interested powers. At first the French Foreign Minister, Delcassé, resisted this German pressure, but when it was made clear that such resistance would involve war, he was forced to yield. Many Germans were disappointed by this peaceful settlement. "No waiting ten or twenty years for a world war", they argued; "now is the time to settle with France by force." But war in fact was delayed for nine years, partly because the French gave in, but partly because Germany lost her nerve.

The Liberal Party, which had been returned to power in December 1905, carried on their predecessors' policy. Naval and military discussions soon took place between Britain and France, and Britain supported her ally at the conference demanded by the Germans, which was held at Algeciras in 1906. The Germans, finding that Italy supported Britain and that Austria was uninterested in Morocco, were compelled to be conciliatory. Nevertheless by threatening France in Morocco, the one region where England had promised her diplomatic support, Germany unintentionally drew the two powers together and converted the *entente* into a much closer union.

The aggressive nature of German diplomacy towards France, and her Navy Bill of 1906, which planned the building of six battle-cruisers and provided for the widening of the Kiel Canal, forced England to expand her own fleet and to find greater security in the Anglo-French *entente* by a closer understanding with Russia. That German diplomacy provoked Campbell-Bannerman's Government to re-arm and ally with Czarist Russia, two actions most strongly opposed to traditional Liberal policy, showed how incapable the Germans were of foreseeing the consequences of their own acts.

Desirable as it undoubtedly was to reach an Anglo-Russian *entente*, there were many difficulties in the way. England's traditional enmity to Russia, the Anglo-Japanese alliance, Liberal and Labour objections to Czarist autocracy, and disputes in Persia, Tibet and Afghanistan, all had to be considered. By 1907, after many months of negotiations, the British ambassador at St. Petersburg, Sir Arthur Nicolson, who represented all that was best in the old type of diplomat, had settled most of the outstanding differences. Both sides agreed to leave Tibet alone, the Russians consented to have no dealings with Afghanistan except through the British Government in India, and Russian and British spheres of interest were clearly defined in Persia. These agreements were cemented by the meeting of Edward VII and the Czar at Reval (1908).

As far as Britain was concerned the Anglo-Russian agreement merely cleared up a number of misunderstandings with Russia and helped to preserve the peace of Europe. But the Kaiser regarded the *entente* in a more sinister light. He saw himself as the victim of a conspiracy to "encircle" Germany. This suspicion and resentment led him in 1908 to attempt to break up the new alliance just as he had attempted to break up the Anglo-French *entente* in 1905.

While the Liberal Government sought security in better understanding with Russia, it also attempted to ease international tension by suggesting disarmament. The Germans, however, seeing in this proposal an attempt to perpetuate British naval supremacy, refused to consider it. Consequently Haldane at the War Office overhauled the British army, organized it as an expeditionary force, and established a general staff to plan operations and co-operate with the French. The navy was even more ruthlessly reformed by

Sir John Fisher. Since Germany, rather than France or Russia, was the potential enemy, naval bases were built on the North Sea, the disposition and relative strength of our Far Eastern and Mediterranean Fleets were altered to increase the effectiveness of the Home Fleet, and the construction of bigger and faster battleships of the Dreadnought class was begun in 1905.

In 1908 Europe was divided into two hostile camps: the Triple *entente* and the Triple Alliance. Given the formation of this rival group of powers, given the atmosphere of suspicion, mobilization and competitive armament, given the Balkan rivalry of Austria and Russia and given the fact that a war started by any one power would inevitably involve the others; it is hard to see how conflict could have been averted. It is also perhaps difficult to blame one power exclusively for the outbreak of hostilities in 1914.[1]

### 3. *The Period of Crisis, 1908–1914*

The period from 1908 to 1914 was one of repeated crises, any one of which might have started a war. The Bosnian crisis (1908), the Agadir crisis (1911) and the series of crises arising from the Balkan wars (1912–1913) were all tided over. But in 1914 statesmen proved powerless to localize a dispute between Serbia and Austria.

In 1878, at the time of the Congress of Berlin, Austria had occupied Bosnia-Herzegovina, which had previously been part of the Turkish Empire. In 1908 a revolution occurred in Turkey, a constitutional monarchy was established, and the administration was revitalized. Fearing that the Turks would attempt to recover Bosnia-Herzegovina, Austria in 1908 formally annexed the territory, thereby repudiating the Congress of Berlin. Serbia, the champion of the Slav peoples in the Balkans, realizing that the provinces were eager to become part of a great Slav state, determined to declare war on Austria and prevent the annexation. Serbia, however, could only wage war effectively with Russian assistance, and when the Czar was informed by the Kaiser that such support would immediately

---

[1] See page 206 for details of the clause, in the Treaty of Versailles, which forced Germany to accept the responsibility for beginning the war.

bring Germany into the war against her, he was forced to tell the Serbians that they would have to act alone. Consequently Serbia was compelled to climb down and recognize the annexation.

This German diplomatic victory was really a disaster in disguise. Without loss of prestige Russia could never again afford to be conciliatory over Serbia, as the events of 1914 were to show. Moreover Russia from that moment "regarded the consolidation of the *entente* as a matter of life and death". The Czar told Nicolson that the crisis had only served to strengthen the *entente*. "We must", he said, interlocking his fingers with significant emphasis, "keep closer and closer together". As the Anglo-French *entente* had been strengthened rather than weakened by German attempts in 1905 to destroy it, so also the Kaiser's plan to break up the Russian alliance achieved exactly the opposite result.

The whole period from 1908 to 1914 was one of constant peril, but certain crises stand out sharply against a background of rearmament, suspicion and fear. The Agadir crisis, for example, although trivial in itself, agitated the entire western world. In 1911 a French expedition occupied Fez in Morocco. Then, in response to appeals "from certain German merchants", the Kaiser sent a warship, the *Panther*, to Agadir, on the Moroccan coast. The Germans next told the French that they could do what they liked in Morocco provided Germany were compensated for not interfering by being given practically all the French Congo. Lloyd George, in a famous speech at the Mansion House, told the world in general and Germany in particular, that Britain would stand by France in any Moroccan dispute. Surprised by Britain's firm attitude, the Germans withdrew most of their demands and reached an agreement with France. But they neither forgave nor forgot this humiliation.

In 1912, Montenegro, Serbia, Greece and Bulgaria, members of the Balkan League, declared war on the Sultan, having first obtained the full approval of Russia. The moment was carefully chosen. Turkey in 1909 had gone to war with Albania which had rebelled against her rule, and in 1911 had tried to prevent Italy from seizing Tripoli. Turkey realized that she was utterly unable to repel the Italian invasion. Consequently she resigned her claim to Tripoli, renamed Libya by the victor, in the Treaty of Lausanne (1912).

Exhausted, defeated and demoralized, the declining Turkish Empire fell an easy prey to the Balkan League.

After several serious defeats, the Sultan appealed to the European powers who had interests in the Balkans. A truce, and a conference held in London, followed. The Turks, however, rejected the terms suggested, restarted the war and were again overwhelmingly beaten. At the ensuing peace they lost all their territory in Europe, except Constantinople itself. Soon the victors began to quarrel among themselves over the division of the spoils, and a second Balkan war began, between Greece, Serbia and Rumania on the one hand, and Bulgaria on the other. Bulgaria suffered the same fate as Turkey and by the Treaty of Budapest (1913) was deprived of much of her territory.

Serbia emerged from these two wars enriched by the spoils of victory, and filled with nationalist aspirations which, if successful, would involve the destruction of the Austrian Empire. Tension in the Balkans was high. Bulgaria and Turkey longed only for revenge. Serbia had grown ambitious and arrogant. Austria, frightened of Slav nationalism, was determined to yield no further. These two wars had not become European, partly because the Balkan League were so swiftly victorious that neither Russia nor Austria had time to intervene, and partly because Germany refused to give Austria all the support she expected. "I think" the Kaiser told the Archduke Ferdinand, the heir apparent to the Austrian Empire, "that you are rattling my sabre a little too loudly".

The final crisis began on June 28, 1914, when the Archduke Ferdinand and his wife were murdered by a Bosnian student, Gabriel Princip, at Sarajevo. His revolver was discovered to have been made in Belgrade, the capital of Serbia. Princip belonged to a secret terrorist organization known as the "Black Hand". This Society, dedicated to the encouragement of Slav nationalism and prepared to use any means to further it, had the general support of the Serbian Government, although it is unlikely that it knew in advance about this particular outrage. The Austrians decided to make the murder the pretext for crushing Serbian influence in the Balkans.

On July 2nd the Austrians told the Germans that they intended to send an ultimatum to Serbia; they did not, however, explain how

EURO

ESTONIA

Riga
LATVIA

LITHUANIA

°Vilna

AST
USSIA

°Tannenburg

Brest-Litovsk

°Warsaw

R   U   S   S   I   A

0          300
Miles

UKRAINE

eschen

GALICIA

KIA

BESSARABIA

TRIA-

Budapest

HUNGARY

TRANSYLVANIA

Temesvar

ROUMANIA

Bucharest

BLACK     SEA

OVINA

SERBIA

P. Danube

DOBRUDJA

ENEGRO

ALBANIA

BULGARIA

THRACE

Bosphorus

Constantinople

MACEDONIA

Salonika

Corfu

GREECE

Dardanelles

ANATOLIA

°Smyrna

T   U   R   K   E   Y

ORE 1914

excessive and provoking its demands were going to be. The Kaiser assured the Emperor that he could rely on German support. The Austrian ultimatum was delivered at Belgrade on July 23rd. The Serbians accepted all the terms of the ultimatum except the last, which demanded that Austrian representatives should be present at the trial of those concerned in the Archduke's murder. On July 28th Austria declared war on Serbia, allegedly because her ultimatum had been rejected, but really because she could not afford to lose the opportunity to attack Serbia whose nationalist propaganda was undermining her empire.

The day after the Austrian declaration of war, Russia began to mobilize. She had often supported Serbia in the past, and she was frightened by the enormous extension of Austrian power in the Balkans which would inevitably follow if Serbia were left to her fate. Germany attempted to prevent the war spreading. Urgent telegrams were sent to Austria "immediately and emphatically" recommending mediation. But although the Kaiser insisted that he declined "to be irresponsibly dragged into a world war" his objection came too late. On July 31st Germany sent Russia an ultimatum demanding demobilization within twelve hours and the next day the two countries were at war. Under the terms of the Dual Alliance of 1894 France was now obliged to come to her ally's assistance. The Germans, whose strategy entirely depended upon defeating France quickly before the Russian "steam roller" got under way, could not afford to wait for the moral advantage of appearing to be the victim of French aggression. On August 3rd Germany declared war on France.

Neither the 1904 *entente* with France nor the 1907 agreement with Russia bound Britain to any action in the situation which had arisen. Both Liberal and Conservative statesmen had repeatedly hesitated to bind future parliaments to definite pledges, particularly to pledges involving war. For some hours the French remained in doubt as to what action Britain would take. But the Germans left us no choice.

In order to avoid a war on two fronts, Germany had to defeat France as quickly as she had done in 1870. The weakest part of the French defence was along the Belgian frontier and consequently the main attack would have to involve the violation of Belgian neutrality. This took place on August 3rd. As we had guaranteed Belgian neutrality in 1839 by the Treaty of London Sir Edward Grey, the Foreign Secretary, telegraphed an ultimatum to Berlin, which expired, unanswered, on the night of August 4th.

The issue at stake was a very simple one, however involved and complicated the origin of the war might be. Germany had threatened our independence and our empire, by building a great fleet. She had attacked Belgium, whose coast was traditionally regarded as our first line of defence. Like Louis XIV and Napoleon, the Kaiser attempted to make himself supreme in Europe and upset the balance of power. It was to maintain that balance that we went to war.

## 4. The Great War, 1914–1918

The German high command had several years previously decided, if war came, to follow the Schlieffen plan. This proposed an advance through Belgium, an overwhelming attack on the French left wing, followed by the capture of Paris. The Germans could then attack the French right wing from the front and the rear simultaneously. A British Expeditionary Force, consisting of five divisions commanded by Sir John French, had been landed in France by August 20th. The Germans having shattered the gallant Belgian army, drove the allies back to the river Marne. The fall of Paris seemed imminent. But the impetus of the attack was over and by the end of September the Germans had been forced to retreat to the Aisne. Both sides began to dig themselves in, and except for the German break-through in 1918, the western front as then established remained much the same for the rest of the war. It was essential for Britain, if she were to retain her control of the Channel and keep her communications with France open, that the Germans should be forestalled in their attempt to capture the Channel ports. The Battle of Ypres, lasting several months, was fought to protect them. Although the "first hundred thousand" suffered devastating casualties. the Channel ports were saved.

The Battles of the Marne and Ypres frustrated the German plan to outflank the allies and to capture Paris by attacking through

Belgium. Early in 1915 both sides constructed a line of trenches from the Swiss frontier to the English Channel. Meanwhile, the Russians, who had invaded East Prussia at the very beginning of the war and had thereby diverted German troops from the western front, had been disastrously defeated by Hindenburg at the Battle of Tannenberg (August 1914). Although the Russians did the allies a great service in exhausting the enemies' manpower, they won very few victories, as their armies were ill-equipped and badly led.

In October 1914 Turkey joined Austria and Germany, hoping to destroy Russian influence in the Balkans. With Turkey as an enemy our communications with Russia were severed, and Egypt, the Suez Canal, and our oil supply from Persia were threatened.[1] The theatre of war was now enlarged to include the Middle East. Italy joined the allies in May 1915, but the price we had to pay in the secret Treaty of London to secure her support later proved a great embarrassment to us at the Treaty of Versailles.

As the war on the Western Front appeared to have become a deadlock, many people suggested that the best strategy was to find weak points elsewhere. What was the use of a frontal attack on the enemy's stronghold, which held out little hope of success, when there were so many back doors, some perhaps unguarded, through which it might be entered? The soldiers tended to advocate the concentration of all forces on the Western Front, particularly the French generals whose country would suffer if the Germans broke through, while politicians like Lloyd George and Winston Churchill recommended an attack in the east. An expedition was sent to the Dardanelles in 1915. This was intended to capture Constantinople, to join up with the Russians and to induce Bulgaria and other Balkan powers to support the allies. Despite unsurpassed gallantry, the Gallipoli campaign failed. The generals in the West were half-hearted, the essential element of surprise was lost, and the forces which could be spared were too small to achieve decisive results. Bulgaria, anxious to join Austria and Germany in obliterating Serbia, seeing the evacuation of the allied armies from Gallipoli, hesitated no longer and joined the Central powers. British casualties

[1] Persian oil was particularly important as the latest type of battleships such as the *Warspite* were oil-burning.

in the expedition numbered 112,000 men. On the Western Front a quarter of a million men were killed in the battle of Neuve Chapelle, a heavy price to pay for a few miles of mud and craters. The great autumn offensive of 1915, planned by Joffre, achieved practically nothing at immense cost. The British were held in the Battle of Loos, and the French at Vimy Ridge. In December, Sir John French was replaced by Sir Douglas Haig as Commander-in-Chief of the British Expeditionary Force.

The great German attack on Verdun, a part of the French sector and a position of great strategic importance, was launched in February 1916; 400,000 Frenchmen were killed to effect the proud boast "They shall not pass". On July 1st the promised British offensive was launched on the Somme and continued until the end of October. On the first day of the attack there were 100,000 casualties, and by the end of the year Britain had lost half a million men. Nobody had been able to end the stalemate in the West and it was becoming clear that the defensive power of barbed wire, pill boxes and machine guns, surpassed the offensive force of the weapons of either side, including poison gas, first used by the Germans early in 1915. Useless as this slaughter seemed to be, "the German army", by Ludendorff's[1] admission, "had been fought to a standstill and was utterly worn out". Throughout 1916 the Russians did much to divert the enemies' attention and resources. In June, for example, a Russian victory over the Austrians at Bukovina, forced the Germans to withdraw troops from the Somme.

During the winter of 1917 the Germans retired to the Hindenburg line, devastating the country before it and sowing it with land mines. The French, now commanded by General Nivelle, who replaced Joffre at the end of 1916, began yet another great and disastrous offensive. So appalling were their casualties, that their army mutinied and Nivelle was replaced by Pétain who, with a mixture of tact and severity, managed to retrieve the situation. Haig, in order to give Pétain time to restore the morale and discipline of his army, began

---

[1] In 1914 the Supreme German Commander was Falkenhayn. He was replaced by Hindenburg. Ludendorff, the Quartermaster-General, was the real director of German strategy. The Germans, who staffed the Turkish and Austrian armies, had a great advantage over the allies in their unified command, and interior lines of communication.

the Passchendaele offensive. During this campaign, tanks were used successfully for the first time at Cambrai. The result, as usual, was a small gain achieved at enormous cost. In Paris a political revolution took place. The Government, accused with some foundation of treachery and defeatism, was taken over by Georges Clemenceau, "the Tiger", and a new vitality was soon evident in the French war effort.

The future in October 1917 seemed sombre. The Italians were defeated by the Austrians at the Battle of Caporetto, and over three-quarters of a million men were captured, or deserted. Worst of all, the Russians made peace with the enemy. The Czarist Government was hopelessly corrupt and inefficient, communications broke down, the supply of munitions was inadequate, and men were sent to the front unarmed. In March 1917 Revolution broke out, and the Czar abdicated. After seven months of confusion, Lenin and Trotsky took over the government in October. Their first action was to come to terms with the Germans in the Treaty of Brest-Litovsk. The German armies hitherto engaged on the Russian front were now sent to the West, where a decision was imperative. America had come into the war in 1917, ostensibly because her merchant shipping had been attacked in the Kaiser's unrestricted submarine campaign. The real reason was that President Wilson (1856–1924) thought that Britain and France might otherwise be defeated, a result which neither he nor the American public were prepared to accept.

Early in 1918 Ludendorff began the offensive which was intended to end the war. The first attack fell on the British Fifth Army, which within three days was all but annihilated. By June the Germans were back on the Marne and Paris was once again threatened. But in August the tide of battle turned and in less than a month the Germans were in full retreat. With the Hindenburg line pierced, with Austria and Bulgaria suing for peace, the chance of German victory vanished. The Kaiser abdicated and fled to Holland. At eleven o'clock on the morning of November 11, 1918, the "cease fire" sounded, and the enemy surrendered on the understanding that the ensuing peace would be made in accordance with President Wilson's fourteen points.

The final victory owed much to British naval supremacy. The

struggle at sea began with tracking down German cruisers, such as the *Emden* and *Dresden*, which did a great deal of damage before they were sunk. The only major engagement of the whole war was the Battle of Jutland, fought in May 1916. The British loss was heavier than the German, three battle cruisers sunk with all hands, but the enemy fleet never put to sea again in force. In 1917 the Kaiser ordered an unrestricted submarine campaign, designed to starve Britain into surrender. In April of that year the allies lost 900,000 tons of shipping. However, food rationing, American help, the convoy system and the valour of our seamen, combined to deal with the emergency. One of the most daring exploits of the war, the storming of the submarine base at Zeebrugge, took place in 1918.

If much of its work was unspectacular, the navy, nevertheless, rendered indispensable services. Throughout the whole war no troopship was lost through enemy action. The navy enabled us to blockade the enemy, so that starvation and lack of war materials almost as much as military defeat, compelled them to surrender. It enabled us to import food, despite submarines and raiders. Finally it kept the German navy bottled up in harbour, except for its short escapade in 1916.

The Great War was different from any previous war in the area it covered, in its cost, and in the casualties it involved. The British alone lost nearly a million killed. It has been calculated that between 1914 and 1918 nine million men were killed, thirty million wounded and fifty thousand million pounds spent on war. Four empires were destroyed during the course of the conflict, while machine-guns, tanks, poison gas, submarines and aeroplanes added new horrors to war. It is little wonder that in 1919 men hoped that they had just finished a "war to end war". Twenty years later the veterans of the Marne, Ypres and the Somme, lived to see the shattering of this dream.

## CHAPTER X

# ENGLAND IN THE TWENTIETH CENTURY, 1901–1960

## 1. The Framework of a New Age

THE nineteenth century transformed the face of England, altering suddenly and drastically a way of life that had been much the same for centuries. Most of the social problems created by this upheaval were handed on for the new century to tackle. In many cases the solution had been foreshadowed by the pioneer work of the Victorians themselves; in many more it had been indicated in the writings of the more thoughtful and far-seeing among them. But the practical task which faced the twentieth century was the creation of a new system of society in which the state would have to do more and more for the individual which in the past he had either been left to do for himself or had had to go without. The result of this new policy is what is now called "The Welfare State".

To deal with all aspects of the Welfare State would be impossible, since the precise limit of the State's responsibilities towards its citizens is still a matter of debate and likely to remain so. But, apart from Education, which will be dealt with separately, the backbone of the system is the National Insurance Act of 1946 which unites the three most important spheres of State benevolence—Public Health, Old Age Pensions and Unemployment Relief. To trace the growth of these three and to study the development of State Education is to master the essentials of the Welfare State.

Public Health had already been the subject of legislation during the nineteenth century (for details see Chapter I). But the Victorian Acts were simply designed to establish conditions in which it was possible to be healthy: Public Health meant sanitation and a decent water supply. The provision of medical care for those who could not afford it was still left to private charity. By the turn of the century a few progressive towns had begun to supply free milk and medical advice to expectant mothers, and the Education Act of 1902 had made some provision for the regular medical inspection of children. But the first real step towards a comprehensive State medical service was Lloyd George's National Insurance Act of 1911. This measure, an imitation of Bismarck's social legislation in Prussia, compelled both workman and employer to pay a regular contribution to a National Insurance Fund. Those doctors who entered the scheme were given a panel of workmen and paid at a uniform rate for attending them, regardless of how little or how much medical attention each patient required. Hospital treatment was free and the difference between the incomings and outgoings of the Fund was to be made good by the taxpayer. This system continued with minor alterations and extensions until 1946 when another National Insurance Act carried matters a great deal further by making all medicines, spectacles, false teeth and so on available to anyone without any charge. The service was extended to cover dentists and ophthalmologists and all hospitals were brought under the control of the Minister of Health. The alarming rise in the cost of the Health Service has been explained as a natural consequence of its increased scope. But there is probably more truth in the contention that the sudden and sweeping changes in the methods of administration which formed part of the Act have resulted in a great deal of extravagance. In any case serious doubts have been expressed on the possibility of maintaining the health services at their present level and already certain charges have been re-introduced.

The introduction of Old Age Pensions in 1908 was also the work of Lloyd George. Seldom can so much unhappiness have been averted at so slight a cost. The threat of the workhouse no longer haunted those who felt themselves becoming too infirm to work. The bill owed its passage through a Liberal House of Commons and a Tory House of Lords solely to the fact that it was an elementary measure of mercy and humanity, for it contained a principle that few Liberals and fewer Tories could approve, the principle of redistributive taxation. That is to say, the State was taking upon itself to redistribute the national income by taking money away from the rich (by means of taxes) and giving it to the poor (in the form of pensions). This principle is now admitted to some extent by all political parties, but in the first decade of the century it was favoured only by the Socialists. It should be noted that the National Insurance

Act of 1911 had a contributory basis. Thus the principle was discreetly camouflaged, although in fact the whole National Insurance Scheme involved redistributive taxation, since the benefits paid out exceeded the premiums received by about twenty million pounds a year, and this sum had to be provided out of taxation. Though Old Age Pensions were gradually, and generally belatedly, increased to meet the rising cost of living and the qualifying age was reduced, there was no change in principle until 1946, when they were included in the National Insurance Act of that year.

The third cornerstone of the Welfare State is Unemployment Relief. The handling of this issue has caused more bitterness, controversy and frustration than any other in the domestic politics of this century. A limited provision for it was made by way of experiment in the National Insurance Act of 1911. This applied only to workmen in certain specified industries and the benefit was restricted to six weeks in any one year. This was called the "covenanted benefit"—that is, a benefit to which the workman was entitled in return for the premiums he had paid. Anything that the State might pay him beyond this was an uncovenanted benefit, to be given at the discretion of the government of the day, not claimed as of right by the unemployed man. This timid approach to the problem was accepted as adequate chiefly because the period was one of full employment and the distress caused by lack of work, if acute, was not widespread. But after the war it was a different story. Rapid demobilization flooded the country with labour which industry could not absorb. Many of the export markets, lost when British factories turned over to war production, had gone for ever. The war had prevented British manufacturers from modernizing their plants, and some of their rivals could employ labour at rates far cheaper than any on which a British workman could live. The outlook was black. By 1921 there were one and a half million unemployed in this country and though there was a partial recovery, the numbers rarely sunk far below a million until the outbreak of the Second World War, rising in the worst year of the slump (1931) to three million.

The Insurance Act of 1920 added about eight million to the four million working people already insured by the Act of 1911 and the

Munition Workers Act of 1916. But the covenanted benefit was soon exhausted and the Government instituted a system of uncovenanted benefit, offensively called the "dole", which was intermittent instead of being continuous. In the intervals when it was suspended the unemployed had to apply to the Poor Law authorities for relief. Insult was added to misery rather than admit the right of the unemployed to benefits they had not paid for. In 1924 the first Labour Government abolished the distinction between covenanted and uncovenanted benefits and made both continuous. The right of a man who could not find work to be maintained by the State was at last fully admitted. But there were still causes of bitterness. An application for relief could be arbitrarily dismissed on the grounds that the applicant was "not genuinely seeking work". Accusations were made that the Conservative Government applied this provision unfairly, especially after the General Strike of 1926. It was done away with by the second Labour Government elected in 1929 and thereafter Unemployment Relief became automatic. The amount payable has been increased by the National Insurance Act of 1946.

It might be well to say something about the origin of this Act of 1946 to which reference has been made throughout this chapter. The claim of the Labour party that the Act is all their own work is an exaggeration. The measure as it stands is indeed theirs: but the bulk of the provisions are based on the Report drawn up by Sir William (now Lord) Beveridge for the wartime Coalition Government, a document accepted by the Liberal, Labour and Conservative parties as the keystone of post-war social policy. What is distinctively Labour about the Act is the machinery devised for working it. It has been well said that democracy can only work where all the main parties are agreed on fundamentals. The Welfare State is built on five years of national unity, not on the results of one general election.

The story of how the State came to take a share in providing education for its citizens is a great deal more complicated. A swift glance backward is necessary if the reader is to understand the significance of twentieth-century progress in this field. In the eighteenth century very little provision was made for the education of the poor. The grammar schools, mostly of indifferent quality, scattered up and down the country, offered a grounding in Latin and a possible opening at the University to those of moderate means. But elementary education was practically non-existent until the Evangelical Movement stirred the Nonconformists into founding elementary schools towards the end of the century. This in turn awoke the national Church to unaccustomed activity and the excitement of competition stimulated both sides. This is probably the only period in our history in which sectarianism has been anything but a stumbling-block to the progress of education. In 1833 the Treasury made a small annual grant to both Nonconformist and Church of England schools. After this first hesitant step the State did nothing more until the Reform Bill of 1867 made the spread of education a necessity. As Robert Lowe remarked: "We must educate our masters." Accordingly in 1870 W. E. Forster introduced an Education Bill which, though it was badly mauled in its passage through Parliament, at least made a beginning. The most important provision was for the creation of a new local authority, the School Board, which was to be elected by the ratepayers. In districts where there were no elementary schools the Boards, with Treasury assistance, were to set them up. By the so-called Cowper–Temple clause religious teaching in such schools was to be strictly undenominational. That is to say, children were to be taught the Bible but were not to have the advantage of any doctrine by which they could relate the many difficulties and apparent contradictions to each other. They were, so to speak, to be given the pieces of a jig-saw puzzle which it was well known none but the most brilliant could solve unaided. This arrangement satisfied no one, and was only adopted because the fierce sectarianism of Anglican, Roman Catholic and Nonconformist rendered all other solutions of the problem impossible.

Where there was already a denominational school the local Board was given powers to subsidize it out of the Treasury grant but was not allowed to interfere with the religious teaching. This again caused widespread dissatisfaction among the zealots of the contending faiths. But considering all the fuss that had been made about the Act it had been allowed to do little enough. Elementary education was still not compulsory (it was made so in 1880) and it was not free of charge. Worse still, nothing had been done for secondary education.

On the whole the Act worked as its authors intended: but its inadequacy became ever more obvious, and in 1902 a new Act was passed by the Conservatives under the leadership of A. J. Balfour. The School Boards were abolished and the local authorities of County and Borough took their place. This meant a great reduction in the number of bodies responsible to the central authority, which, in its turn, had been greatly strengthened by the creation in 1899 of the Board of Education. The administrative machinery of the new Act was thus far more efficient. In addition the new Board had in the person of Sir Robert Morant (1863–1920) the ablest civil servant of the day. The religious question was left more or less alone, but great anger was caused by the provision that the subsidy paid to denominational schools should come partly out of the Treasury grant and partly out of the rates. The stark reality of transferring money straight from the pockets of Nonconformist ratepayers to the local Roman Catholic or Church of England school appalled, where the same process conducted through the mysterious labyrinths of taxation had merely irritated. Secondary education was also, for the first time, subsidized out of the rates on condition that a certain number of free places were reserved for the most promising pupils from the elementary schools. The path thus opened to higher education was not in fact a wide one, since the provisions concerning it left almost complete freedom to the local authorities, who were generally more interested in lowering rates than in raising intellectual standards.

Nevertheless the Act was a great advance and the opportunities it created were exploited to the full by able and public-spirited civil servants. In 1906 free meals were provided for poor children, and in 1907 a school medical service was introduced. The value of expanding the secondary education of the country was impressed on all responsible people by the war. Not only was war itself more technical and complicated, it was on a far larger scale; and officers had to be found for the vast new armies. Consequently, Lloyd George invited H. A. L. Fisher, a distinguished academic figure with no experience of politics, to become President of the Board of Education. Fisher accepted and devoted himself to the framing of the Education Act of 1918 which is usually associated with his name.

The Act of 1918 was in the grand style. In elementary schools all fees were abolished and the leaving age raised to 14. The employment of children was totally forbidden under the age of 12 and severely restricted thereafter. For those who did not go on to a secondary school "continuation classes" amounting to not less than 320 hours a year were to be provided up to the age of 18. This last provision proved, in effect, a dead letter as it was one of the first victims of governmental economy. In secondary education the free place system was greatly extended and local authorities were compelled to provide a uniform minimum number. Finally Fisher raised the salaries of the school teachers and instituted the Burnham Scale: he increased the contribution of the Treasury, where a subsidy was paid jointly with a local authority, to a minimum of 50 per cent. All this cost a great deal of money. The Education estimates which had been nineteen million pounds in 1918 had risen to forty-three millions by 1920. It was on this score, not on the question of religion which Fisher had prudently left untouched, that this great measure was attacked.

In 1922 teachers' salaries were reduced; the raising of the school leaving age was postponed, and the scheme for nursery schools was dropped. The continuation classes, as we have seen, were scrapped and the opportunities for secondary education were restricted. Nevertheless the Act still remained on the Statute Book, at once an inspiration and a reproach. As England recovered from the depression of the early twenties and the slump of the early thirties more money was made available for education, but the whole Act was never put into effect. In 1944 it was superseded by the Butler Act, called after R. A. Butler, who was President of the Board of Education in Winston Churchill's Coalition Government.

The Act of 1944 contained much of Fisher's Act that had never been put into force. The school leaving age was raised to 15 with the prospect of it reaching 16 as soon as the necessary facilities were available. Part-time education up to the age of 18 was to be made compulsory and without fee. The reduction of the size of classes in elementary schools was given urgent priority and to achieve this a real attempt was made to attract an adequate supply of men and women into the teaching profession. Salaries were raised and new Teachers' Training Colleges set up. On the administrative side the number of local authorities was again reduced and the power of the Minister to deal with recalcitrants was strengthened. In providing for secondary, technical and adult education the sky, it appeared, was the limit: or so one might gather from the following passage in the Act:

"The schools available for an area shall not be deemed to be sufficient unless they are sufficient in number, character and equipment to afford for all pupils opportunities for education offering such variety of instruction and training as may be desirable in view of their different ages, abilities and aptitudes, and of the different periods for which they may be expected to remain at school, including practical instruction and training appropriate to their respective needs."

The results of the working of this Act cannot possibly be estimated yet, if only for the reason that post-war difficulties have prevented it from being fully carried out. Certainly it is difficult to imagine an Act in which the State undertakes more for the individual. The most convincing criticism of it is that the best energies of the academic profession and the limited resources of the Government are being scattered on the broad ranks of the second-rate instead of being concentrated on the small number who show exceptional promise and ability. Whether such criticism is well or ill founded time will show.

## 2. *Modern Britain, 1901–1960*

The England of Edward VII was a comfortable place for the well-to-do. Taxes were low and the wealth concentrated in the hands of a few was still increasing. The gaiety, frivolity and heedlessness of Edwardian high society put a sheen on the surface of the age. Hardness and vulgarity have always a certain glitter. Like the eighteenth century the period has a beery, racy flavour; in the upper ranks of society the best-dressed men and women in the world are making charming conversation amid the popping of champagne corks and in the background there is always the graceful music of a waltz: in the lower ranks an unbelievable number of public houses are disgorging a multitude of drunken workmen who reel home to the strains of the latest music-hall favourite: in between are the thick ranks of respectability, the clerks, the skilled workmen, the small business men, who visit the music hall but certainly do not whistle the tunes in the street. To descend from generalities to facts, prices were low and goods abundant. But the purchasing power of the working man was slightly less than it had been in the nineties, and living conditions in the large towns were still appalling. The barrier of class distinction remained formidable, although the Labour party had begun to send workmen into Parliament and the Liberal party had included one or two in their great administration of 1905.

In spite of the apparent tranquillity of Edwardian England there was an undertone of anxiety. Abroad the colossal armaments of Germany would have been alarming even if that country had been under wiser rulers than the Kaiser and his undesirable advisers. As it was, war was a great deal more than an unpleasant possibility. At home some serious strikes had shown that a violent collision between capital and labour could not be ruled out. Moreover England was just beginning to lose her position of unchallenged industrial supremacy among the nations of the world. All this was disturbing and to make matters worse the Irish question seemed to be coming to the boil again. But no age is without its worries and if the worst came to the worst would it, after all, be so very terrible? Only a few could foresee the huge scale and the extended duration of modern war, which could include battles like Passchendaele and the Somme, when sixty thousand Englishmen died in one day, and still go on for four years. Still fewer foresaw the depression and unemployment of the post-war years and the bitterness bred between class and class. The Edwardians may have been uneasy and apprehensive now and then, but in the main they felt a sense of security and peace such as we can barely conceive. The efficient barbarism of the dictator state and the indiscriminate mass slaughter of modern war would have seemed to them like a nightmare. We may justly take pride in a more humane and intelligent social system and may claim that it is not our fault if we have had to build it where typhoons and tornados are an ever-present threat. All the same we cannot help envying the less enlightened inhabitants of a more temperate zone of history.

The horrors of the first world war were made more terrible by being unexpected. In 1939 most people had a pretty clear idea of what they were in for: but in 1914–1918 it came as a surprise and thus threw people off their balance. Throwing stones at dachshunds and refusing to listen to the music of Beethoven were regarded by many normally sane persons as signs of patriotism.[1] In such an atmosphere of emotion and hysteria the restraints of reason and convention were roughly pushed aside. Much that was sensible and much that was silly was toppled over by the impartial torrent. Formality was everywhere at a discount: in small matters like dress, for instance, the lounge suit superseded the frock coat for business and the tail coat for pleasure on all except ceremonial occasions. The cheapness and good quality of ready-made clothes made it possible for a poor man to dress in much the same style as the well-to-do, thus removing the oldest and most obvious class-distinction. Not only was it now permissible for a gentleman to smoke in the presence of a lady, but ladies themselves began to smoke. Dinner parties were no longer the principal method of entertaining; their place was taken by the cocktail party where everybody talked to everybody else at the top of their voices and drank large quantities of gin, a spirit hitherto regarded as low and coarse. But the biggest change of all was in the position of women. As all available men were wanted at the front women took their place in the factories and on the land. They even went into uniform and undertook various auxiliary duties in the armed forces, to say nothing of nursing. The old fiction that a woman was a timid, helpless creature not to be allowed outside the safe limits of a home except under constant male protection was exploded and there could be no going back. This was an advance from which society has gained at every point.

A less happy consequence of the war has been the loosening of the marriage-tie and the great increase of divorce. The immediate cause was the great number of wartime marriages which went on the rocks. In ordinary times a man and a woman do not join them-

[1] When Winston Churchill said that he was surprised to see Morley drinking German wine, he replied: "I am interning it."

selves together for life on the strength of a passing attraction. But the war years were not ordinary; during the worst period of the war the average expectation of life for a young man going to the front was three weeks, and to demand prudence in such circumstances is to ask altogether too much of human nature. Divorce had been legally possible since 1857 but the Church had forbidden it and society had frowned on it. Now the disapproval of society has changed to acquiescence and some Churchmen have mitigated the uncompromising hostility on which their doctrines and liturgy insist. Once the principle has been accepted there is no logical stopping-place short of making marriage a temporary contract terminable by the consent of both parties. Sir Alan Herbert's Matrimonial Causes Act of 1937, which simplified and rationalized previous legislation, has been attacked for making divorce easier. The injustice of such attacks is evident. All that laws can do is to embody the prevailing opinion in a workable code. The only way to banish divorce is to convince people of the truth of Christian teaching on the subject. Such a change of heart can only be effected by the Church and not by Parliament.

The appearance of our country has altered greatly since the end of the first war. Except for the replacement of slums by trim new housing estates the change has not been for the better. The bus and the motor-car have made it unnecessary for people to live together in towns and villages and the ensuing ribbon development has ruined much of the landscape. The decay of English taste in architecture, which started with the industrial revolution, has defaced nearly all our towns with shops and cinemas of vulgar design and odious materials. Advertisements have drowned the quiet tones of English town and countryside with loud and jarring colours. In London the destruction of our architectural heritage proceeded merrily for the twenty years between the wars. But the most tragic of all these processes has been the slow strangulation of the great country houses by death duties and ever increasing taxation. The country house is the symbol of English civilization. From the days of Elizabeth to the death of Victoria it is difficult to think of any great Englishman who is not associated with some country house. These houses are the visible links which bind our history together and to the making of them went all that was most distinctively

English in the artistic talent of the nation. Now many of them have gone beyond recall and those that are left owe their survival to the courage and public spirit of their owners or to the magnificent efforts of voluntary bodies such as the National Trust. This age, in which so much lip-service has been paid to the importance of art, has shown one of the blackest records of neglect and vandalism.

The standard of living throughout the whole Western world has risen fast and far since the end of the second world war. In Britain the great majority of people are much better fed, clothed and housed than they were a generation ago. Education and medical care are provided on a scale that few would have believed possible at the beginning of the century. All this has changed the life of the people in a thousand ways, not least in the matter of recreation. Radio and television claim by far the greater part of those hours that the modern Englishman devotes to enjoyment. The music hall is practically extinct; the theatre flourishes only in London; and the cinema, which drew immense audiences during the nineteen-thirties and forties, has lost much of its following to television. Spectator sports such as league football, horse-racing and greyhound-racing still maintain their popularity. County cricket enjoys rather less support than it did but show-jumping attracts large crowds and is eagerly followed on television. The effects of this new medium reach far beyond the field of entertainment; politics, education, the press, all have been or soon will be deeply affected by it.

Of all means of communication the cinema and television make the smallest demands on the intelligence and the imagination. Their immense success in the last few decades has led to some doubts of the value of universal education. On the other hand there has been a constant increase in the demand for books all over the country; in London and the big towns the audiences at the ballet and the opera grow steadily larger, and more and more people go to listen to good music. The great increase of leisure which has resulted from the shortening of the working week since the end of the second world war is a fact of crucial significance in the social history of our time. Whether this leisure will be used creatively or wastefully it is far too early to judge. All that the historian can say with confidence is that the opportunities of self-improvement offered to the Englishman of 1950 are far richer and wider than his forbears ever had.

## CHAPTER XI

# ENGLISH POLITICS, 1902–1918

## 1. *The State of Parties in 1902*

BETWEEN 1896 and 1900 the leadership of the Liberal party changed hands twice. In 1896 Rosebery resigned because his policy was more imperialistic than that of the majority of his followers. In 1898 his successor, Harcourt, threw up his post in a sulk and Campbell-Bannerman became leader of the party. These changes in Liberal leadership to some extent reflected a deep rift in the Liberal ranks, which opened up, curiously enough, just at the time when the Irish Nationalists had reunited their Parnellite and anti-Parnellite factions under the leadership of John Redmond. The Liberal party was divided between the supporters of Campbell-Bannerman, an old-fashioned Gladstonian Liberal opposed to an adventurous foreign and colonial policy; the Liberal imperialists, Asquith and Grey, who wished to convince the nation that the Liberals could be entrusted with the fortunes of the empire; and the radical Liberals, consisting of men like Morley and Lloyd George, who were regarded as "pro-Boers".

The Conservatives in 1902, unlike the Liberals, were a united party. Chamberlain's conversion to tariff reform was in fact about to split it, but after its victory at the khaki election it looked as if the party would survive its seven years of office without difficulty. Chamberlain was by far the most popular and powerful figure in the Government. It was he, rather than Salisbury or Balfour, who committed the Conservatives to imperialism, and his influence guaranteed that Disraeli's and Randolph Churchill's policy of Radical Toryism should not be smothered by the inertia and apathy of Salisbury and Balfour. The fact that the Conservatives retained office for ten consecutive years with a majority of over 120, and that their victories at elections depended upon the working man's vote, is a measure both of the decay of Liberalism and of Chamberlain's success in persuading the country that the Conservatives were not a party of vested interest, aristocracy and privilege.

In 1901 only two Labour candidates were returned at the general election. Nevertheless the founding of an Independent Labour Party (I.L.P.), resolved to improve upon the traditional alliance between Liberal and working-class politicians, was soon to become of immense importance. The failure of the new Labour party at the khaki election was partly the reward of their pro-Boer sympathies and partly the result of trade union preference for the Liberal party. At the general election of 1906, 53 Labour members were returned, and only 18 years later Ramsay MacDonald became the first Labour Prime Minister.[1]

## 2. Balfour's Ministry, 1902–1905

The first and greatest achievement of Balfour's ministry was the Education Act of 1902. Previous Education Acts had been haphazard in their approach and suffered from three main defects. First, no civilized country spent so little on education as Great Britain; per head of population, Switzerland annually spent twelve times as much; and by 1902 it was felt that Britain was being handicapped in her struggle to maintain industrial supremacy by the greater efficiency not only of German but French and American education. Secondly, there was the problem of Church schools. In 1902 the ever-increasing cost and standard of education was making it almost impossible for the Churches to make both ends meet. It was clear that such schools would either perish from want of money or would have to be supported like the State schools from the rates. The High Churchmen in the Conservative party, particularly Balfour's own cousins, Lord Cranborne and Lord Hugh Cecil, were anxious that the Government should come to the rescue of the Church schools and thus prevent the whole country being brought up on undenominational religion. The third defect which the 1902 Act set out to remedy was that no provision had been made in 1870 or subsequently for secondary education. Many schools abroad had remedied the omission on their own initiative, but in 1901 the

[1] For a fuller discussion of the origins of the Labour Party, see pages 173–6.

courts decided that school boards had no statutory powers to spend the ratepayers' money on secondary education.

The Act of 1902 put Church schools on much the same financial footing as State schools; it transferred the responsibility for education from school boards to committees of County and Borough Councils, and it empowered but did not compel such committees to see that some secondary education was made available free of cost. The County Councils, under the general supervision of the Board of Education, proved to be more enterprising and enlightened bodies than the previous school boards, which were only too often narrow-minded and provincial in outlook. As was intended, the Act led to a great improvement in education. Teachers were better paid, clever children whose parents had little money now had some chance of getting to a university, and many new universities were soon established (e.g. at Leeds, Bristol and Reading).

Although this measure has proved to be one of the greatest of the twentieth century, it aroused enormous opposition at the time. Nonconformists fought the Act tooth and nail in the House of Commons while its provisions were still being debated, and when it became law some went to prison rather than pay rates to Church schools. A few Conservatives, particularly the Nonconformist Chamberlain, were uneasy about helping Church schools from rates. The Tory and Whig parties, from which the Conservatives and Liberals had evolved, began their history with religious disputes. The struggle between Church and Dissent had enlivened party politics even in the nineteenth century, but the bitter religious controversy provoked by the 1902 Education Act has never since been revived. Social and industrial questions now divide the parties, and religion owing to its general decline throughout the country provides only a minor cause of dispute. Thus the alliance between the Liberals and Nonconformists has gradually lost its significance, which may partly account for Labour victories at the Liberals' expense.

Already in 1902 scattered groups of Liberals, separated from each other by imperial disputes, had joined together in opposition to Balfour's Education Act. In 1903, Chamberlain, by adopting tariff reform, completed the work of Liberal reunion, while at the same time dividing his own party. In 1846 Peel had split the Conservative party on the question of the Corn Laws, in 1886 Gladstone had split the Liberals on the Irish question, but Chamberlain alone has the distinction of successively dividing both the parties, the Liberals in 1886 over Home Rule and the Conservatives in 1903 over Protection.

Chamberlain was converted to Protection because he thought that it was an essential means of keeping the Empire together. In 1902, at the time of Edward VII's coronation, the fourth Colonial Conference was held,[1] which urged the establishment of a system of imperial preference. Free Trade had been very much to our advantage so long as our industries were pre-eminent. When towards the close of the nineteenth century competition from Germany and America became severe, when our own country was being flooded with cheap foreign goods, while foreign markets were excluding our manufactures by high tariffs, the idea of protection became more attractive. In the changed environment of the twentieth century, in which the world was plunged into economic war, Chamberlain doubted whether free trade was an up-to-date weapon. Might it not—like an ancient blunderbuss—explode in its owner's face? Only by protecting our industries from foreign competitors and giving preferential treatment to our Empire, could we hope to maintain our trade at a high level.

The Liberals, when they heard that Chamberlain had abandoned free trade, made the most of the fact in order to unite their own supporters. "There had been an almost religious element about the preaching of free trade in the days of Cobden and Bright; it was advocated not merely as a set of sound precepts from the gospel of Mammon, which would make us all richer, but as a kind of economic footnote to the Christian message of peace and goodwill among men."[2] Tariffs were regarded as likely to lead to war, while free trade was thought to produce international understanding.

[1] In 1887 the year of Queen Victoria's first jubilee, the Prime Ministers of the self-governing colonies, who had to come to London to take part in the ceremony, met together to discuss questions of Imperial Defence. Another Colonial Conference was held in 1897, at the time of the Diamond Jubilee, and subsequently such meetings became regular.

[2] G. M. Young, *Portrait of an Age*.

Chamberlain in September 1903 resigned from the Cabinet in order to be able to advocate Protection from a free platform. Balfour, who tried to make "tariff reform" an open question, nevertheless dismissed Ritchie and Lord Balfour of Burleigh from the Cabinet, because they were too ardent free traders. In October the Duke of Devonshire resigned as his sympathies lay with Ritchie on the question of protection. The Prime Minister lost the support of both Free Traders and Protectionists by his havering.

Many working men were very suspicious of tariff reform, which they regarded as a capitalist conspiracy. Although Chamberlain insisted that "tariff reform meant work for all" the opponents of the scheme were widely believed when they said that protection would lead the country back to the misery of the "hungry forties". The campaign against free trade came at a time when enthusiasm for the Empire was declining and indeed the Boer War had shown the nastiest aspect of imperialism.

Balfour realized that at the next general election the Conservatives would have no chance of victory if they remained divided on the question of protection. Early in 1905 he produced a formula "on half a sheet of note paper", to which Chamberlain somewhat reluctantly agreed. Balfour's plan suggested that a colonial conference should be summoned to discuss protection, and that a system of retaliatory tariffs should be devised. In other words without accepting Chamberlain's thesis that protection was desirable in itself he was prepared to give it limited support. In December 1905 a new crisis arose in the Conservative party because Chamberlain, who had never been happy about Balfour's compromise, had begun to say that tariff retaliation necessitated and implied a general tariff. The Prime Minister, partly to avert this newly threatened division in his party, and partly because he thought that the Liberals were once again quarrelling among themselves, resigned. He hoped thereby to do what Gladstone did in 1885, to force the opposition to form a minority government which would discredit itself before the next election.[1]

[1] Gladstone resigned in 1873 but Disraeli then refused to form a ministry (see page 91), whereas under similar circumstances, Salisbury accepted office in 1885 (see page 99).

### 3. The Liberals and the Lords, 1905–1914

When Campbell-Bannerman accepted office in 1905 his party was not nearly as disunited as Balfour had hoped. It is true that when Campbell-Bannerman announced his support of a "step by step" policy of Home Rule, Rosebery had retaliated in a speech at Bodmin that "emphatically and explicitly and once for all" he would not serve under that banner. In the long run, however, this did more harm to Rosebery than it did to the party. The Liberal Cabinet of 1905 was undoubtedly a ministry of all the talents: Morley, Bryce, Harcourt, Haldane, Lloyd George, Winston Churchill, and Asquith were members of the Government which, since it combined the Whig, the Radical and the Gladstonian Liberals, revealed the extent of Liberal unity.

In 1906 the Liberals went to the country and the election proved the greatest disaster the Conservatives ever suffered. Balfour and a great number of his colleagues were defeated. The final figures of those elected were 377 Liberals, 53 Labour members, 83 Irish Nationalists and only 157 Conservatives. Balfour was soon returned at a by-election for a safe London seat, but Chamberlain was struck down by paralysis and retired from politics. This landslide was the result of Nonconformist opposition aroused by the Education Act of 1902, the working class reaction against the Taff Vale decision (see page 174), the electorate's suspicion of tariff reform and the very effective use the Liberals made of a colonial grievance. After the Boer War the gold mining industry of the Rand suffered from a serious labour shortage. In 1904 a labour force of 50,000 was imported from China. The Chinese were enlisted on the understanding that they would have to work for a fixed minimum period of time to cover the cost of their transport to South Africa, and when they arrived in Africa they were segregated in compounds like prisoners. The English Socialists regarded such use of foreign labour as a capitalist trick to keep down the wages of free workmen, and the Liberals stirred up the intense moral indignation of Englishmen against what they described as "Chinese slavery".

Although the election of 1906 gave the Liberals the clearest possible mandate (their majority over all parties was 80) the

Conservatives could still frustrate their designs through the House of Lords. The Lords, as a predominantly Conservative body, had not opposed a single piece of legislation between 1895 and 1905. Between 1893 and 1895 they had thrown out several important Liberal measures (e.g. Gladstone's second Home Rule Bill 1893, an Employers' Liability Bill 1894, etc.). At that time, however, the Liberal majority depended upon the support of the Irish party, and the Conservative victory in 1895 was probably rightly regarded as vindicating the Lords' use of their veto.

Balfour, when he wrote in 1906 to the Conservative leader in the Lords, Lord Lansdowne, saying that the Lords might be "strengthened rather than weakened" by rejecting Liberal measures, clearly did not see how the situation differed from that of 1893. That the Conservatives intended to use their majority in the Upper House was made clear from the start. "Whether in power or in opposition" Balfour told his dejected followers after their great defeat, "the Unionist party will still control the destinies of the country." The Lords, by using their power of veto unscrupulously in the interest of one party, disclaimed the chief justification of their existence, their alleged impartiality. Consequently it was not long before the Liberals revived the old cry of "mend them or end them". Disraeli, who had prevented the Lords throwing out Gladstone's measures between 1868 and 1874, provided a much better precedent for Balfour than the freak conditions of Gladstone's last ministry.

It was obvious that a Government with such a majority must try to do something about the grievances which they had been elected to remedy. Both in opposition and during the election they had attacked Balfour's Education Act, the Licensing Act (1904) and "Chinese slavery". Now that they were in power they brought forward measures to improve the Conservative legislation and to end a number of long-standing abuses. In 1906 they attempted to remove Nonconformist grievances about rate-supported Church schools in an Education Bill which they eventually dropped because it was so mutilated in the Lords. In the same year they passed a measure abolishing plural voting, a practice which was clearly in the Conservative interest as the plural voter was necessarily a man of property.[1] This bill, together with a couple of bills dealing with land reform, was thrown out, and a Small Holdings Bill and an Irish Eviction Bill (1907) were destroyed, in effect, by amendments. In 1908 the Government introduced a Licensing Bill designed to reduce the number of public houses in England. Since the days of the Newcastle programme the Liberal party had concerned itself with the problem of temperance which so deeply engaged the Nonconformist conscience. Consequently the whole drink industry contributed generously to Conservative funds and the public houses radiated Conservative propaganda. The Licensing Bill was also thrown out by the Lords, although one or two by-elections suggested that in this instance they reflected the will of the electorate better than the Government.

In 1908 Campbell-Bannerman retired owing to ill-health and died soon after. He was succeeded as Prime Minister by Asquith, and among other Cabinet changes Lloyd George became Chancellor of the Exchequer. At the time of this change in Liberal leadership, the party not unnaturally was exasperated. A large number of their measures had been rejected or mutilated by the Lords, in spite of the fact that they had the largest majority the Commons had known for nearly a century. It was in order to find a way out of this impasse that Lloyd George produced his famous budget. The budget "was like a kid, which sportsmen tie up to a tree in order to persuade a tiger to its death; and at its loud, rude bleating the House of Lords began to growl". Not only was the 1909 budget designed to provoke the Lords into suicidal folly, but it breathed the spirit of what was then the entirely new principle that the budget should be used to reduce inequalities between rich and poor. The Chancellor's budget was anyway likely to be drastic because he had to find money to pay for an old age pension scheme promised by Asquith the year before, to build eight new dreadnoughts, and to reduce the income tax of taxpayers with families.

The "People's Budget" of 1909, which then appeared to the Conservatives to be a revolutionary measure and which was advocated and opposed with hysterical intensity, seems absurdly mild

---

[1] Those who had a University degree or owned business premises in a constituency other than their own, retained a second vote until 1948.

compared with a modern budget. A bottle of whisky was to cost 4s. instead of 3s. 6d., a tax was imposed on all licensed premises, motor-cars and petrol were taxed for the first time, income tax was increased from 1s. to 1s. 2d., a very small super-tax was levied on incomes of over £3,000, and to goad the Lords to fury and at the same time to gratify the Radicals and the Labour party, a small land tax was introduced. The budget could not have fulfilled its purpose better. The attack on that great prop of Conservatism, the liquor industry, the destruction of the argument that tariff reform was the only way to increase revenue, the feeling that it was a socialist budget inspired by class hatred, and the final provocation of a land tax, entirely deprived the Lords of their judgment. Just in case at the eleventh hour they began to see the light, Lloyd George made a series of speeches well calculated to make them reckless.

Edward VII, alarmed by the prospect of a constitutional crisis, which would inevitably arise if the Lords rejected the budget, tried to persuade Lord Lansdowne to prevent his colleagues throwing out the measure. But no argument could persuade the peers to withhold "its legislative hand", and "noble statesmen" did "itch to interfere in matters which they did not understand". Consequently the budget was rejected in the Lords by 350 votes to 75. If only the Conservatives had been a little more patient the Liberals would most probably have been defeated at the next election, particularly as so many of them were pacifists at a time when public opinion was increasingly demanding that strong measures should be taken against Germany. Asquith, after passing a vote of censure on the Lords, dissolved Parliament. The election held in January 1910 was fought over two issues: should the budget pass? "Shall Peers or People rule?" The result of the election was not nearly as decisive as the Liberals had expected. 275 Liberals were elected as opposed to 273 Conservatives. Consequently 80 Irish Nationalists and 40 members of the Labour party held the balance of the house.

If the Liberals were to stay in office they could only do so with Irish support. The fate of the English constitution was in the hands of the declared enemies of the country, and the price they demanded for their support was of course Home Rule. The Irish had already voted against the budget in 1909 because they objected to the duties on spirits, and they argued that if they were to vote against their consciences they would expect a considerable reward.

In May 1910 Edward VII died after a short illness, and at the suggestion of his successor, George V, a constitutional conference was arranged. Early in 1910 the Lords had passed the budget, but it was very doubtful whether they would accept any reduction of their powers. The King hoped that some compromise might be arranged between the parties on the reform of the Lords, because, if they failed to reach agreement, the only way in which such a reform could be passed through the Lords itself was by a very considerable creation of Liberal peers. The King was anxious to avoid using his prerogative in this way because it would greatly reduce the prestige of the Second Chamber. The negotiations broke down because the Conservatives, although prepared to reform the House of Lords, were not ready to reduce their powers to an extent which might allow the Home Rule Bill to pass. The Liberals, on the other hand, because they had pledged themselves to Home Rule in order to secure Irish votes, could not possibly leave the Lords with power to maintain the Union.

The Prime Minister then told the King that there was only one way out of this deadlock, and that was that the King should promise to create a sufficient number of peers to carry the Parliament Bill. Naturally both George V and Asquith hoped that the mere threat of such a large scale creation would suffice to bring the peers to their senses, as had happened in 1832. The King consented to use his prerogative, if necessary, to carry the measure, but only after another general election had shown that it was the will of the electorate that the Lords should be reformed. Consequently a second election was held in December 1910 and the result was much the same as before. 272 Liberal, 272 Conservative, 84 Irish Nationalist and 42 Labour members were returned. This constituted a clear majority in favour of the Parliament Bill which nothing now could avert.

The Parliament Bill was presented to the Lords in May 1911. Some Conservative peers, nicknamed the "hedgers", felt that the time had come to climb down, and advocated the policy of the Duke of Wellington in 1832. On that occasion the peers opposed to the Reform Bill had abstained from voting. But Lord Halsbury,

Lord Willoughby de Broke and others refused to admit that they were beaten and were resolved to die hard. "Let them make their peers", said Curzon, "we will die in the last ditch before we give in." Curzon, in spite of coining this phrase, which gave the "die-hards" the alternative title of "last ditchers", when he discovered that the Liberals had secured the King's consent to the necessary creations, played a leading part in the struggle to ensure that the bill should pass the Lords. In the end the "hedgers" triumphed and the Parliament Bill passed by 131 votes to 114, after some 29 Conservatives had voted for the Government rather than see their House ruined by a deluge of Liberal peers. The Conservatives, after this defeat, made Balfour the scapegoat for disasters which were largely the result of their own perversity. In 1911 Balfour resigned his leadership of the party and was succeeded by Bonar Law.

Despite the fact that the Parliament Bill made it impossible for the Lords to reject a measure for more than two years, they soon had occasion to use their restricted powers. In 1911, in fulfilment of their promises to Redmond, the Liberals introduced the third Home Rule Bill, which the Lords rejected. In the same year the Government brought forward a National Insurance Bill designed to insure working people against sickness and unemployment. As the scheme was a contributory one, the Conservatives maintained that it was depriving the poor man of his wages. Lloyd George retaliated by saying that it was "9d. for 4d." (4d. was the proportion deducted from wages, 3d. was contributed by the employer and 2d. by the State). The measure, although an excellent one as far as it went, was not popular with the electorate, who seemed to share the Conservatives' dislike of "licking stamps".

### 4. Social Unrest, 1902–1914

The Industrial Revolution created social problems very much faster than it could solve them. On the whole the nineteenth century was an era of improvement, increasing wages, and full employment; although after 1870, owing to the competition of America and Germany, periodic slumps and trade depressions caused widespread misery. The growth of Trade Unions, strikes like the great dock strike (1889), and the creation of the Labour party, were all symptoms of social unrest. In the seventies and eighties mid-Victorian prosperity suffered a check, and although it returned in the nineties and continued down to 1914, the discontent created in the previous period of lower wages and threatened unemployment, was not forgotten. The feeling arose that there was something wrong with the capitalist system, that although the franchise had been extended, the voter was only confronted with candidates whose interests were those of the capitalist whatever their party might be, and that life would be a great deal better and fairer for the working man if he returned to Parliament members of his own class, pledged to reorganize industry on socialist lines.

The doctrine of Socialism, derived from the writings of Karl Marx, is that the State should own the means of production, distribution and exchange, that industries and essential services should be nationalised, that capitalism is a passing phase containing within itself the seeds of its own destruction, and that just as slavery inevitably gave way to serfdom, and serfdom to wagedom, so capitalism will crumble away leaving a classless society. The Socialist, like the Calvinist, thinks that destiny is on his side. History, according to Marx, has predetermined the destruction of capitalist society and the triumph of the Proletariat, and all that the Socialist need do is give it a helping hand to ensure that the process is as quick and as painless as possible.[1]

Socialist ideas in this country were spread by the Social Democratic Federation (S.D.F.), founded in 1884, and the Fabians. The founder of the S.D.F., Hyndman, was an old Etonian and played cricket for Sussex. In a book called *England for All* he pointed out that less than a quarter of the £1,300,000,000 worth of goods made every year went to the workers.

It took a very considerable time for Socialist ideas to filter through the Trade Unions. But in 1893 some Trade Unionists met at Bradford and decided to set up an Independent Labour Party,

---

[1] Marx's socialism would today be called "communism" to distinguish it from less radical forms of socialism. Many socialists only wish to nationalize selected industries and, although anxious to see wealth more equally distributed, are not necessarily opposed to limited differences of income.

committed to Socialism. It was hoped that one day the party would become strong enough to exert an influence on the Liberal and Conservative parties by holding the balance of the house, as the Irish Nationalists had done. In 1900 the Independent Labour Party was transformed into the Labour Representation Committee, with Ramsay MacDonald (1866–1937) as secretary. At the khaki election two Labour members were returned. Thus in the very first year of the new century a new party was begun, consisting of many familiar elements: working-class politicians, co-operatives, Trade Unions, and Socialists. Within fifty years of its formation the Labour Party had destroyed the Liberals. The Liberals, no longer the party of the Left, no longer distinct from the Conservatives as a social and economic force, appeared to an increasing number of electors to be superfluous.

Ramsay MacDonald, the secretary of the Labour Representation Committee, at first found it very hard to persuade working men to vote Labour rather than Liberal. However, the Taff Vale Case (1901) which struck a blow at the very heart of Trade Unionism, persuaded many people that industrial problems would always be decided in favour of the employer, unless Labour was powerful enough in the House of Commons to protect the interests of the working class. Some employees of the Taff Vale South Wales Railway Company were guilty of "tumultuous picketing" and the Railway Company decided to prosecute the men's trade union, the Amalgamated Society of Railway Servants. The case was contested all the way to the House of Lords, where the Company were granted £23,000 damages against the Union. The precedent established by the Taff Vale dispute implied that a Trade Union was to be held responsible for the illegal activity of any of its members. Balfour appointed a Royal Commission to examine the legal position of Unions, thus postponing the need for further action until its report was ready.

The Commission eventually concluded that legislation should be introduced reversing the Taff Vale decision, but that Trade Unions should remain liable to prosecution if illegal acts were committed by their members. The Labour Party was very suspicious of the law courts and very reluctant to leave them any discretion. It recalled how the Trade Union Acts of 1825 and 1867 had been reversed by judicial decisions in 1867 and 1901. When Campbell-Bannerman in 1906 introduced a Bill to give effect to the Commission's report, the Labour Party, now 53 strong in the House of Commons, demanded that the Unions should be given far more extensive immunity. The Prime Minister surrendered, and even the Lords dared not alienate the Unions by rejecting the Bill.

How well founded was Labour's suspicion of the law courts was shown by the Osborne Judgment (1909). This established the principle that Trade Unions could not lawfully devote any part of their funds to political purposes. Since Labour members were dependent on Union funds to keep them alive[1] it was essential for them to reverse the Osborne Judgment, as they had reversed the Taff Vale decision. In 1913 a Trade Union Act was passed making it legal for Unions to use their funds as they chose. Despite the considerable achievements of the Labour Party some of the working class were not satisfied. They thought that Parliamentary action was too slow, and that the Labour siege of capitalist strongholds might last as long as a century. Tom Mann between 1910 and 1914 was an active exponent of these views. The aims of the working class, he maintained, would best be fulfilled by violence, unofficial and general strikes, if need be by revolution. Industries should be run by the workers rather than by capitalists or even the State.

The view that "direct action" (e.g. strikes) rather than parliamentary agitation is most likely to achieve the workers' aims, and that those who work in an industry should own and manage it, is known as "Syndicalism". Syndicalism came to England from France and was first translated from theory into action by the Seamen's and Firemen's Union in 1911. Encouraged by their successful strike the Dockers followed suit and got the "Dockers' Tanner" raised, in some cases, to 8d. an hour. The success of the latter strike was partly the result of the amalgamation of local unions into the great National Transport Workers' Federation, which meant that strikes dislocated the industry on a far greater scale than before, and that it was no longer possible to break strikes by employing other workmen in the same trade, but in a different union.

---

[1] Although payment of members had been advocated in the Newcastle programme the practice was not established until 1911.

In 1911 Railway workers struck for higher wages, and to get their Unions recognized by their employers. The Government intervened and settled the dispute, because, as a war might be started over the Agadir incident at any moment, it was essential to have the railways running properly. In 1912 the Miners' Federation of Great Britain called upon all workers in the coalfields to strike for higher pay. A million men responded, creating havoc in a large number of dependent industries. Many of their demands were granted, but only after they had been forced by an Act of Parliament to accept arbitration. The 1914 war put an end to this period of strikes. Trade Unions, by combining into large-scale Federations, enormously increased their bargaining power and infected their members with the idea of working-class solidarity. It is, however, possible for Trade Unions to exert a pressure on the Government not far removed from political blackmail, and since a Union is likely to represent a minority interest in relation to the total electorate, the tendency of such pressure may be anti-democratic.

The years between the Parliament Act and the war witnessed an extraordinary outbreak of "direct action" in spheres other than industry. Rebellion in Ireland and the Suffragette movement both implied contempt of Parliament, for both depended upon force and violence rather than debate. The Suffragette movement began in earnest in 1903, when Mrs. Pankhurst founded the Women's Social and Political Union. Its aim was to put women on an equal footing with men, and in particular to win them the vote. When a bill framed to extend the franchise to women was dropped in 1910 the Suffragettes resorted to every sort of expedient to keep their case in the public eye and to bring pressure on the Government. They burned houses, smashed windows, shouted at the King in a theatre, chained themselves to railings, and those who were sent to prison for such crimes made martyrs of themselves by refusing to eat. In 1913 a Suffragette was killed when she hurled herself at the King's horse running in the Derby. The Government could scarcely yield to such irregular pressure. It was the work which women undertook in the war and the way in which they then proved themselves able to do men's jobs, rather than their courageous antics before the war, which finally persuaded the House in 1918 and 1928 to give them the vote.

In 1913 "direct action" in Ireland nearly precipitated a revolution. The Conservatives, who could no longer depend upon the Lords to destroy Home Rule, took up Ulster's cause in the hope that it could be used as a stick with which to beat the Government into submission. Ulster did not want Home Rule in the least, particularly as it would involve one of the most violently Protestant countries in the world being ruled by Roman Catholics. In 1912 Bonar Law said that he would go to any length to maintain Ulster in the Union, and Sir Edward Carson, the leader of the Ulster Unionists, began drilling an army to resist Home Rule if necessary. By 1914 ammunition was being landed in Ulster, paid for by English Unionists; sections of the regular army had mutinied at the prospect of being used to suppress an Ulster rebellion; and the South had begun to recruit Irish volunteers to enforce Home Rule on the North. For a time the world crisis distracted the attention of both sides, but discontent was not extinguished. Below the surface smouldered passions and resentments which were soon to set Ireland alight.

## 5. *The War Cabinets, 1914–1918*

The Liberals, whose slogan "Peace, Retrenchment and Reform" was a just description of their policy, were by tradition and instinct the most inappropriate party to be responsible for the conduct of the war. Public confidence in the Government, however, was greatly increased by the appointment of Lord Kitchener as Secretary of State for War (August 6th, 1914). The British Expeditionary Force sent to France was rightly known as "Kitchener's army" since he was largely responsible for its recruitment, training and equipment. In 1915 two crises shook the Government and forced Asquith to broaden its basis by admitting Conservatives into the Cabinet. The first was a "shell scandal" exposed and partly invented by the Press. Trench warfare demanded artillery attacks on an unprecedented scale. In the forty-eight hours before the battle of Neuve Chappelle, British gunners fired more shells than had been used in the entire South African War. According to *The Times* this created a shortage of shells and "Men died in heaps upon the Aubers Ridge, because the field guns were short, and gravely short, of high explosive shells".

The second crisis was provoked by the First Sea Lord, Admiral Fisher. In May 1915 he resigned because he disagreed with Churchill, then First Lord of the Admiralty, on the extent of naval support for the expedition to the Dardanelles. The Conservative opposition, who had hitherto restrained their criticism of the conduct of the war for fear of "giving aid and comfort to the King's enemies", now told the Prime Minister that it was "the duty of the opposition to oppose" and oppose they would, unless the Government became a coalition. After much argument Asquith replaced six Liberal ministers by five Conservatives and one Labour member.

In forming the new coalition ministry Asquith was forced by the Conservatives, much against his will, to deprive both Churchill and Haldane of office. As both men were largely responsible for the preparedness of our fleets and armies at the outbreak of war, the Conservative insistence upon dismissing them showed both ingratitude and folly. In this Cabinet reconstruction, Lloyd George was given the newly formed Ministry of Munitions, which in effect put him in control of a considerable part of the industry of the country, while Fisher, whose resignation had precipitated the crisis, retired into obscurity.

Lloyd George soon came up against serious labour problems. In order to obtain the maximum output of war materials, women and other volunteers new to industry flocked patriotically to the factories. This large-scale use of unskilled workers, "dilution" as it was called, necessarily involved abandoning Trade Union conditions. Many Trade Union leaders feared that all their hard-won privileges were to be flung away on the pretext of emergency conditions and that it might be extremely difficult to recover them after the war. In order to deal with these grievances and prevent industrial disputes the Government in 1915 introduced a Defence of the Realm Act (D.O.R.A.), which gave it the power to take over factories and control labour; and a Munitions of War Act, which forbade strikes and suspended Trade Union restrictions for the duration. The standard of life of the working class improved greatly during the war, partly because overtime work increased wages, and partly because wives and daughters became wage earners instead of financial liabilities. The Labour Party was determined that this higher standard of living should continue in peacetime. The Trades Union Congress of 1916 passed a resolution in favour of the nationalization of vital industries, because they believed that it was wartime State control which had secured the general improvement in conditions.

By the end of the war we had spent well over £10,000,000,000 and lost ships and cargoes valued at £750,000,000. In order to foot this gigantic bill income tax was raised from 1s. 2d. to 6s., foreign investments were sold, death duties increased from 8 per cent to 40 per cent and the national debt rose to a total of £8,000,000,000. If the war cost us sums of money previously never dreamt of, the cost in men killed and wounded was horrifying. In May 1916 the Universal Military Service Act ensured a constant flow of men to the front. At home Zeppelin raids which began early in 1915, and the growing food shortage caused by the success of Germany's submarine war, led to the black-out and food queues. 1916 was, in some ways, the worst year of the war. In June Kitchener was drowned on his way to Russia and in Ireland the Sinn Fein rebellion broke out.

The policy of violence advocated by the Conservatives in their effort to exclude Ulster from the provisions of the Home Rule Bill, inevitably encouraged the Irish Nationalists to abandon strictly constitutional agitation. The preoccupation of England with the war, and promise of support from Germany, encouraged the Irish to rebel in April 1916. The Sinn Fein[1] movement, which had begun as an academic attempt to study Gaelic and encourage its use, became during the early years of the war a fanatical republican organization from which was developed the Irish Republican Army (I.R.A.). The rising was limited to Dublin and was easily suppressed, but the cause had succeeded in providing itself with martyrs and thereafter flourished. Fifteen leaders of the Revolution were executed, as was Sir Roger Casement, who was captured after landing from a German submarine. These reprisals provoked the bitterest hatred of England, although in fact the authorities were lenient. From then onwards the Parliamentary Home Rule Party was regarded as timid and outmoded and the sympathies of Irishmen were given to the Sinn Fein.

The war on the Western Front had apparently reached a deadlock,

[1] Sinn Fein is Gaelic for "ourselves alone".

and food shortages at home aggravated the situation. Then the Press, towards the end of 1916, started a campaign in which they held Asquith responsible for the succession of disasters which made it so bleak a year. Slowly the Conservatives came to the same conclusion as the *Daily Mail*, that Lloyd George was the man to save the situation. Considering how much he was hated and feared by the Conservatives, as a dangerous Radical and as the author of the 1909 budget, no greater compliment could have been paid to his genius and energy than that even his opponents should at length have discovered that he was indispensable. Lloyd George resigned in December, dissatisfied with the general conduct of the war. Asquith thereupon retired and George V sent for Bonar Law, who failed to form a Cabinet and advised the King to send for Lloyd George.

Lloyd George had always believed that a peacetime Cabinet was too large and unwieldy for total war. Consequently when he became Prime Minister he established a war "directory" consisting of himself, Bonar Law, Curzon, Milner and Henderson (Labour). When necessary, ministers of departments, service experts and others, were summoned to meetings of the War Cabinet. In 1917 Dominion Prime Ministers were summoned to attend its meetings and in the same year General Smuts was added to the Directory. In March 1918 the Germans made a desperate attempt to end the war. Asquith and 106 other Liberals suspected that our withdrawal in face of the enemies' advance was partly due to Lloyd George's incompetence. Consequently they opposed a vote of confidence in the Government. At the general election (1918) these followers of Asquith were singled out for destruction and very few of them retained their seats. This split in the Liberal party sealed its fate and it never again obtained a majority in the House of Commons. Lloyd George in 1918 introduced two great measures unconnected with the war: the Representation of the People Act, which gave women of 30 and over the right to vote,[1] and Fisher's Education Act.[2] Unfortunately post-war slumps made the Education Act too costly to carry out and many of its provisions were abandoned.

[1] In 1928 women were given exactly the same right to vote as men, i.e. women were given the vote at the age of twenty-one.
[2] See page 156.

## CHAPTER XII

# THE AIMS AND METHODS OF GOVERNMENT
## 1832–1950

### 1. *The Growth of Democracy*

A FRENCH aristocrat, the Marquise du Deffand, once remarked about the legend of St. Denis, who is said to have walked two leagues carrying his head in his hands, "the distance is nothing; it is only the first step which counts". In 1832 the first step towards democracy had been taken, and although the journey to universal franchise was to take ninety-six years to complete, the great Reform Bill was undoubtedly *le premier pas qui coute*.

Lincoln, in the famous Gettysburg address (1864), said that democracy was "government of the people, by the people and for the people". There are, however, many other definitions and traditions of democracy. The Athenians regarded themselves as democrats although their vast population of slaves had no political rights whatever. Napoleon and Hitler claimed that they ruled democratically, as did Stalin. Whereas the English tradition of democracy maintains that if you have government *by* the people, then *ipso facto* you will have government *of* and *for* the people, the dictators believe that representative government is inefficient and that it is enough to govern *for* the people—although perhaps occasional plebiscites may be held to prove that the dictatorship is supported by public opinion.

In so far as a democratic State is one whose government is carried on *by* the people, the history of English democracy is the history of the extension of the franchise. By 1928 every man and woman over 21, who was not incapacitated by being a lunatic, prisoner, peer of the realm, or a peeress in her own right had the right to vote. This universal franchise, which had been the main demand of the Chartists, was achieved by five Acts of Parliament: the Reform Bills of 1832 (see Vol. I, page 295), 1867 (see page 46), 1884 (see page 97), 1918 and 1928 (see opposite).

*Approximate number of Electors added by the Reform Bills*

| Number of electors before the Reform Bill | | Number of electors at the first election after the Reform Bill | |
|---|---|---|---|
| 1831 | 400,000 | 1833 | 650,000 |
| 1866 | 1,000,000 | 1868 | 2,000,000 |
| 1883 | 2,600,000 | 1885 | 4,400,000 |
| 1918 | 8,000,000 | 1918 | 21,000,000 |
| 1928 | 23,500,000 | 1929 | 28,500,000 |

The right to vote, by itself, was not enough. The vote was value-less if the voter was not completely free to vote as he wished, uninfluenced by any form of pressure. The extension of the franchise did not put an end to bribery. Even after 1832 Mrs. Disraeli could still write a letter to Sir Robert Peel in which she remarked "they will tell you at Maidstone that more than £40,000 was spent through my influence alone". More formidable even than bribery was the intimidation made possible by open voting. Not only was the elector liable to be insulted and injured at the hustings, but he might well be dismissed from his job or evicted from his house for failing to vote as his employer or landlord wished. The Ballot Act of 1872 (see page 90) put an end to this particular abuse, and each successive extension of the franchise made it more and more difficult and expensive to bribe the electorate. Moreover the whole tone of morals and politics changed so completely in the first thirty years of Queen Victoria's reign that eighteenth-century methods of influence were no longer tolerated by public opinion.

The various Reform Bills of the nineteenth and twentieth centuries, by establishing universal franchise, ensured that British democracy should involve government *by* the people, in the sense that they were able to elect their own representatives. But throughout the nineteenth century most Members of Parliament were drawn from the upper class. In the first reformed Parliament of 1833, 508 members were landowners. In Palmerston's second ministry (1859–1866) there were three dukes. Of the ten Prime Ministers of the Queen's reign, six were peers, one was the son of a duke, one was a baronet, one was made a peer, and only Gladstone was a commoner (peers: Melbourne, Derby, Aberdeen, Palmerston, Salisbury, Rosebery;

son of a duke: Lord John Russell; baronet: Sir Robert Peel; created a peer: Disraeli). Five of these Prime Ministers were educated at Eton (Melbourne, Derby, Gladstone, Rosebery and Salisbury). It is clear then that the Reform Bill of 1832 and the subsequent reforms of the nineteenth century did not flood the House of Commons with irresponsible agitators as many of the opponents of these measures anticipated; although the Duke of Wellington on seeing the members of the first reformed Commons remarked "I never saw so many shocking bad hats in my life".

After 1832 the great political families were compelled to open the doors of their most exclusive London club, the House of Commons, to merchants, industrialists and bankers. But the new middle classes had no intention of throwing out the old members altogether, or of electing working men. A narrow land-owning oligarchy had merely been broadened so as to include men enriched by the industrial revolution. Whereas in 1832 66 per cent of the House of Commons were landowners or had interests in land, by 1900 77 per cent had interests in industry. Economic changes in the country had gradually led to equivalent changes in the composition of the House of Commons.

So long as members of the House of Commons were unpaid, a working man could not possibly afford to be elected. But in 1911 salaries for members were introduced so that anybody, whatever his income, might stand for Parliament. It was not enough merely to pay members, it was also necessary to limit the expenses of candidates at elections. The Representation of the People Act (1918) provided that each party could only spend 6d. per elector in counties, and 5d. in towns. In 1948 the Act was revised according to the recommendations of the all-party Speaker's Conference of 1944. In boroughs the parties may now spend £450, plus 1½d. for every name on the electoral roll, and in counties £450 plus 2d. for every voter.

By 1928 the long struggle for parliamentary democracy had ended. The Reform Bills of the nineteenth and twentieth centuries, the payment of members and the secret ballot, had won for every Englishman the right to vote for any candidate without fear or favour, and the right to stand for Parliament without wealth or connections. Yet at the moment of its triumph democracy began to appear to millions of people all over the world to be an empty shell. The aim of the victorious allies in 1918 was, according to President Wilson, "to make the world safe for democracy", yet by 1939 only a few democracies remained. Elsewhere Communism, Fascism and other forms of dictatorship had been acclaimed. This reaction from democracy was largely owing to the belief that political rights (e.g. the right to vote, freedom of speech, the right to stand for Parliament) were a sham. The right to vote, for example, had become the right to choose between two or possibly three party candidates, whose policy was dictated to them by party headquarters, which in their turn took their orders from the vested interests which supplied the party funds.

He who pays the piper tends to call the tune. Political parties, whether supported by big business or by Trade Unions, must frame their policy to please their backers. A party candidate at a general election, if he is to have the moral and financial backing of his party, must toe the party line. Many voters, who disagree with the policy of all parties, regard casting their vote merely as a choice of evils. The right to choose between two evils, to support a party over which one has little control, whose policy appears to be determined behind one's back, is not as gratifying as might be expected. The real reason behind the long battle for the franchise was that a vote was thought to give those who had won it economic power. The Chartists in 1848 had demanded male suffrage, not so much as an end in itself, but as a means of securing better wages and social justice.

The vastness of the modern party machine, the ever increasing complexity of government and the bewildering immensity of the nation's finances, have made it very difficult for the man in the street to take any part in government or indeed to understand it. Given one vote among many thousands, allowed only to choose from two or three candidates, having no real control of the policy of the party of his choice, he regards democracy as a shabby trick to give him a sense of power without the reality, to fob him off with meaningless political rights. Equality before the law and equal political rights both sound very fine, but are not worth much in face of economic inequality. My right to sue the Prime Minister for libel, my right to publish a newspaper, my right to hire the Albert Hall and address an audience thousands strong, my right to start a political party, what are they worth if I only earn a few pounds a week?

Karl Marx (see page 173) as early as 1848 had been telling the working man that he was a "wage slave". The rich and the provileged, so Marx argued, tried to tell him that England was the land of the free. But freedom was really only freedom for the rich. The freedom of the poor was the freedom to work long hours for miserable wages, or starve. Freedom could only be made real by being interpreted in economic terms. Only when the working man gained a financial equality with the capitalist would political equality have any significance. It was because the democracies established after the 1914–1918 War all over Europe failed in the economic sphere that whole peoples were prepared to sacrifice political rights which had become meaningless to them in return for more substantial advantages, such as security, employment and higher wages.

As in the animal kingdom, so in the political world the condition of survival is continual adaptation to an ever changing environment. The ends and aims of politics may be constant; the democratic ideals of government for the people, by the people, of the people, may in themselves be eternal; but the means to secure these ends must change as the world changes. The Welfare State is a contemporary experiment to achieve democratic ideals while changing and adapting the means to secure them.

## 2. *The House of Lords*

The Reform Bill of 1832 had only been carried against the bitter opposition of the House of Lords (see Vol. I, page 291). In the nineteenth century the Lords rejected the Home Rule Bill and only withdrew their opposition to the third Reform Bill (1884) at the last moment. Nevertheless the struggle between the two Houses of Parliament only reached an acute stage after 1906. The Second Chamber was mainly Conservative, despite the large number of Liberal Governments throughout Queen Victoria's reign. In 1906 the Liberal Campbell-Bannerman became Prime Minister with a very considerable majority in the House of Commons. Balfour, the leader of the opposition, encouraged the Lords to throw out a number of important Liberal measures, including Lloyd George's 1909 budget (see page 169). The House of Lords by so flagrantly using their power of veto in the Conservative interest, despite the unequivocal mandate of the Liberal party, forced the Liberals to reduce their powers in the Parliament Act of 1911 (see pages 170-2). By this Act the peers were only enabled to delay a measure for a period of two years, and they were not able to amend or veto a bill certified by the Speaker as a money bill. The Parliament Act of 1911 was only passed by the Lords because the King promised the Prime Minister that he would create a sufficient number of peers to carry the bill should it be rejected. Once again, as in 1832, the royal prerogative proved itself to be the safeguard of democracy. In 1949 the Lords' power of obstruction was reduced from two years to one.

It is hardly surprising that Liberal and Labour Governments should be anxious to reduce the powers of the House of Lords, as a second chamber is bound by its very nature to be conservative in spirit. The Parliament Act of 1911 stated in its preamble that one day it was "intended to substitute for the House of Lords a second chamber constituted on a popular instead of hereditary basis". Yet no Government since 1911 has shown any desire whatever to destroy the House of Lords. This is partly because it does so much useful work in revising and amending bills sent to it from the House of Commons and partly because it is able to debate important issues without regard to the popularity of views expressed. Speakers in the House of Commons are often reluctant to express views objectionable either to their party or to the electorate, whereas members of the House of Lords are uninfluenced by fear of party whips or general elections. Moreover the Lords have now learnt the lesson of the Parliament Act, that their survival depends upon their ability to remain impartial. Consequently when a Labour Government came into power in 1945 and inaugurated a period of intense legislation, the Lords were prepared to swallow nearly all that they were offered, except the Nationalization of the steel industry and the Parliament Bill (1947) restricting their power of veto to one year. In 1945 the Marquis of Salisbury made a speech in which he stated that he believed that "it would be constitutionally wrong, when the country had so recently expressed its view (i.e. at the general election, 1945) for this House to oppose proposals which have definitely been put before the electorate". The two measures which the Lords rejected between 1945 and 1950 were rejected on the grounds that the Government had received no mandate[1] for them from the electorate.

### 3. The Monarchy

When Queen Victoria came to the throne the prestige of the monarchy was at a very low ebb. George III's attempt to revive the influence of the Crown had met with disaster. When George IV died *The Times* obituary stated "There never was an individual less regretted by his fellow creatures than this deceased king". The Duke of Wellington described his successor, William IV, as "a silly, bustling old fellow, who can by no possibility comprehend the scope and meaning of anything". Queen Victoria herself went through a long period of unpopularity, mainly owing to her retirement from public life after the death of Prince Albert. It was felt that her mourning for the Prince was carried to a morbid extreme. For forty years after his death she had his evening clothes laid out in his room and his wash basin filled with hot water. In 1871 a pamphlet was published entitled *What does she do with it?* It expressed in respectful language the feeling of many of the Queen's subjects that she was not justifying the expense of her court and family, and that she could well reduce the Civil List by meeting some of its expenses from her own private fortune of £5,000,000.

Partly owing to the influence of Disraeli, the Queen in the last thirty years of her reign emerged from her retirement and republican feeling immediately disappeared. When her long reign closed on January 22, 1901, she had given her name to one of the greatest ages in our history and had made the monarchy not only respected but loved. The influence of Queen Victoria is very hard to define,

[1] See Glossary.

as it was exerted almost exclusively behind the scenes. Certainly all her ministers regarded her views with the greatest deference. They realized that their own experience of power was inevitably discontinuous. Not one of them was Prime Minister for more than six consecutive years, but the Queen held office for more than sixty years without a moment's break.

Despite all the limitations on the royal prerogative accumulated after two centuries of struggle, the Queen's constitutional powers were still very considerable. "Not to mention other things, the Queen could disband the army; she could dismiss all the officers; she could dismiss all the sailors too; she could sell off all our ships of war and all our naval stores; she could make peace by the sacrifice of Cornwall, and begin a war for the conquest of Brittany. She could make every citizen in the United Kingdom, male or female, a peer; she could dismiss most of the civil servants; she could pardon all offenders." Such at any rate was the view of Walter Bagehot, one of her subjects.[1] Fortunately the Queen did not avail herself of all these opportunities.

The extent of the Queen's activities, however, was amazing. She insisted on seeing every Foreign Office dispatch. Lord Palmerston said that in 1848 alone she read through 28,000. Every important order sent to the Channel Squadron had to be submitted to her, and she was extremely annoyed when the Admiralty made additions to the Queen's Regulations without consulting her first. No appointment of a colonel in the army could be made without a long written explanation to the Queen. She even wrote to the editor of *The Times* asking him to write articles "pointing out the *immense* danger and evil of the wretched frivolity of the lives of the upper class". Her influence and experience of foreign affairs was a great asset to all her ministers. Most of the rulers of Europe were her relations, and foreign policy often became little more than an extension of family affairs. At times during the eastern crisis, 1876–1878, the Queen telegraphed hourly to Disraeli, such was her concern; and in 1861 she and Prince Albert helped to avert war with America. As head of the Church she was personally responsible for the appointment of Tait to the Archbishopric of Canterbury in 1868, despite Disraeli's

[1] Walter Bagehot, *The English Constitution.*

disapproval, and the Public Worship Regulation Act of 1874 was introduced partly at her instigation.

In constitutional theory the sovereign is impartial; in real life, however, a king or queen must necessarily have personal political views. Queen Victoria, although she began life as a Whig under Lord Melbourne's influence, very soon, like the House of Lords, took the Conservative side in politics. In religion she was of Broad Church views. Nevertheless just as the Speaker of the House of Commons should remain impartial while performing his office, so also should the sovereign. This the Queen did not always succeed in doing. When she heard of the death of General Gordon she sent the Prime Minister, Gladstone, the following uncoded telegram: "These news from Khartoum are frightful, and to think that all this might have been prevented and many precious lives saved by earlier action is too frightful." After the general election of 1880 the Queen tried to persuade Hartington to form a ministry rather than Gladstone in whom she said she "never could have the slightest particle of confidence after his violent, mischievous, and dangerous conduct for the last three years". There were times clearly when she allowed her own prejudices to become more apparent than was wise.

During her lifetime Queen Victoria refused to let the Prince of Wales take a prominent part in politics or diplomacy. Whenever her ministers suggested employment for the Prince, she refused to permit it. Yet despite the Queen's low opinion of his talents, he was both successful and popular when he came to the throne. His visit to Paris in 1903 was a personal triumph. Both Lord Lansdowne and the French President, M. Poincaré, spoke of the powerful impulse the visit had given to the Anglo-French alliance of 1904. Edward VII's handling of the crisis of 1909, when the Lords threw out Lloyd George's budget, showed that he had inherited all his father's tact and judgment. George V soon after he came to the throne was faced with the same crisis, which was ultimately solved by the passing of the Parliament Act of 1911. If anything the episode strengthened the monarchy, in that the royal prerogative had enabled the will of the electorate to be made effective despite the opposition of the House of Lords.

## 4. *The Extension of the State's Activities*

"It is one of the finest problems in legislation", wrote Burke in 1795, "and what has often engaged my thoughts while I followed that profession, what the State ought to take upon itself to direct by the public wisdom, and what it ought to leave, with as little interference as possible, to individual discretion." The political philosophy of the early part of the nineteenth century was that of *laissez-faire*, but even before Queen Victoria came to the throne it is possible to detect the faint whispers of a very different creed— collectivism. By the end of the century collectivism was driving *laissez-faire* to the wall and in order to understand this battle of principles, it is first necessary to examine these doctrines a little more closely.

Those who believed in *laissez-faire* believed that the best governed country was the least governed country. The middle class, which won political power in 1832, regarded a great many of the laws on the statute book as bulwarks of the privilege of the landed aristocracy, and as mischievous meddling on the part of the Government in the everyday life of the citizens. If these restrictions could be removed, if trade was made free and if each man was permitted to seek his own good in his own way, then, it was argued, the country would be happy and prosperous.

> "The good old rule,
> Sufficeth them, the simple plan,
> That they should take who have the power
> And they should keep who can."

The duty of the Government was to preserve law and order, to protect the country by maintaining the army, the navy and a police force. *Laissez-faire* required the Government to hold the ring and let private enterprise work out its own salvation; and it assumed that Governments could really do very little more.

> "How small of all that human hearts endure,
> That part which kings or laws can cause or cure."

The fundamental principle of the collectivist is faith in the benefits to be derived from the action or intervention of the State, even when it limits the sphere of individual liberty. The State is regarded as a wiser judge and a stronger servant of a man's interest than the man himself. The struggle between collectivism and *laissez-faire*, carried on in the nineteenth century in the economic and social sphere, had already been waged in the sixteenth century in the religious sphere. Then Protestants began to demand that the individual should be left to work out his own salvation in his own way, without the guidance of the Church. Roman Catholics, on the other hand, insisted that without the corporate aid of the Church man was too frail to stand alone. It is therefore natural that the chief support of economic *laissez-faire* was derived from Nonconformity, and one of the main props of governmental paternalism was the party of "Church and King".

Although belief in *laissez-faire* was undoubtedly predominant in the first half of the nineteenth century, it was not without critics. Dr. Arnold (1795–1842), the famous headmaster of Rugby, spoke of *laissez-faire* as "one of the falsest maxims which ever pandered to human selfishness under the name of political wisdom—I mean the maxim that society ought to leave its members alone, each to look after their several interests". Arnold had no use for the argument that life was a race in which the runners should be unhandicapped. People, he insisted, "are not equal in natural powers, and still less have they ever started with equal advantages. Knowing that power of every sort has a tendency to increase itself, we stand by and let this most unequal race take its own course, forgetting that the very name of Society implies that it shall not be a mere race, but that its object is to provide for the common good of all, by restraining the power of the strong and protecting the helplessness of the weak".

Arnold's views, although they eventually won acceptance, were not typical of the time (1838). Macaulay's review of the poet Southey's essay on "The Progress and Prospects of Society" reflected far better the opinion of his age. Southey believed that moral evils were largely of man's own making, and that therefore they could be prevented by the activity of the State. "He conceives", says Macaulay, "that the business of the magistrate is not merely to see that the persons and property of the people are secure from attack, but that he ought to be a jack-of-all-trades—architect, engineer, schoolmaster, merchant, theologian, a Lady Bountiful in every parish, a Paul Pry in every house, spying, eavesdropping, relieving, admonishing, spending our money for us, and choosing our opinions for us. His principle is, if we understand it rightly, that no man can do anything so well for himself as his rulers, and that a government approaches nearer and nearer to perfection, in proportion as it interferes more and more with the habits and notions of individuals."

Although it is easy enough to define the ideas of collectivism and *laissez-faire*, it is difficult to attribute them to one or other of the parties in the State. Also it is necessary to consider whether we are speaking of the period from 1832 to 1870 or the period from 1870 onwards. On the whole, it is true to say that the Liberals supported *laissez-faire*, that the Conservatives were often prepared to accept collectivism, while the Socialists actively welcomed State control. Nevertheless both parties and individuals tended to maintain incompatible principles. They spoke the language of *laissez-faire*, while acting as collectivists. This confusion in their minds was the result of their reluctance on humanitarian grounds to pursue *laissez-faire* to its logical conclusion—to leave children to the mercy of ferocious employers, or, having freed the negro, to refuse to interfere in "Yorkshire slavery". The writings of Dickens reveal a confusion of mind which reflect the perplexity of his time. He is "equally ready to denounce on the grounds of humanity all who left things alone, and on the grounds of liberty all who tried to make them better".[1]

After the great Reform Bill of 1832 the newly enfranchized middle class passed a large number of *laissez-faire* laws. The repeal of the Corn Laws (1846), the repeal of the Navigation Laws (1849), the Jewish Relief Act (1858), the Dissenters' Chapel Act (1884), the Marriage Act (1835), the Divorce Act (1857), are all typical measures designed to remove restrictions hitherto imposed on the nation by the Government. The Liberal middle class regarded these laws as limiting liberty and enterprise, and designed only to buttress the vested interest of the aristocracy, the landowner and the Anglican

[1] G. M. Young, *Portrait of an Age.*

Church. Yet even in the period 1832–1870 measures were proposed and some were approved, contrary to the whole philosophy of *laissez-faire*. A series of acts were passed to protect lunatics, animals and children. In 1833 bull-baiting and cock-fighting were made illegal. In 1840 a law was passed prohibiting the employment of children as chimney sweeps. The Factory Act of 1833 is the classic example of a collectivist measure, inspired by humanitarianism, passed at a moment when *laissez-faire* was otherwise triumphant.

The change from *laissez-faire* to collectivism was, as we have seen, partly caused by the humanitarianism of the nineteenth century. The assumption that a workman should be left free to agree with his employer what his labour was worth, was absurd when the workman was a child of six. The Factory Act of 1833 was designed to protect child labour, and *ipso facto* involved an important step towards collectivism. In the second half of the century two other powerful factors were at work which accelerated the transition. The extension of the franchise in 1867 and 1884 meant that Parliament increasingly reflected the opinions and desires of the working class. As the working class wanted Government action to improve the conditions of industry, and as they had always been told first by the Chartists, then by the Socialists, Co-operatives and Trade Unions, that their welfare depended upon State control, it is hardly surprising that the outcome of these Reform Bills was a movement towards collectivism. Only through the intervention of the State could the employer be compelled to limit hours of work, to negotiate with Trade Unions, protect dangerous machinery, insure his employees, or concern himself with their health.

Changes in industry itself, sometimes made the employer anxious for Government aid. As other countries began to compete with us for the markets of the world, the manufacturer and the farmer cried out for protection. While we maintained our industrial lead over all other countries, naturally we wanted free trade. But when after 1870 our supremacy was seriously challenged by Germany and America, equally naturally we started talking about Imperial Preference and protection. In addition to this, the tendency of private enterprise proved to be towards monopoly, and the one man business became the joint-stock company. In the economic jungle of *laissez-faire* only the fittest survived, and the fittest proved to be the concerns which had the most capital behind them. Over one hundred private railway lines were gradually swallowed up by four main companies, and the same tendency was at work among newspapers. In this monopolistic stage of industrial development competition was restricted as far as possible to foreign countries and to foreign markets. Not only did the industrialist often turn to the State to protect him, but the working man, confronted by this vast accumulation of capital, more and more needed the assistance of the Government in disputes with his employer. The Labour politicians at the beginning of the twentieth century soon began to demand that these great monopolies should be nationalized. To them the choice appeared to be between privately owned monopolies, acting in their own sectional and private interests, and publicly owned monopolies responsible to the public.

The Factory Acts of 1833 and 1844, the Education Acts of 1870 and 1880, the Conspiracy Act, 1875, the Employers' Liability Act, 1880, the Workman's Compensation Act, 1897, the Irish land laws of 1870 and 1881, the Act of 1848 setting up the Board of Health, to mention only a few of many hundred statutes, were all collectivist measures. Particularly in the last twenty-five years of Queen Victoria's reign this collectivist spirit was abroad, both in the House of Commons and in local government. In 1890 Sidney Webb wrote that "the practical man, oblivious or contemptuous of any general principles of social organization, has been forced, by the necessities of the time, into an ever-deepening collectivist channel. Socialism, of course, he still rejects and despises. The individualist town councillor will walk along the municipal pavement, lit by municipal gas, and cleansed by municipal brooms with municipal water, and seeing, by the municipal clock in the municipal market, that he is too early to meet his children coming from the municipal school, will use the national telegraph system to tell them not to walk through the municipal park, but to come by the municipal tramway. . . 'Socialism, Sir', he will say, 'don't waste the time of a practical man by your fantastic absurdities. Self-help, Sir, individual self-help, that's what's made our city what it is.'"

At the present day, living as we do in an age of collectivism, many people look back with nostalgia to the glorious era of private enterprise, and they infer that *laissez-faire*, which made Britain the "workshop of the world" is the solution to most of our present problems. Unfortunately methods appropriate to the expanding economy of nineteenth-century England, are not necessarily applicable to the very different circumstances of our own times. World-wide competition, monopolies, and unemployment on a vast scale, have all forced collectivism upon us, and confronted us once again most forcibly with Burke's problem: "What the State ought to take upon itself and what it ought to leave to individual discretion."

## 5. *The Machinery of Government*

The extension of the activities of Parliament led to an increase in the duties of the Prime Minister. As early as 1844 Peel complained of the difficulties of the office. "I defy the Minister of this country", he wrote, "to perform properly the duties of his office, to read all that he ought to read, including the whole foreign correspondence; to keep up the constant communication with the Queen and the Prince; to see whom he ought to see; to write with his own hand to every person of note who chooses to write to him; to be prepared for every debate; to do all these things, and also to sit in the House of Commons eight hours a day for 118 days."

Perhaps the main difference between the Prime Ministers of the nineteenth century, particularly towards the end of the Queen's reign, and those of the reign of George III, was that they had to consider the electorate as well as the sovereign and their majority in the House of Commons. Bute (1713–1792) had depended entirely upon the King's support for his office. Gladstone, despite the Queen's disapproval and efforts to prevent it, became Prime Minister because the country wanted him.[1]

The various Reform Acts of the nineteenth century, by making political parties more dependent upon the electorate, inevitably altered methods of electioneering. Persuasion and propaganda replaced patronage and corruption. Gladstone was the first Prime Minister to understand the necessity of addressing meetings all over

[1] See the 1880 election, page 94.

the country, although the Queen, and many politicians brought up before the passing of the great Reform Bill, strongly disapproved of his doing so. Derby, a statesman of the old school, referred contemptuously to the "balderdash and braggadocio in which Gladstone had been indulging on his stumping tour", and Gladstone's Midlothian campaign was described by Selborne as "a precedent tending in its results to the degradation of British politics, by bringing in a system of perpetual canvass, and removing the political centre of gravity from Parliament to the platform". Nevertheless the new methods prevailed, and by wireless and television it is now possible for politicians to address a considerable proportion of the electorate.

Not only the Prime Minister but the whole party organization had to turn its attention to the electors. In the eighteenth century the only party organization that existed, existed in Parliament itself. After 1832 local organizations were set up in the constituencies to ensure that all who had the right to vote had their names on the electoral register. In 1868 the Conservatives affiliated their local associations into a National Union with a central office in Whitehall. Nine years later the Liberal party formed the National Liberal Federation, modelled on Joseph Chamberlain's "Caucus" in Birmingham. The growth of these organizations outside Parliament, while undoubtedly stimulating public interest in Parliamentary proceedings, has tended to limit the independence of members. What Burke told the electors of Bristol in 1774 is too often forgotten today. "Your representative owes you, not his industry only, but his judgment; and he betrays, instead of serving you, if he sacrifices it to your opinion."

The difference between the Liberal and Conservative parties in the nineteenth century was partly an economic one. Before the Reform Bill all parties recruited their supporters from the nobility, gentry, mercantile and professional classes, and it is difficult to distinguish an absolutely clear-cut difference of economic interests between them. By the beginning of the nineteenth century a new economic interest appeared, that of industry, the railways and finance, which was, broadly speaking, represented by the Liberal party. As commerce and industry increased their strength in the

House of Commons, the Conservatives became less and less the party of land and their economic interests became much the same as those of their opponents.

By 1900 it was no longer true, either that the Conservatives were the party of land, or that there was any appreciable economic difference between the parties in the House of Commons. In the years when the parties represented distinct and opposing economic interests, there were radical differences in their policies. As the economic differences disappeared so it became harder to differentiate party programmes. The Reform Bill of 1867, the Conspiracy Act of 1875, and the Workmen's Compensation Act of 1897, at first sight look like Liberal measures, but in fact they were all the work of Conservative Governments. It is perhaps partly because the Liberal party ceased to represent a fundamentally different economic interest from that of the Conservative party, that the Labour party, representing an altogether new interest, has stolen its thunder.

The continual extension of the activities of nineteenth-century Governments involved the growth of bureaucracy.[1] The beginnings of all this are contained in the Factory Act of 1833, since it appointed inspectors to see that its provisions were carried out. In the twentieth century, government departments and local government departments have been given increasing authority to make their own rules and regulations, or to carry out in detail general principles laid down by Parliament. Such "delegated legislation" is regarded by many people as a sinister threat to Parliamentary democracy since it involves the surrender by Parliament of its legislative and executive functions. On the other hand it is argued that the increasing complexity of government necessitates administration by experts, and that the most that Members of Parliament can do is to indicate in general terms what is to be done.

In the nineteenth century the Civil Service, upon which so many of the executive functions of government depend, in common with most other institutions, came under the hand of Liberal reformers. As Parliament and local government had become democratic, it was only natural that the Civil Service should be made to open its doors to all comers, instead of providing a last resting place for eighteenth-

---

[1] Between 1890 and 1910 alone the number of civil servants doubled.

century patronage. In 1870 the Civil Service, except the Foreign Office, was thrown open to public competitive examinations, thus, in theory, establishing the principle of the career open to talents. In fact, however, only those who had had an expensive education had any real chance of success in these examinations.

Liberalism, Democracy and Collectivism, are forces which between them have completely altered the political life of the nation, and set a great gulf between us and the eighteenth century. The conflict and influence of these principles is nowhere better illustrated than in the history of the development of local government. Before the Reform Bill the local government of England was carried on by Justices of the Peace, who were unpaid country gentlemen, responsible for administering the law, licensing public houses and looking after roads, paupers and prisons. The towns were either governed by Justices of the Peace, or if they were among the 178 boroughs (i.e. towns which had been granted a royal charter) by a Mayor and Corporation. One of the first reforms demanded by the newly enfranchised middle class in 1832 was the reform of local government. In the country and in the towns local government was in the hands of small self-elected oligarchies. In the city of Newcastle, for example, the municipal franchise was possessed by thirty-six people. The Municipal Reform Act of 1835 provided a uniform system of local government, in which the middle class were to be represented, in which dissenters could hold office, and which would end for ever the rule of a "shabby mongrel aristocracy".

In 1848 a Public Health Act set up a department at Whitehall with powers to compel local authorities to adopt sanitary measures. This was the first of a series of acts whereby government departments compelled local government to maintain a standard insisted upon by the State, leaving the administrative details to local knowledge and initiative. A good example of this interaction between Whitehall and the municipalities is Disraeli's Artisans Dwelling Act (1875) which required town councils to appoint a Medical Officer of Health, empowered to buy slum sites and rebuild. The Local Government Acts of 1888, 1894 and 1929, the Town Planning Act of 1932, and the National Insurance Act of 1946, have all involved giant strides towards collectivism. The achievements of local government in the last century have been remarkable. The death rate has been halved; infant mortality reduced by three-quarters; typhus, small-pox and cholera, once only too common, are now rare diseases, and illiteracy has been almost abolished.

Oddly enough at the moment only about 40 per cent of the electorate bother to vote in municipal elections. In general elections at least 70 per cent of voters go to the poll. Considering that local government is responsible for our water supply, drainage and sewage, many of our hospitals, food inspection, our schools, museums and libraries, our roads, our bridges, our buses, our parks, and our police, it is curious that many electors who are concerned enough to vote for a member of Parliament, do not apparently care what local councillors they have.

The complexity of modern life is the resultant of the industrial revolution, the democratic ideals of the French Revolution, the traditions of English law, Parliament, and the political revolution of the seventeenth century. The nineteenth century witnessed the transformation of an oligarchy into a democracy, and of an individualist into a collectivist state. All these great changes were effected within the framework of ancient parliamentary and monarchical institutions, and their remarkable power of adaptation enabled them not only to survive but to prosper. It would be a great mistake if, dazzled by the splendid achievements of the Victorian age, we persuaded ourselves that our future greatness depended upon preserving nineteenth-century institutions and methods. Our greatness then was produced by a series of changes in our industrial and political life without parallel in our whole history, for prosperity and civilization are the fruits not of perpetual regrets for the past, but of continual and fearless advance.

## CHAPTER XIII

# FOREIGN POLICY, 1918–1950

## 1. The Versailles Settlement

THE Treaty of Versailles has been universally execrated and that fact alone speaks volumes for its merits. Few people abuse what is self-evidently wrong or foolish, and when we come across something which was apparently equally hateful to French Marshals and English Pacifists, to German Nazis and English Liberals we may hesitate before joining in so inharmonious a chorus. Before considering the wisdom or unwisdom of what was done at the Peace Conference a brief survey of Europe in 1919 reveals the limits of what it was possible to do. Russia was in a state of chaos, too weak to help or hinder any general settlement of European problems, but the Government which was emerging had announced its intention of furthering violent revolution in all the countries of the world. The Austro-Hungarian Empire was in the sad condition of Humpty-Dumpty after his fall. The non-German races of the Empire, Poles, Czechs, Slovaks and Croats, had seized the national independence denied them by the Habsburgs, and Austria itself had expelled the Emperor and declared itself a republic. Alone of the Great Powers east of the Rhine Germany remained united and, in spite of her defeat, a country whose recovery was certain. Of the victorious allies France had suffered terrible losses in life and property and, lacking Germany's industrial strength and rising birth-rate, lacked her resilience. Italy, threatened with revolution, thought only of acquiring territory from the conquered states with which to satisfy her ever larger, ever hungrier population. Britain, to all appearances as strong as ever, had been gravely weakened; the delicate mechanism of international trade had been smashed by the war and many of her old export markets were closed to her. Finally across the Atlantic the Congressional elections of 1918 had shown that the American people were heading once again for a policy of isolation. The situation that faced the Peacemakers was, in its barest essentials, this: Russia was out, Germany was down, the long-repressed nationalism of Central and Eastern Europe had blown the Austro-Hungarian Empire sky-high, Italy was for grabbing all she could get away with, France and Britain, dangerously shaken by the war, were determined to make Germany pay, America had repudiated the internationalist foreign policy of her President, Woodrow Wilson.

To build a lasting peace on such foundations was difficult; indeed some have said that it was impossible. The task was complicated by a clash of personalities: Clemenceau, dry, brilliant and sceptical, Wilson a generous but rigid idealist unsuited to the give-and-take of negotiation, Lloyd George a master of all the arts of diplomacy but lacking Wilson's vision and Clemenceau's knowledge of Europe. Clemenceau's over-riding idea was to win security for France by weakening Germany; Wilson in his famous Fourteen Points, on the basis of which Germany had surrendered, had promised that the peace was not to be a punitive one but an attempt to build a world-wide family of nations. Lloyd George agreed with Clemenceau in seeking to make the Germans pay "the uttermost farthing" in Reparations and with Wilson in setting up an international organization which would reduce armaments and outlaw aggression.

The actual settlement was a compromise. The principle of self-determination, which Wilson championed, was recognized in the new states of Czechoslovakia, Hungary, Yugo-Slavia and Austria which took the place of the Habsburg Empire. Poland returned to the map of Europe and was granted access to the sea by means of a corridor which separated East Prussia from the rest of Germany. Alsace-Lorraine was given back to France. The other territorial changes of the treaty cannot be defended on Wilson's principles. Italy received the German-speaking South Tyrol and parts of the Dalmatian coast which were predominantly Croat. Rumania took Transylvania from Hungary and the Dobrudja from Bulgaria for no better reason than that she had been on the winning side. Similarly Belgium obtained the small German provinces of Eupen and Malmedy and France the rich industrial valley of the Saar with the provision that its eventual sovereignty was to be decided by plebiscite

The shaded portion indicates new states, and ter

underwent a change of political sovereignty.

in 1935. Germany's possessions oversea were confiscated and put under a League of Nations mandate, which was in most cases entrusted to Great Britain, and the port of Danzig was put under direct League of Nations control.

The Reparations issue was never brought to a satisfactory conclusion. A Commission was set up to fix the amount in consultation with the Germans. In the event, the French brushed aside German objections and demanded an impossible figure. To cut short a long and tedious history Britain and America lent Germany enormous sums to rehabilitate her economy so that she could pay. However, this scheme was robbed of its fruits by the slump and in 1932 when it was finally agreed to cancel all further reparations Germany had paid out far less than she had received in loans. Thus the country it was intended to penalize had been the only beneficiary, and resentment and ill-feeling had been created all round.

The most original, and to many the most hopeful, feature of the settlement was the adoption of the League of Nations covenant as an integral part of the treaty, binding on all signatories. Briefly this meant that the nations who signed the covenant (and this soon included many who had no share in framing the Versailles settlement) agreed to submit all international disputes to arbitration. If any nation rejected arbitration and committed an act of aggression against one of the members of the League, the other members bound themselves to break off all economic relations with the aggressor and to give all the help they could to the victim, including, if necessary, armed support. This was the classic theory of the War of All against One which is the most obvious method of deterring aggressors and outlawing war. In practice it is difficult to apply and the League started off under such handicaps that it would never have been a simple and easy matter. In the first place the two remaining great powers of Eastern Europe, Germany and the Soviet Union, were not admitted to membership until 1926 and 1934 respectively.[1] Worse still the United States, whose President had been the father of the institution, never became a member as the American Senate refused to ratify the Treaty of Versailles. This had the most unfortunate effect on France who had only agreed to include the League

[1] Germany withdrew in 1933 after Hitler's rise to power.

covenant in the Treaty in return for promises of an Anglo-American guarantee for her security. Now she felt that she had been tricked, especially as England insisted that her own promise was conditional on America's. France therefore attempted to win security for herself by maintaining a large army at home and by making military alliances with Poland, Czechoslovakia, Yugo-Slavia and Rumania, the states which owed either their existence, or a great part of their territory, to the Treaty of Versailles and were consequently interested in maintaining it.[1] To many French statesmen the League became a symbol of Anglo-American cant and hypocrisy, of the Great Betrayal. Italy was dissatisfied with the Treaty and after Mussolini's seizure of power in 1922 she could hardly be considered a supporter of the League, though she remained a member until her Abyssinian venture in 1935. The whole success of the League rested on Britain, who was the only great power to base her foreign policy on its principles. When the testing time came, however, her practice was not equal to her profession.

These are the main outlines of the Treaty of Versailles, which set the scene for the next twenty years of the European tragedy. Apart from the cession of a great part of Silesia to Poland, Germany did not suffer any territorial loss that she could not reasonably expect. The reparations that she was made to pay, as distinct from those demanded, were very mild. She was allowed a professional army of 100,000 men and a token navy, but no air force or submarines. Her unity and her industrial power were not destroyed. It was not a harsh peace. Nevertheless there were aspects of the peace and of the manner in which it was made which the propagandist, skilled in exaggeration and distortion, could use to misrepresent its real nature. The Germans had not been admitted to the peace Conference in Paris and the Treaty could therefore be described as a Dictated Peace. The adjective "Dictated" is charged with emotional associations—the victor's jackboot on the prostrate body of his victim, etc. etc. It was of little use to point out that the Treaty itself was a perfectly reasonable one. Most people, and especially most Germans, tend to think with their emotions rather than with their reason, a fact of which Hitler made the fullest use. Another

---

[1] These states were known collectively as the Succession States.

feature of the Treaty with which Hitler and his friends made great play was the War-Guilt clause (Article 231).

"The Allied and Associated Governments affirm and Germany accepts the responsibility of Germany for causing all the loss and damage to which the Allied and Associated Governments and their nations have been subjected as a consequence of the war imposed on them by the aggression of Germany and her allies." To most Englishmen and Frenchmen this seemed a fair and obvious statement of the truth but few Germans saw the matter in this light. It was an insult, possibly justifiable as a statement of historical truth, but serving no useful purpose. In the German mind it was quickly confused with the reparations issue and helped to create a general sense of injustice. Because little fighting had taken place on German soil the idea that the German army had never been defeated soon became prevalent. An elaborate myth was invented and eagerly believed to the effect that Germany had surrendered, while still undefeated, on the basis of Wilson's Fourteen Points, but the treacherous allies had denied Germany access to the Peace Conference, had convicted her of War Guilt without a fair hearing, and had sentenced her to loss of territory and payment of reparations.

That such a glaring falsification of recent history should gain currency among a defeated people is not surprising, but what is truly astonishing is that the German myth was soon widely accepted in England. It seems that after the passions aroused by war have begun to cool the English are affected by a sort of spurious pacifism which makes them recklessly indulgent to their ex-enemies and grossly unfair to their allies. Thus by the middle twenties sympathy for Germany was commonly expressed in this country, together with severe disapproval of French militarism and the French system of alliances. To be lectured by England for trying to defend the settlement that had cost such incalculable suffering to achieve was too much for the French to bear. Anglo-French relations were often strained and the one sure way of avoiding catastrophe, namely a common Anglo-French foreign policy, was not followed until it was too late.

## 2. The Twenties

From the fall of Lloyd George in 1922 to the collapse of France in 1940 Britain had only three[1] Prime Ministers, Baldwin, MacDonald and Neville Chamberlain, all three mediocrities who knew little of foreign affairs. The Foreign Secretaries during the same period were more numerous but not more distinguished, except for the Socialist Henderson and the Conservatives Curzon and Eden, none of whom were in office long enough to have any appreciable influence on British foreign policy. The leadership was third-rate, and the Labour and Conservative parties who put up with it deserved no better. Nor did the electorate who put up with them. The differences between the two parties on foreign policy were small. Both professed a belief in collective security within the framework of the League and both shirked the difficulties of putting it into practice. The Labour party, strongly influenced by its pacifist traditions, consistently demanded a reduction in armaments and when in opposition voted against the Service estimates. The Conservatives, wiser in theory, were as foolish in practice. Few of them took the League policy seriously, especially when it involved risks, and they shut their eyes to the ugly fact of German re-armament under Hitler. Those who, like Churchill or Eden, wanted a real policy of collective security—Arms and the Covenant, to quote Churchill's slogan —were disregarded. Both parties were equally unwilling to risk unpopularity by bold action but it must be remembered that it was the Conservatives who were in power for most of the period and during all the crucial years after 1933.

The ten years that followed the Treaty of Versailles seemed peaceful enough. On the initiative of the United States a Naval Conference was held at Washington in 1921–2 at which the leading naval powers agreed to scrap a large number of their capital ships and not to replace them. In Europe this left the Royal Navy in a position of unchallengeable superiority while in the Pacific the power of the United States, Great Britain and Japan was to be in the ratio 5 : 5 : 3. The Washington Naval Treaty also involved the abrogation of the Anglo-Japanese Alliance of 1902 and the

---

[1] Not counting Bonar Law's six months of office in 1922–3.

establishment of a looser treaty of mutual co-operation between America, Britain, France and Japan. This arrangement was by no means pleasing to the Japanese, who considered themselves slighted and let down by the British. The position of the peaceful, pro-Western politicians in Japan was appreciably weakened.

In 1923 the Italians bombarded and occupied the Greek island of Corfu on the flimsiest of pretexts. Greece at once appealed to the League and after some diplomatic interchanges the Italians evacuated the island. The affair is a small one, but the fact that Italy remained unrepentant and was treated with anxious sympathy by Britain and France was not an encouraging sign for the future. On the other hand the Locarno Pact which was signed in 1925 by Germany, France, Great Britain and Italy seemed a very hopeful document. Briefly it reinforced the Versailles settlement with mutual guarantees, recognized the French alliances with the Succession states and arranged for arbitration over points still disputed between Germany and her eastern neighbours. The participation of Germany in the discussions as an independent and equal state reassured many who had doubted the stability of the peace treaty. This sense of stability was short-lived. The Wall Street crash of October 1929 reverberated to the other end of the world and the thirties opened with despair. All over Europe there were armies of unemployed, and in Germany they reached the staggering figure of six millions. Desperation and hunger are the richest breeding-grounds for totalitarianism. The Communist and Nazi parties with their promises of an easy, immediate remedy for unemployment grew daily stronger. The World Economic Depression was if not the parent at least the midwife of Hitlerism.

Hard on the heels of the Depression came the first real test of the League of Nations. In October 1931 Japan whose government was now controlled by the militarists, invaded Manchuria and occupied the country without difficulty. The League at once sent out a commission under the chairmanship of Lord Lytton to find out the rights and wrongs of the matter. The Lytton report which was adopted by the League, with Japan alone dissenting, found that China was the rightful owner of the territory in question and that an act of aggression had been committed. Japan promptly resigned from the League and the world waited to see what the League would do next. According to Article Sixteen of the Covenant Japan should have been solemnly cursed with bell, book and candle and excluded from any commercial relations with the other member-states who, in their turn, should have prepared themselves for the possibility of a war against her. In fact nothing of the sort happened. Of the great powers who were in a position to bring military and economic pressure to bear on Japan neither Russia nor America were members of the League. It was perfectly obvious that if anything was to be done Great Britain would have to do it alone. Without Russian and American help the British could not hope to achieve a decisive result while the risks involved to British possessions and trading interests in the East were tremendous. So apart from condemnation of the Japanese action the League did nothing. In the circumstances it had no alternative. Japan, elated by her easy success, went on to invade China proper and confidence in the League as a bulwark against aggression was everywhere reduced.

## 3. The Thirties

The lesson of these events was not lost upon Hitler. Appointed Chancellor of Germany in January 1933 he lost no time in suspending the constitution and in butchering his political enemies with great thoroughness and brutality. Europe was at first deeply shocked by this sudden display of bestiality, and those who had read the manifesto of the Nazi party and Hitler's own book *Mein Kampf* were filled with alarm. In these documents the aims of Hitler's subsequent foreign policy were openly stated. The violent overthrow of the Versailles settlement, the incorporation of Austria, Czechoslovakia, Danzig and parts of Poland in the German state, the destruction of any power or group of powers who could challenge German supremacy in Europe—all were there for those who cared to read them. Why, it may reasonably be asked, was Hitler allowed to get away with it? France was still ready to act and Mussolini was frightened that Germany might supplant Italy as the arbiter of South-Eastern Europe. With such an overwhelming preponderance of power could not a still unarmed Germany have been brought

to heel? The answer is emphatically yes. The principal reason why
Hitler was not stopped in time was the slothfulness, ignorance and
political cowardice of Baldwin and his supporters. The attitude of
the Conservatives towards Hitler's Germany was a curious blend of
incompatibles. They did not like his violent methods and his persecution of the Jews but they approved of the same methods when
applied to German Communists and hoped that the new régime
would be a firm barrier against Bolshevism. The fact of German
re-armament was for long regarded as a bee in Churchill's bonnet
and officially denied by Government spokesmen in spite of the most
convincing proofs. When at last forced to re-arm and to admit that
Germany was dangerously stronger than this country, Baldwin
defended his previous inaction by blaming the pacific mood of the
people he had lulled into a sense of false security. It is a dismal
record.

The Stresa Conference of March 1935 between Britain, France
and Italy produced little beyond a general re-affirmation of the
Locarno treaty of 1925, with the important difference that Germany
was no longer a supporter but an avowed opponent of Locarno.
Italy's adherence to the Stresa front, which the French set great store
by, was owing to her fear of German designs on Austria. It proved
to be short-lived. In October the Italians invaded Abyssinia, ostensibly because of a frontier dispute which was then before the League
but in reality to acquire a colonial empire on the cheap. Britain and
France were now torn between loyalty to the League and a desire
not to offend their ally. Laval, the French Foreign Minister, who
disliked the League found the decision easy and adroitly manœuvred
the havering British into a pro-Italian position. For once this was too
much for British public opinion. There was a great outcry and
Baldwin dropped Sir Samuel Hoare from the Foreign Office, re-
placing him by Eden. In the League, Britain headed the party which
called for economic sanctions against Italy. If these had been properly
applied the Italian forces could have been brought to a standstill
since Italy was entirely dependent on foreign countries for her
supplies of oil. Mussolini let it be known that he would consider
any interference with his oil supplies as an act of war. In view of
the French attitude this meant in practice that the British Medi-

terranean Fleet would have to take on the new and powerful Italian Navy. This the British Cabinet were not prepared to do although the Commander-in-Chief at Alexandria was confident of success. In order to save the League's face sanctions were imposed but did not include the one vital material—oil. The Italians went on to win an easy victory against their ill-armed opponents and the net result was the alienation of Italy from the Stresa front, a feeling of mutual distrust and resentment between Britain and France and, of course, a further setback for the League.

Germany had been a delighted spectator of this exhibition bout of Western bungling and in March 1936 she re-occupied the Rhineland which had been declared a demilitarized zone in the Treaty of Versailles. France immediately prepared to mobilize and called on Great Britain to support her in demanding and, if necessary, enforcing an immediate withdrawal of the German troops. Now, if ever, was the time to strike. Hitler had already denounced the clauses of the Versailles Treaty which forbade German re-armament, and the remilitarization of the Rhineland was clear proof that he meant every word that he had written in *Mein Kampf*. Yet the balance of power was still on the side of the West. The French Army was large, well trained and well equipped, though lacking the modern weapons the Germans were to have in 1939. The Germans on the other hand were virtually defenceless. It takes a long time to translate a re-armament programme into actual arms. The Panther tanks which were to rumble, in a few short years, all over the continent of Europe had not yet come into production and the bombers which were to pulverize so many fine cities were still on the designer's drawing-board. The British Cabinet, however, refused to support the French Government in any action it might take against this gross violation of the Versailles Treaty, although Britain was bound by the Locarno Pact to co-operate with France in just such a case. It was argued that Britain could not be expected to go to war to stop German troops marching into what was, after all, German territory; that appeasement was the best policy for reducing the Germans to a more peaceful frame of mind, and so forth and so on. Unhappily the French, who were quite strong enough to have dealt with the situation on their own, allowed themselves to be dissuaded. For many French politicians this marked a turning-point. They saw that the last chance to stop Germany without a full-scale war had been thrown away and they began to think of making what terms they could with the new masters of Europe.

In 1937 Baldwin retired from the Premiership. His successor, Chamberlain, was more conscientious but had even less knowledge of European affairs than his late chief. Worst of all he was stiff in his opinions and disinclined to listen to his Foreign Secretary or his expert officials. Convinced that he could arrange a settlement by personal contact with Hitler and Mussolini he rebuffed an approach from President Roosevelt which might have meant an ending of the American policy of isolationism. This was too much for Eden who resigned in the spring of 1938. Shortly after Eden's resignation Hitler annexed Austria, a move which Mussolini was powerless to prevent. From this point the association between Germany and Italy —the Rome–Berlin Axis as it was called—became indissoluble and was soon strengthened by the adherence of Japan. The Soviet Union, whom Hitler had consistently attacked in the most violent language, had been growing more and more alarmed by the rise of German power, and after the *Anschluss*[1] she approached Britain and France with a suggestion of a defensive military alliance. Public opinion in England favoured such an alignment, but the Cabinet was contemptuous of Russia's military strength and distrustful of her politics. France, who already had a pact with the Russians, should have been more eager to develop this alliance which, if it could not dethrone Hitler, might at least keep him in check. But the spirit of defeatism was already numbing her power of decision. What was the use of taking arms against a sea of troubles? One's allies could never be relied on when it came to the point. Better cultivate the friendship of Italy and sit tight behind the Maginot Line. After all there was still a good chance that Hitler might go for Russia and leave the West alone. So matters continued to drift in a sea of waking dream until they grounded on the coast of Bohemia in September 1938.

The Czechoslovak state which had been created at Versailles con-

[1] The German word for the annexation of Austria.

tained upwards of three million Germans, mostly concentrated in the area adjoining the Czech-German and Czech-Austrian frontiers. These Sudeten (or Southern) Germans disliked being included in a non-Teutonic state and Hitler and his friends took advantage of their resentment to demand the cession of the Sudetenland to Germany. If Czechoslovakia yielded she would be left with an indefensible frontier and her extinction could only be a matter of time. If Czechoslovakia fell, the French system of alliances with the Succession states and the best hope of co-operation with Russia fell with her. France declared that she would honour her pledges to Czechoslovakia and Britain implied in the strongest terms that she would stand by France. Russia again suggested an alliance with the Western powers and promised assistance to the Czechs. This time it looked as if Hitler would have to fight. However, Chamberlain saw a solution that the wisest heads had overlooked. He would fly to Berchtesgaden and have a personal interview with Hitler. The result of this meeting was the Munich agreement signed by Germany, France, Britain and Italy by which the Czechs were forced to give the Germans all they had asked, in exchange for a guarantee of their reduced territories and a pledge from Hitler to Chamberlain that Germany and Britain should never go to war. It was the most devastating defeat that the Western powers had suffered and the most shameful betrayal by France of a brave and powerful ally. Chamberlain described Czechoslovakia as "a far-off country of which we know nothing", but Churchill pointed out that she had an army several times as large as the British, equipped with the most modern weapons. When in March 1939 the Germans proceeded to occupy the rest of Czechoslovakia the Appeasement policy was done for, but Czech industry and above all the Skoda works, one of the largest arsenals in the world, was in the hands of the Nazis.

Britain and France had administered a resounding snub to the Soviet Union by failing to invite her to the Munich Conference. Half-hearted attempts were now made to take up the Soviet suggestion of military talks and a Western delegation was actually sent to Moscow, though the rank of its members hardly suggested any serious intentions. By this time, however, the Russians had other fish to fry. Like Mussolini they had become convinced that Britain and France would never stand up to Hitler unless directly threatened, and consequently they began to negotiate with Hitler on their own account. The Western reply to the German breach of the Munich agreement was to guarantee the territorial integrity of both Poland and Rumania, which showed a fine disregard for the facts of geography and strategy as both countries refused to admit Russian troops to their defence, even if the Russians had been willing to come. To desert Czechoslovakia and then fight for Poland was the final touch of idiocy.

### 4. The Second World War

In August 1939 Hitler concluded a non-aggression pact with the Soviet Union and at once demanded the return of Danzig and the Polish corridor to Germany. There were the usual frontier incidents, the same raving speeches, the same promises that this was the last demand Germany had to make. The only difference was that this time there was no Munich. In September we declared war on Germany. From then until Russia and America entered the war we had no foreign policy except to try to keep the neutrals as favourably inclined towards us as possible. But by 1943 it became clear that we should win, and discussions took place with the Americans and Russians concerning the settlement to be made after the war. At the great conferences at Teheran (1944) and Yalta (1945) Roosevelt, Stalin and Churchill agreed to re-establish the frontiers laid down at Versailles. The only substantial alteration was that Poland was to give up her eastern Russian-speaking provinces to the Soviet Union in exchange for East Prussia, from which the German population was to be expelled. When the states of Eastern and Central Europe were liberated temporary governments representing every shade of political opinion were to be set up until it was possible to hold free elections. Germany was to be disarmed and occupied for an unspecified period by the allies. To replace the old League a new international organization known as the United Nations was formed in which the special position and responsibilities of the great powers were recognized by membership of a small, inner committee called the Security Council. It was hoped that this device would avoid the unwieldiness which had made the League so ineffective. Finally Britain, America and Russia declared their readiness to co-operate in peace as in war.

This halcyon prospect soon faded. Even before the end of the war the Russians had shown a cynical contempt for the agreements concluded at Yalta regarding the governments of the liberated countries. By the end of 1946 all the countries east and south-east of Germany and Austria with the single exception of Greece, were ruled by men who took their orders from Moscow. The difficulty of conducting relations with a great power which is also the head-quarters of an international revolutionary party has been abundantly demonstrated. The volley of abuse and threats which the Russians hurled at their allies and the readiness they showed to exploit the economic dislocation of the West for subversive ends provoked a reaction. In 1947 the American Secretary of State, General Marshall, made his great offer of help to the countries of Europe which was eagerly taken up by the British Foreign Secretary, Ernest Bevin. Since that date the foreign policy of this country has been based on the idea that it is only by working with the Americans that we can secure Europe from a Russian invasion and avert the economic misery which breeds totalitarianism.

The period in British diplomacy covered by this chapter is a sad one. The systematic terror of the police state and the mad destructive-ness of modern war have reduced the margin of error in foreign policy to a razor's edge. Blunders cannot be retrieved. It is all the more tragic that the leadership of our country in the decisive years before the war should have been in such nerveless and incompetent hands.

## CHAPTER XIV

# THE CHURCH OF ENGLAND, 1832–1960

## 1. *The Church in 1832*

THE Church of England at the time of the Reform Bill appeared to be at its last gasp. In the State and in society a powerful wind of reform was blowing; the last traces of the eighteenth century had all but vanished. But in the Church nothing had altered: the idleness, the ignorance, the bland worldliness of the clergy, the toadying of churchmen to politicians from whom they expected preferment, all these disfigurements of the Church were as abundantly present in the twenties and thirties as they had been a century before. It is true that the Evangelical Revival had left behind it a small body of energetic and conscientious clergymen but by far the greater body of Evangelicals had left the Church. The movement itself was showing signs of faltering. It was losing the simplicity and warmth that had attracted so much popular support. More and more the Evangelicals were becoming a party in the State and in the Church, with the narrowness and bitterness of a party. The timidity and slothfulness of the eighteenth-century clergy had robbed the Evangelicals of their chance of reviving the national church. Since their time no new force had arisen which seemed capable of the task. Dr. Arnold, the great headmaster of Rugby, was expressing the opinion of most intelligent observers when he said in 1832 "The Church as it now stands, no human power can save." What had been good enough for the eighteenth century would not do in the nineteenth.

What was needed most was leadership, and if one runs one's mind's eye along the episcopal bench of 1832, a body which had excited public opinion against it by voting almost solidly against the Reform Bill, one is struck by the lack of outstanding men. The two archbishops, Howley of Canterbury and Vernon Harcourt of York, were good men and competent administrators but they are remembered as the last two archbishops who lived in the style of a great feudal overlord, attended by a large retinue and dispensing lavish hospitality. Blomfield, Bishop of London, was perhaps the ablest—during his tenure of the See of London he built two hundred new churches and tightened the discipline of his clergy—but even he was uninspiring. Speaking in the House of Lords a year after his elevation to the See of London, he apologized for taking a different line in a debate from that taken by the statesman to whom he owed his bishopric. This cringing before the power of the State was typical of the higher clergy of the day and explains why men felt they had to look elsewhere for spiritual leadership.

There were in the Church at this time three main parties or schools of thought. The most numerous were the High Churchmen. This term had had in the seventeenth century, and was soon to have again, a deep meaning. But at the time of the Reform Bill it meant little more than a blind conservatism and a determination at all costs to hold on to that special relation between church and state which is called "Establishment". The contemporary nickname for these men, the "two-bottle orthodox", suggests a mixture of conventional religion and port-drinking conservatism. Of the Evangelicals something has been said already and it is not necessary to say more here, except to emphasize their practical Christianity and spiritual quality. The third body of opinion, young and ill-supported as yet but rapidly growing in importance, was that headed by Dr. Arnold of Rugby. Arnold sat loose to creeds and formularies and was ready to admit every kind of Dissenter to full membership of the Church. He saw the essence of Christianity to lie in its moral teachings while the mysterious side of religion (Sacraments, the priesthood, etc.) meant nothing to him. He stands in the line of Latitudinarians[1] and connects them with the "Modern Churchmen" of our own time.

## 2. The Oxford Movement

In 1833 a new force began to make itself felt. This was the revival of the teaching of Laud and the seventeenth-century High Church-men. Briefly, this teaching was that the English Church had broken

---

[1] So called because they believed in extending the bounds of the Church to the widest latitude.

with Rome not on matters of faith and doctrine but on the question of obedience to the Pope. Thus, in the High Church view, the English Church was still a part of the Catholic Church, though not under the jurisdiction of Rome. In matters of doctrine and ceremonial she must therefore accept the authority of the Early Church as expressed in the writings of the Fathers and the decisions of the Councils: as regards the power of the priesthood and the nature of the Holy Communion, High Churchmen and Roman Catholics held views which were practically the same. To say that the High Churchmen were Romanizers would be untrue; but they were firm opponents of the teachings of Luther and Calvin and consequently deplored the power which the State had obtained over spiritual things, more especially as the State, in the early 1830s, appeared to be on the way towards rejecting Christianity.

What touched off the movement[1] was the proposal brought before Parliament in 1833 to abolish ten Irish bishoprics. The merits of this scheme do not concern us. It was seen by many apprehensive Churchmen as the first step towards Disestablishment, towards the secularization of Church property, towards the destruction of the Church by the free-thinking Philosophic Radicals[2] who seemed to be carrying all before them. In July 1833 Keble, the Professor of Poetry, protested against the proposal in a sermon preached before the University of Oxford. This sermon, which was latter published under the title *National Apostasy*, was always regarded by Newman (1801–1890), the greatest of the Oxford leaders, as the starting point of the movement. Meetings followed and manifestos were drawn up which were published under the title of *Tracts for the Times*. The early tracts were brief, clear statements of the old High Church tradition already outlined. The authors saw the weakness and shallowness of contemporary churchmanship; they saw, too, the powerful threat from what they called "Liberalism"—which could be roughly defined as that belief in inevitable progress which makes

[1] Sometimes called the Anglo-Catholic Revival but more usually the Oxford Movement because its leaders were all members of that University. Contemporaries sometimes styled its followers "Puseyites" (after Dr. Pusey, one of the leaders) or "Tractarians" because they published their views in tracts. But by the end of the century they were generally called High Churchmen.

[2] See pages 21 ff.

men feel that the Kingdom of Heaven can be realized on earth without any reference to God. A collision between religion and "Liberalism" could not be averted. The aim of the tract-writers was to show churchmen what were the real fundamentals of their case and to urge them to put their defences into repair.

The stir roused by the tracts was widespread; and no wonder, for their authors were among the ablest and most learned men of the day. But it was in Oxford itself that the movement grew and flourished. Never has an English university known such a sudden flowering of all that was best in mind and character. The leaders of the movement, Keble, Newman and R. H. Froude, had qualities seldom found in combination: the sensibility of the poet, the brilliance of the intellectual, the transparent goodness of the saint. Free from pettiness, self-seeking, or meanness, they stood out in strong contrast to the sleepy irritability of the two-bottle orthodox who occupied the chief seats in the synagogues of Oxford. Almost every young man of promise who came up to Oxford in the ten years that followed 1833 came under the influence of the movement and, though many in later life reacted from it, nearly all of them remembered with affection and veneration the name of its greatest figure—Newman. The subtlety of his thought and the beauty of his prose still attract a greater number of readers than any other Victorian writer on religious topics. But it was through the sermons he delivered from the pulpit of St Mary's, the University church, that he exerted his greatest influence. The indefinable grace of his appearance is conveyed to us in the fine drawing by Sir William Richmond, and in the memory of his congregations his voice was the most beautiful they ever heard. The attraction of his character shines from a hundred memoirs and biographies. When he left the Church of England for the Church of Rome in 1845 it was generally assumed that the movement would collapse, so great was his personal ascendancy.

The core of Newman's thought was his rejection of rationalism —that is, the view that reason is the only guide to truth, the only touchstone by which it can be recognized. In his eyes no system of religious thought could stand firm unless it were founded on axioms whose truth was not open to question—in a word, on dogma. To him, the Church was a society founded and charged by Christ with the especial duty of preserving and interpreting truth: she was enabled to perform this task by the divine grace transmitted to her ministers at their ordination. As Christ only founded one society endowed with these special powers, the idea of unity and continuity was obviously essential. Was the Church of England a part of the One True and Catholic[1] Church or was she not? If she was not, then she was leading men away from truth and from salvation. If she was, then in spite of the hostility of her Thirty-Nine Articles[2] towards the Church of Rome, she had yet infinitely more in common with the Roman Catholics than she had with those Christians who rejected the whole idea of Catholicism. Newman and his friends were certainly not pro-Roman: but they emphasized the distinction between the theory of the Roman Church, which on examination they found admirable, and her practice, which, together with most Englishmen of their day, they regarded as superstitious and deplorable.

This distinction, however, was one which the higher clergy, backed by the overwhelming weight of public opinion, were unable or unwilling to grasp. Matters came to a head when in 1841 Newman claimed that the Thirty-Nine Articles could be interpreted in a Catholic sense. The Evangelicals who had at first shown some sympathy with the movement now moved into decided opposition, so that Church and nation presented a united front of hostility to the Tractarians. They were accused of reviving the worst aspects of medieval religion, priestcraft and superstition. Newman, in particular, was execrated as a Roman Catholic traitor within the Church

[1] This word means primarily "universal". Confusion is often caused by using it as a synonym for Roman Catholic. It is applied in this book to any Church which claims continuity with the early, undivided Church.

[2] The Thirty-Nine Articles of Religion approved in 1562 state the position of the English Church in the doctrinal controversies which were then agitating Europe. In conformity with Elizabeth's policy of compromise and toleration they were so framed as to allow the widest possible interpretation of disputed points. They were not a comprehensive, or even a coherent, statement of a system of theology but a series of isolated, and as far as possible ambiguous, rulings. Dr. Johnson's judgment of them is perhaps worth quoting: "Some have thought it necessary that they should all be believed; others have considered them only to be articles of peace, that is to say, you are not to preach against them." Up to 1865 every English clergyman had to subscribe to them in their entirety. Nowadays an assent to their general sense is enough.

of England, ready to open the gates at a signal from the Pope. The University of Oxford was narrowly prevented from censuring the work of its most distinguished member and bishop after bishop denounced his views. In the face of all this he abandoned his leadership of the movement, gave up writing and preaching and retired to a life of contemplation so that he could examine more fully his own position and that of the Church of England. In his retirement he saw little of his old friends but his company was eagerly sought out by the younger and hotter heads of the movement who would be satisfied with nothing less than complete submission to Rome. Their enthusiasm and the coldness of his own Church gave a decisive turn to his thought. In 1845 Newman became a Roman Catholic.

To the enemies of the movement it seemed that the battle was won. Newman's example was followed by many others, and those who remained loyal were numbed by a sense of defeat. Of those who had stood in the front rank only Keble was left, as Froude had died young. Nevertheless in spite of some defections the second rank held firm. In Dr. Pusey, the Professor of Theology, the movement had the most learned and perhaps the most respected member of the University, and though he was not a leader, he proved an invaluable rallying-point. The movement went on steadily expanding its influence and by the opening of the twentieth century it was the most active force in the Church.

What, in the long run, did the Oxford Movement do for the Church of England? In the first place it taught clergymen to look on themselves as priests of God instead of as the religious officials of the state. This higher conception of his function does much to explain the superiority of the modern parson over his eighteenth-century counterpart. Secondly, it emphasized the importance of tradition and authority in matters of belief and thus checked the tendency of Christian teaching to become nothing more than the indiscriminate baptizing of the fashionable ideas of the day. The foundation of theological colleges and the better instruction of the clergy have been the direct results of this. Lastly, by stressing the duty of worship it restored beauty and dignity to the services of the Church and helped to remedy the neglect and decay into which so many churches had fallen. Curiously enough it was through this that the movement was enabled to overcome the hostility of public opinion. As a natural consequence of their revival of the Catholic view of the Church many High Churchmen began to revive Catholic ceremonial. This was not only unpopular but contrary to the explicit instructions of the Church authorities. Some High Churchmen remained defiant and in order to deal with them Parliament passed the Public Worship Regulation Act of 1874. But, as with the suffragettes, the spectacle of high-minded people being imprisoned for a point of principle caused a revulsion of feeling. The bitterness and vindictiveness of the extreme Low Churchmen defeated their own ends.

### 3. Modernism

The direct antithesis of the Oxford Movement was that school of thought which is sometimes called Modernist and sometimes Broad Church. The views of Dr. Arnold who was its first leader have already been outlined. Liberal and rationalist, it had allied itself with the conservative orthodox churchmen against Newman and his friends but after 1845 it soon called down on its own head the wrath of authority. The aim of the movement was to re-state Christian truth in a form which would be acceptable to the scientific spirit of the day. How this could best be done was by no means clear, but there was a general agreement that the first step was to throw overboard the traditional, the mysterious and the supernatural. Dogma was at a discount; reason would reveal the way. The Bible was not entitled to any special reverence as containing the Word of God: it was a document, and should be handled like other documents. Thus if some passage could be shown to be incompatible with the facts of history or the laws of nature, then that was that. It was no good talking about poetic truth or the use of natural symbols to illustrate spiritual realities. A thing was either literally and historically and scientifically true or it was false. If such an approach to religion is carried to its logical conclusion, it is not hard to see what that conclusion will be.

Trouble began in 1860 with the publication of *Essays and Reviews*. This book contained essays written by seven authors, most of them clergymen. Two or three of the essays contained views which seemed hard to reconcile with a belief in Christianity and one at least was written in an offensive, sneering manner. There was a great outcry. Two of the clerical authors were convicted of heresy in the ecclesiastical courts and suspended, but the Judicial Committee of the Privy Council reversed this decision on appeal. This setting aside of a decision of a Church court on a matter of doctrine by a body mainly composed of laymen who need not even be members of the Church caused further excitement. The High Churchmen and the Low Churchmen combined to resist the affront done to the Church by the State. The offending volume was synodically condemned by the bishops and though this action was ridiculed by the Lord Chancellor the matter was allowed to rest there.

This series of events is typical of all the controversies of the nineteenth-century Church, whether the case was one of a High Churchman indulging in fanciful ritual or a Broad Churchman dispensing with the creeds. The disciplinary machinery of the Church was hopelessly inadequate. The usual ending of a case which had dragged on for months, or perhaps years, was the exact point from which it started. Nothing was achieved and the maximum of anger and party-spirit was generated in the achieving of it. The futility of trying to reach a decision on disputed points of worship or belief at last brought the extremists on either side to be more tolerant of each other. But all this is a digression from the Modernists.

To describe the growth and development of Modernism is impossible for, unlike the Evangelicals or the Tractarians, the Modernists had no common creed. The very thing that united them, a belief in change, in progress, in evolution, was of its nature bound to separate them. Some, like Frederick Temple, later Archbishop of Canterbury, reached a position differing little, if at all, from orthodoxy. Many became agnostics. Others swung uneasily in between.

As a separate party they have been in the present century a declining force. That bold confronting of intellectual and critical objections, which was their most valuable contribution, has been absorbed into the main stream of English churchmanship. In this sense Gore and William Temple, whom we shall consider in the next section, were modernists. But Modernism as a distinct school of thought was an essentially nineteenth-century thing. It sprang in large measure from that general questioning of established ideas and beliefs which was the especial characteristic of the nineteenth century in almost all European countries. In fact it was from Germany that the Modernists drew the bulk of their ideas and arguments. The critical examination of the text of the New Testament by German scholars and the teaching of German philosophers formed, as it were, their front line; but their communications and supply lines stretched back over the same territory as those of "Liberalism" to the belief in inevitable progress and in the essential goodness of man expressed by the French philosophers of the eighteenth century.

## 4. The Growth of Unity

Both the Evangelical and the Oxford Movements had injected vitality into the Church. In whatever else they disagreed both were at one in reviving the art of popular preaching, in putting new life into church services and in bringing religion to the people instead of waiting for the churches to fill themselves. To borrow the phrase of a late Victorian archbishop, "The danger that the Church of England might die of its dignity" was by the sixties a thing of the past. The new danger was that the Church might be split by the violence of internal controversy. The High Churchmen, disgusted at the supremacy of State authority in spiritual matters which the Judicial Committee of the Privy Council seemed to assert in its decisions, were growing less and less attached to the Establishment and on several occasions there were threats of secession. On the other hand Low Church leaders such as Lord Shaftesbury were fanatical in their loyalty to the State connection and in their horror of giving ground to anything that smacked of Rome. Listen to Lord Shaftesbury in the House of Lords: "The vote has produced more anger, grief and consternation in the country than any vote that is recorded in the whole history of Parliament. It has very seriously injured your Lordships' position. It has still more seriously injured the position of the Bishops, and the safety of the Established Church." What on earth is he talking about? He is talking about a microscopic amendment to the bill for disestablishing the Irish Church which would allow the Roman Catholic clergy to take over some of the vacated parsonage houses.

To hold back such headstrong men demanded leadership that was strong, tactful, and above all, fair. More than ever the qualities required in an archbishop of Canterbury were those of a statesman. In 1868 the appointment of Archbishop Tait answered the need. Tait, the first Scotsman to become Primate of All England, had been brought up as a Presbyterian and to the end of his life he remained a moderate Low Churchman. But he detested partisanship, and the truly Christian consideration and kindness that he showed towards those whose opinions he could neither share nor understand raised the standing of his office and encouraged men to a more comprehensive view. Time and again he faced bitter unpopularity by refusing to come down on one side or the other in disputes where the feeling aroused seemed to him out of proportion to the issues involved. All his life he maintained a keen interest in politics, both English and European, and even in his busiest days as archbishop he invariably read the political news before turning to ecclesiastical affairs. Without being in the least worldly he had a wider knowledge and understanding of the world than most clergymen of his day and he was more concerned with the practical task of applying Christian remedies to the social evils of his time than with controversies about doctrine or ceremonial. As archbishop he attended the debates of the House of Lords more regularly than his predecessors and the weight and shrewdness of his speeches reminded the nation of the advantages of the Establishment. In an emotional and excitable age he possessed the un-Victorian virtues of calmness and restraint.

Not the least of Tait's contributions to the building up of a central tradition in the Church of England was to emphasize that she herself was the centre of a communion which stretched round the world. The two greatest English missionary societies had been founded at the end of the seventeenth century, the Society for Promoting Christian Knowledge in 1698 and the Society for Propagation of the Gospel in 1701. The Evangelical Revival and the Oxford Movement led to the foundation of several more, and the sense of guilt and shame awoken by the propaganda of the Anti-Slavery

Movement inspired a great missionary campaign in Africa. Besides the new missionary Churches, English settlers had taken their national Church with them: there were flourishing Churches in Canada, Australia and New Zealand, and even after the War of Independence the Protestant Episcopal Church of America maintained its connection with the mother Church. The doctrinal controversies which caused so much division at home had spread to the daughter Churches and in the early sixties the Bishop of Cape Town had deprived the Bishop of Natal on the grounds of heresy. The legal problems involved in this action were extremely complicated, but it was widely felt that the Anglican communion as a whole ought to meet and discuss the rights and wrongs of it. Accordingly in 1867 the first Pan-Anglican Conference consisting of bishops from America, the colonies and missionary Churches not under British rule met at Lambeth. Tait, who was then Bishop of London, was instrumental in restraining the Conference from taking any rash or irretrievable action in this intricate and difficult affair and when as archbishop he summoned the second Lambeth Conference in 1878 he guided it to its true function of witnessing to the unity of the Christian faith by seeking common solutions to common problems. Such has been the path trodden by all subsequent Lambeth Conferences.

Tait was followed at Canterbury by a succession of wise and statesmanlike archbishops, Benson, Frederick Temple, Davidson and Lang who pursued substantially the same policy. Under their leadership the unity Tait had hoped for became a fact and though there were, and still are, High, Low and Broad Churchmen, there is less party-spirit and less wrangling than there was a hundred years ago. More and more in our century the leading churchmen have concentrated on the problems of common, everyday life and have emphasized that Christianity is for

Seven whole days, not one in seven.

The incursion of Christian leaders into the social and economic controversies of our time has not been universally popular nor always well-judged; but few will deny that the very fact that the Church has something to say on labour relations, on the right use of wealth and a hundred other such topics is an encouraging sign of vitality. The gibe that the Church of England is simply the Conservative party at prayer has lost its sting. The two most influential figures in the twentieth-century Church, Bishop Gore and Archbishop William Temple, were both supporters of the Labour Party.

The vigour with which these two leaders championed the cause of social justice made a deep impression on the public mind. But both Gore and Temple regarded this work as just one aspect, and that perhaps not the most important, of what they stood for. Both were thinkers of unusual depth and power, and no priest since Newman in the early days of the Oxford Movement had taken such a leading part in the intellectual life of the time. Gore (1853–1932), who was a lifelong High Churchman, tempered the complete reliance on authority of the old High Church school with an appeal to reason and a qualified readiness to accept the conclusions of Biblical scholarship. The tension between authority and private judgment is one of the most fundamental characteristics of Christianity and one of its most difficult problems. To enter into that vast subject here would be far beyond the scope of this book, but those who wish for a clear statement of the essentials should read the preface to Bernard Shaw's *St. Joan*.

Archbishop William Temple (1881–1944) is among the greatest of all English churchmen. Himself the son of an archbishop, he belonged to that central tradition of Anglicanism which binds High, Low and Broad churchmen together by showing them how much they have in common. The qualities that made him the supreme spiritual leader of his generation are easier to recognize than to define. The firmness and breadth of his understanding, the complete absence of sentimentality from his approach to religion, his refusal to score debating points over his opponents, above all, the gentleness, charity and transparent honesty of the man stand out at once. The extraordinary clarity of his mind and the simplicity of his nature combined in a remarkable power of exposition so that, although one of the most devout and unworldly of men, it was among the down-to-earth, matter-of-fact people of the Northern industrial towns that he achieved some of his greatest success. His death after only three years as Archbishop of Canterbury was directly caused by overwork and the loss to Church and nation was as unexpected as it was severe.

The question is frequently asked nowadays whether England is a Christian country, and the asking of it is regarded as a telling rebuke to the Established Church. It is generally followed by another: "Why doesn't the Church of England do something?" By the term "Church of England" the questioner usually means the clergy, as the lay members of the Church are, for some unexplained reason, excused from this vague but extensive duty. These questions are chiefly interesting for the assumptions they imply in the minds of those who put them. Apparently England was till recently a nation of devout and practising Christians served by an untiring clergy whose learning and energy kept scepticism and unbelief at bay. How little relation this inspiring picture bears to the facts anyone who reads the history of the last two centuries can see. The laxity of the eighteenth-century Church, the disputes and agitations of the nineteenth-century revivals are happily forgotten. But it will be of no service to replace these facts by nostalgic fancies: and it will be less than just to the real achievement of great and good men.

## 5. *Roman Catholics and Dissenters*

The changes that have come over the Roman Catholic and Dissenting bodies during this period have been considerable. The Roman Catholics in 1832 were a small, retiring and exclusive community. Cowed by three centuries of more or less severe persecution and excluded until 1829 from taking any part in public life, they mixed little with their non-Roman fellow countrymen. Although their priests were trained in English colleges on the Continent, they held aloof from the main stream of European Catholicism, cherishing the independence of an isolated outpost in hostile territory. Proud, conservative and exclusive, they were by no means disposed to welcome the flood of converts who left the Church of England after the apparent collapse of the Oxford Movement in 1845. Nor were the converts satisfied with what they found. One of the most distinguished of them, W. G. Ward, genially remarked that "Speaking in argument with English Catholics is like talking with savages". The Reconstitution of the Hierarchy in 1850—that is, the re-introduction of Roman Catholic Diocesan Bishops under the Cardinal Archbishop of Westminster—marks the dividing line between the old and the new type of English Roman Catholic. The old aristocratic type resented this intrusion on their independence and some even went so far as to join the Church of England. But these defections have been insignificant compared with the steady growth in numbers, in power, and in prestige of the English branch of the Roman Church. Of those who regularly attend a place of worship each Sunday at least as many are Roman Catholics as members of the Church of England, although a much larger proportion of the population describe themselves as belonging to the English Church. The success of the Roman Church in this respect can be attributed partly to the large number of Irish immigrants, Roman Catholics almost to a man, and partly to the zeal and thoroughness with which Roman Catholic parents educate their children in the faith. The flow of converts from the Church of England and the Nonconformist bodies has not been large.

The part played by the Nonconformists in keeping England out of revolution in the hard years that followed the defeat of Napoleon has already been emphasized. As the century advanced their power steadily increased, reaching its peak with the ascendancy of the Liberal party. The radicalism of Cobden and Bright found its religious counterpart in Dissent. The hostility towards authority, the insistence on individual spiritual effort and experience, which characterized so many of the Nonconforming sects, tallied with the economic doctrines of self-help and *laissez-faire*. The influence of preachers like Spurgeon (1834–1892) on the national life was enormous. The phrase "England's Nonconformist conscience" dates from the nineteenth-century hey-day of Dissent.

To trace the history of the various denominations of Baptists, Congregationalists and Methodists over the last hundred years would perhaps try the reader's patience a little far; a few crude generalizations are all that can be attempted. After the death of the Wesleys at the end of the eighteenth century the Methodists tended to split into separate groups and so remained until there was a general reunion in 1932. This was but one aspect of a wider movement towards coalition. Early in this century a Free Church Council was set up with power to speak for Nonconformity as a whole, and the last twenty years have witnessed a great improvement in relations with the Church of England. One important result of this has been that the provisions for religious teaching in the Education Act of 1944 were accepted with enthusiasm by Nonconformists and Churchmen alike, a remarkable change from the sectarian battles which had devastated the religious clauses of earlier Acts.[1] All the main Nonconformist bodies have been extremely active in the mission field and, if their influence in this country is less than it was a century ago, it has increased in the world at large.

[1] See pages 154-7.

## CHAPTER XV

# THE VICTORIAN EMPIRE

## 1. The Early Victorian Empire, 1830–1870

To most Englishmen of the Early Victorian age the overseas possessions of their country meant surprisingly little. Their attention was fully occupied by the fast moving changes at home in transport and industry, which offered great and immediate rewards. The steady flow of emigrants to the settlement colonies, which took place in the nineteenth century, was outside the main stream of English life. Nevertheless missionaries, labourers, adventurers, and outcasts flocked to the ports in ever-increasing numbers: between 1815 and 1840 over one million people left the British Isles and after 1847 the Irish began to emigrate in large numbers. Both the Scots and the Irish have played a great part in the expansion of the Empire, the Scots generally settling in remote and undeveloped areas while the Irish have provided cheap labour for the towns. This haphazard exodus of men which continued down to 1930 was not the least important factor in British history in the nineteenth century, though little noticed at the time. It has been estimated that between 1830 and 1930, 7,500,000 British emigrants went to the United States, and about 2,300,000 to Australia and New Zealand.

To the Early Victorians the settlement colonies seemed to be of little value. Australia was peopled with convicts, and the French in Canada and the Dutch in Cape Colony had no racial connection with England. The population of the colonies was small and poor; to businessmen an Empire was only worthwhile if it provided profitable markets. The idea of a self-sufficient Empire regulated by the Navigation Acts made no sense to the aggressive merchant of the forties. The entire world was open to the successful industrialist. Between 1840 and 1860 the firm of Thomas Brassey undertook 170 contracts to provide 8,000 miles of railways in Europe, South America and Asia. No longer did the trader wish to restrict his operations to the limits of an empire: Free Trade was his motto and under its banner he sold English goods as freely to the citizens of Canton and Cologne as to the natives of Africa and Hindustan. Slowly but steadily the old protective laws were repealed or modified, and London became a free port which attracted ships and commerce from every land. The West Indian planters, it is true, complained when they found themselves deprived of their protected market in England, but in general commercial opinion welcomed the change. In 1846 the repeal of the Corn Laws marked the triumph of the manufacturing interest, and when in 1849 the remnants of the Navigation Laws were removed from the Statute Book, their abolition was no more than a parliamentary recognition of a change which had already taken place.

It was small wonder then that many thought the empire to be both unnecessary and expensive. "Our dependencies" wrote Cobden ". . . serve but as gorgeous and ponderous appendages to swell our ostensible grandeur without improving our balance of trade." Contemporary politicians gave them little attention: Melbourne frivolously asked how anyone could be interested in British Columbia where the salmon would not rise to a fly. Until 1854 the Secretary of State for War also controlled colonial administration which shows that the interest taken in the colonies was primarily strategic. Since the office was a stepping stone to higher posts (there were twenty-two secretaries in fifty years), the chief influence was that of the permanent staff. Sir James Stephen (1789–1859), in different capacities, conducted the colonial policy of successive Governments for over twenty years. He regarded the empire as a liability and he hoped that the colonies would achieve independence peacefully. This lack of enthusiasm in London was reflected in the government of the colonies, in the administration of land grants, and in the appointment of incompetent governors and officials. Stephen, like so many of the governing class of the period, was influenced by the Evangelical Movement, whose work resulted in the abolition of slavery in 1833, and the foundation of missionary societies (London Missionary Society 1795, Church Missionary Society, 1790). To these societies the empire offered fertile ground for spreading the Christian gospel, and Stephen's chief concern was to support their activities. The missionaries were passionately opposed to any policy which disturbed the interests of the native peoples and they did much good work, though their interference was often misguided and sentimental. But they did insist that rule over native peoples should be regarded as a trust.

The development of the British Empire in the first part of Queen Victoria's reign was the work of a small band of enthusiasts in England, and the restless initiative of individuals overseas. Men like Gibbon Wakefield, Rajah Brooke, Governor Eyre, Nicholson of India, George Grey (successively Governor in Australia, New Zealand, and South Africa), and Harry Smith, struggled unremittingly against the obstinacy of the home Government; while such missionaries as Bishop Selwyn in New Zealand and David Livingstone in Africa, dedicated themselves to the task of bringing Christianity to the native peoples.

Until the revolt of the American colonies the British Empire had been growing along the northern shores of the Atlantic: the new empire which arose in the nineteenth century lay in the East and South Pacific. In 1788 the first convicts had landed in New South Wales. In 1819 Sir Stamford Raffles had purchased the uninhabited island of Singapore for the East India Company, thereby obtaining the port which became the centre of our Far Eastern trade. At the Treaty of Vienna (1815), England had retained the naval station of the Cape of Good Hope from which our South African empire was to grow. Besides these new possessions, there remained Canada, the West Indian islands, and the Indian territories of the East India Company. The period after 1815 was one of continuous expansion and the English Government, to its disgust, found itself saddled with responsibilities it could not disregard. Only one group of men believed sincerely in the future of the empire and wished the Government to pursue a constructive policy towards it. They were known as the Radical Imperialists and their leader was the obstinate and embittered Edward Gibbon Wakefield (1796–1862), whose early career had been marred by a prison sentence for abducting an heiress. In prison he turned his ability to good use and from Newgate Gaol issued a pamphlet entitled "Letter from Sydney" in which he expressed his belief in the enormous possibilities of the new continent of Australia, if it were constructively developed by the Government. After his release from prison, he founded the Colonization Society and soon collected around him a brilliant group of radicals, including Charles Buller, George Grote, William Molesworth and Lord Durham. Their enthusiasm for colonial development gave them an influence out of all proportion to their numbers. Wakefield's ambition was to persuade the Government to assist settlement colonies throughout the world. Land was to be sold at a high price, thus preventing settlers from buying more than they could cultivate, and the colonies were eventually to govern themselves. It was the Radical Imperialists who forced the Government into occasional action. The appointment of Lord Durham (1792–1840) as Governor-General of Canada in 1838 showed how great was their influence.

Durham was appointed to inquire into two minor revolts which had occurred the year before in Upper and Lower Canada. There were three main causes of these revolts: the conflict of French and British colonists which had only been partially resolved by the division of Canada into Upper and Lower provinces in 1791; the bitterness between the old colonist and the new immigrant; and the conflict between the council nominated by the colonial Governor and the advisory assemblies elected by the colonists. For example, the French, who were in the majority in Lower Canada, complained that the Governor's council consisted largely of British colonists and that the assembly had no control over expenditure. In Upper Canada the class conflict between old and new immigrant was acute and there was particular jealousy over the distribution of land. The rebellions were easily put down and Lord Durham arrived to make a settlement. To avoid bloodshed, he sentenced eight of the ring-leaders to detention in Bermuda. Although this was a wise decision, he had unfortunately gone beyond his powers as Governor-General, which did not extend to Bermuda. Melbourne's enemies, glad of an opportunity to embarrass a falling Government, forced the ministry to repudiate Durham's action. The Governor-General decided to resign and returned home to write his report, which must rank as a document of fundamental importance in the evolution of British Imperialism. In it he recommended that the two provinces of Canada should be united, as the French colonists no longer out-

THE DEVELOPMENT OF CANADA

numbered the British, and that the executive council should be responsible to the assembly which the colonists elected. By these means colonial self-government would be established, though Durham did not intend it to be absolute, reserving to the home Government control of foreign policy, the regulation of trade, Crown lands, and the right to alter the colonial constitution. An Act of 1841 embodied his first proposal but nothing was said of the second. Not till 1847 did a new Governor-General, Lord Elgin, Durham's son-in-law, carry out on his own initiative the policy recommended in the report. From that date responsible government was established in Canada, and it quickly became accepted as the goal towards which every colony should advance. Throughout the rest of the century the powers which Durham had intended the home Government to retain were steadily whittled away.

In the years that followed, Canada continued to expand in size and population, helped by British capital and a bold policy of railway-building. Many Canadians wanted a common government for all the North American colonies and discussions took place between the Maritime Provinces (Nova Scotia, New Brunswick and Prince Edward Island) and the United Provinces of Upper and Lower Canada. The results were embodied in the British North America Act of 1867 which established a Canadian Parliament, consisting of a House of Commons and a Senate. Each province was represented in proportion to its population and retained a legislature and ministry of its own which could deal with certain specified matters. All other business was controlled by the federal Government. More provinces joined the Federation later: Manitoba (1870), British Columbia (1871), Alberta and Saskatchewan (1905) and Newfoundland (1949).

The Radical Imperialists could be proud of their work for Canada but it was in Australia and New Zealand that their influence was greatest. Until the crossing of the Blue Mountains in 1813 and the subsequent development of sheep farming, Australia remained empty and unknown, except for a single colony, New South Wales, merely regarded by the home Government as a dumping ground for convicts. On their own initiative enterprising individuals explored the interior of the continent. Mitchell and MacMillan

travelled southward, Leichhardt set out across the continent never to
be seen again, Eyre arrived in Western Australia accompanied only
by a boy, having lost seven companions on the way. Settlers soon
followed, thereby presenting the Colonial Office in London with
a *fait accompli*. "All schemes of this kind", complained the Under
Secretary, "have been of late years discountenanced as leading

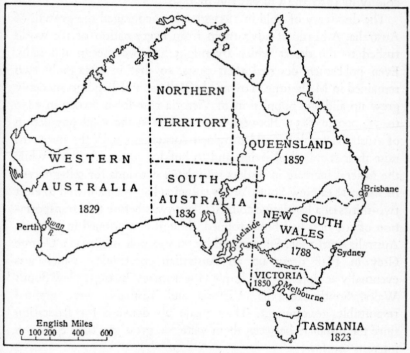

AUSTRALIA 1859

continually to the establishment of fresh settlements and fresh
expense." However, it proved impossible to stop the expansion into
new lands. Sydney, Melbourne, and Adelaide became great ports
handling an ever-increasing export of wool. In 1833, inspired by
Wakefield, the South Australian association was formed to open up
a new province. Before long Wakefield withdrew from the scheme,
disgusted by the low price of land fixed by the colonial commissioners, and for some time the fate of the new province seemed to
justify his pessimism. In 1840 South Australia was almost bankrupt

and only the arrival of George Grey (1812–1898) as Governor saved the situation. Two years later the province became an ordinary Crown colony. Elsewhere on the continent, the home Government was soon forced to deal with the situation created by the thousands of settlers who had pushed out of New South Wales into lands where no government existed. Victoria was recognized as a separate colony in 1850 and Queensland in 1859.

The discovery of gold in 1851 greatly encouraged the growth of Australia. A horde of adventurers from every nation of the world rushed to the desert which overnight had become an Eldorado. Even policemen deserted their posts, so that in 1852 only two remained in Melbourne. Towns like Ballarat and Bendigo suddenly grew up and the population of Victoria rose from 70,000 in 1850 to 333,000 in 1855. Between 1850 and 1860 the total population of Australia trebled. Gold provided Australians with the means to raise their standard of living and to build roads and bridges, while the general increase in settlers stimulated demands for self-government. In 1842 New South Wales colonists had been allowed to elect two-thirds of a legislative council. Two years before this, transportation of convicts had been stopped, though it continued in Western Australia until 1868. Encouraged by the example of Canada, George Grey in 1848 drew up an Australian constitution which was eventually accepted by the home Government. In 1855, New South Wales, South Australia, Victoria and Tasmania were granted responsible government. They made no demand for federation since the distances between them were too great and their common interests too few.

The colonization of New Zealand was systematically discouraged by the Colonial Office. Formally annexed by Captain Cook in 1769, its northern island had become, in the years following, a haven for runaway criminals and a base for whalers and lone traders. In 1814, Samuel Marsden, a clergyman, had founded a mission station there and his missionaries soon complained of the exploitation of the native Maori population by the lawless settlers. Wakefield's attention was drawn to New Zealand and in 1836 he petitioned a select committee of the House of Commons to begin systematic colonization. As he pointed out, English colonists had already settled there in a "most slovenly and scrambling and disgraceful manner". Opposition to settlements in New Zealand came not only from the Government but from missionary societies, who thought that colonization meant ruin for the Maoris. As the Secretary of the Church Missionary Society told the Select Committee, "Though I do not conceive colonization to be necessarily productive of disastrous consequences, yet it has so generally led to that result that there is nothing I should deprecate more than the colonization of New Zealand by this country".

The missionaries won the support of Lord Glenelg (1778–1866), the Colonial Secretary, and the New Zealand Company, founded under Wakefield's influence, received no charter from the Government. However a party of colonists sailed in 1839 and the Colonial Office was thereby forced to appoint a Lieutenant-Governor. The Treaty of Waitangi, negotiated with the Maoris in 1840, acknowledged native ownership of land in return for recognition of the authority of the English Crown, which was given the right of buying such lands as the Maoris wished to sell. Both in New Zealand and South Africa difficulties of colonization were increased by the existence of strong and warlike native peoples: the problem was to do justice to them without doing injustice to the incoming settlers. In New Zealand the situation was complicated by the fact that the settlements were unauthorized by the English Government. Trouble was bound to break out between the Maoris and the colonists, for it was plainly impracticable, whatever the missionaries might say, to recognize the Maoris' absolute ownership of all the land in New Zealand. In 1843 the first of many Maori revolts broke out, and was followed by a more serious one in 1845. At this moment George Grey arrived as Governor, energetically put down the rebellion and set about improving the police, hospitals, and schools. He was assisted by George Selwyn, the first Bishop of New Zealand, who did great work for Maori education.

But the situation still remained difficult. In England, Wakefield had the foresight to conciliate the missionary societies. In 1848 a group of Scotch Presbyterians founded the province of Otago. In 1850 the Canterbury Association under the patronage of two archbishops and seven bishops, sent out 1,500 colonists to establish the province of Canterbury. Between 1847 and 1860 the white population of New Zealand doubled, and by 1859 the Maoris had parted with thirty-two million acres in the south island and seven million acres in the north. The Maori chiefs suddenly saw that their existence was threatened and in 1860 a savage war broke out which was prolonged for nine years by the intransigeance of the New Zealand Government. This was now a government of colonists, since in 1856 they had demanded and received self-government. A previous constitution granted in 1852 had established a united government for the six provinces with a Governor, nominated Council and elected Assembly. The Maoris were allowed votes but their influence was small since their numbers declined from 56,000 in 1858 to 37,000 in 1871. After the end of the war which England had largely financed, the colonists became more reasonable in their attitude to the natives, and New Zealand gradually became peaceful and prosperous.

South Africa, like Australia and New Zealand, developed in a manner unintended by the home Government. Cape Colony, seized from the Dutch in 1806, was only valued as a strategic port of call on the route to India. But difficulties were caused from the beginning by the presence of Dutch settlers (the Boers) and the turbulent native tribes of Zulus and Kaffirs. The Boers believed that they had a right to the land of the interior. Brought up on the stern doctrines of Calvin, they were convinced that the millions of native Africans were bloodthirsty savages to whom no humanity or leniency could be shown. Small wonder then that they scorned the humanitarian views of the English missionary societies which had penetrated Cape Colony as they had done elsewhere. The missionaries regarded the natives as brothers to be converted and their policy seemed to have triumphed with the abolition of slavery in 1833. They considered the Boer attitude towards the natives to be the main cause of unrest: whereas the Boers looked on the missionaries as trouble-makers because they preached that the blacks were their equals. Actually many of the native disturbances were caused by the pressure of raiding Zulu tribes upon the Kaffir peoples who bordered Cape Colony, though the presence of foreigners aggravated the trouble. The home Government wanted to prohibit

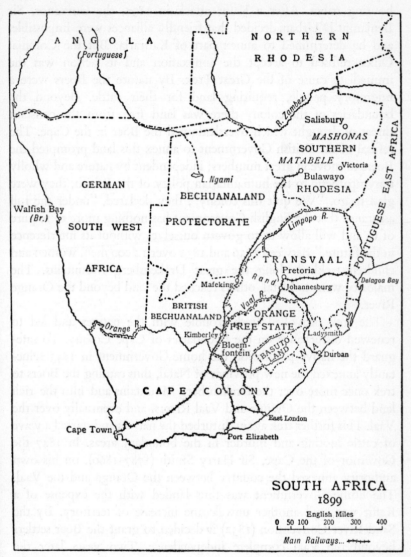

ANGOLA
(Portuguese)

NORTHERN
RHODESIA

R. Zambezi

Salisbury

MASHONAS
SOUTHERN
MATABELE

Victoria

L. Ngami

Bulawayo

RHODESIA

GERMAN

BECHUANALAND

Walfish Bay
(Br.)

SOUTH WEST

PROTECTORATE

Limpopo R.

AFRICA

TRANSVAAL
Pretoria

Rand

PORTUGUESE EAST AFRICA

Mafeking

Johannesburg

Delagoa Bay

Orange   R.

Vaal  R.

BRITISH
BECHUANALAND

ORANGE
FREE STATE

Kimberley

Bloem-
fontein

BASUTO
LAND

NATAL

Ladysmith

Durban

CAPE   COLONY

Cape Town

Port Elizabeth

East London

SOUTH AFRICA
1899

English Miles
0   50  100      200        300        400

Main Railways...

SOUTH AFRICA 1899

expansion, although it encouraged friendly alliances with neigh-bouring tribes. After a Kaffir attack in 1834, the Governor, Sir Benjamin D'Urban, decided that friendly alliances were impossible, and he determined to annex part of Kaffraria. But the Colonial Office refused to accept the annexation and its action was the immediate cause of the Great Trek. By nature the Boers were a migratory people, requiring land for their cattle. Beyond the boundaries of the colony there was land free from the constant threat of drought which overshadowed the Boer in the Cape. The refusal of the British Government to annex this land prompted the Boers to move in great numbers; independent by nature and wholly unsympathetic to the humanitarian policy of the British, they were glad to go. "We quit this colony", they declared, "under the full assurance that the English Government has nothing more to require of us and will allow us to govern ourselves without its interference in the future." Between 1836 and 1839 over 12,000 men, women and children trekked along the great Drakensberg Mountains. The majority went to Natal, others reached the land beyond the Orange River.

The trek provoked fresh trouble with the natives and led to renewed disturbance on the boundaries of Cape Colony. To safe-guard the native population the home Government in 1843 reluc-tantly annexed the new province of Natal, thus causing the Boers to trek once more over the Drakensberg Mountains and into the rich land between the Orange and Vaal Rivers, and eventually over the Vaal. This further trek again disturbed the natives and started a wave of cattle looting and murder in the boundary areas. In 1847 the Governor of the Cape, Sir Harry Smith (1787–1860), on his own authority annexed the country between the Orange and the Vaal. The home Government was thus landed with the expense of a Kaffir war, and another unwelcome increase of territory. By the Sand River Convention (1852) it decided to grant the Boer settlers beyond the Vaal complete independence. Two years later the Convention of Bloemfontein granted the country between the Orange and the Vaal to the Boers, who set up the Orange Free State. By the middle of the century, therefore, the settled area of South Africa consisted of two British colonies, the Cape (granted representative government in 1853) and Natal, and two free Boer republics. Two different European civilizations, the Dutch Calvinism of the seventeenth century and the British Evangelicalism of the nineteenth, had been in conflict with the native Africans and with each other. For the time being a truce had been achieved. But the discovery of gold on the Rand in 1886 added a dangerous element to a situation which the Jingoism of late nineteenth-century Britain would in any case have rendered delicate.

## 2. The Late Victorian Empire, 1870–1901

The year 1870 marks the end of the formative movements which made Germany and Italy into nations, and the beginning of the rapid industrialization of Europe and America. The under-developed areas of the world took on a new importance with the scramble for raw materials and markets. Africa, the islands of the Pacific, Eastern Asia, and the ancient empire of China were all assaulted by aggressive traders. Other European nations were jealous of Great Britain. Her shipping, goods, and money dominated the world. While Europe had been occupied with internal revolutions, British merchants had been supplying the markets of the world, and British pioneers had been acquiring colonies, much to the disgust of their Government. Conscious imperialism played no part in the development of the British Empire for most of the nineteenth century. Humanitarianism and free trade brought the colonies into being; a willingness to grant self-government, and a genuine reluctance to assume further sovereignty conditioned their growth. But after 1870 imperialism became self-conscious and possessive. It forced itself into every uncharted land. It broke into the savage interior of Africa with the same energy as it secured free entry into the ancient civilization of China. Both areas provided trade and raw materials to supply the growing populations and industries of Britain and Europe.

Britain could not ignore the obvious challenge of competing industrial powers. Steamships brought American corn and meat to depress English agriculture, and by the close of the seventies German goods were competing with our own, not only in foreign markets, but even in Britain itself. Long years of prosperity had raised the English standard of living so that everywhere European wages were lower than English, which meant that foreign costs of production were lower too. Dissatisfied merchants and manufacturers clamoured for measures against the unfamiliar foreign competition. The Government was at length forced to act not for imperial purposes, but to maintain its position in Europe. Intervention in Afghanistan, Africa and the South Sea Islands was diplomatic rather than imperial.

Though Britain was unwilling to face the new situation she was at last compelled to change her conception of empire. An aggressive, domineering note crept into English policy. Nevertheless the old humanitarian ideas persisted and developed into the conception of trusteeship for backward peoples, which is the staple of modern British colonial policy. David Livingstone (1813–1873), who spent twenty years exploring Africa in the middle of the century, was interested neither in trade nor flag-wagging but in bringing Christianity and civilization to a barbarous and miserable people.

Disraeli regarded the empire as of use only in the general scheme of foreign politics, and he showed little sense of its other values. His proclamation of Victoria as Empress of India in 1877 was a gesture which marked no real change. His policy towards Afghanistan was directed by the demands of European politics. Though he did as much, if not more, for the empire as any other Prime Minister of the century, he did not understand the growing nationalism of the colonies. The Queen's Jubilees, in which Indian princes, West African chiefs and Canadian mounties took part, emphasized the new imperial spirit. Rudyard Kipling captured the magic of empire in his poems: the flying fishes and the dawn across the Bay of Bengal, the low African moon, the islands where the trumpet orchids blew, the wars where Fuzzy Wuzzy broke a British square. Kipling was the poet of the Tommy, the pioneer, the men whose exploits had brought renown to the British name. The map painted red was the theme of a famous book, *The Expansion of England*, by a Cambridge professor, J. R. Seeley. He maintained that British greatness lay in her colonizing activities and that the time had come for her to pay attention to her settlement colonies. Other publicists playing the part of the Radical Imperialists in a previous generation hammered home the point. Pride replaced indifference. Kinship was felt with the peoples of a far-flung empire who owed allegiance to the same monarch.

It took some years for this new imperialism to grow in England and only after 1885 did it flourish. Gladstone, who became Prime Minister in 1868, had little interest in the empire, and, like the statesmen of the previous generation, he took its dissolution to be matter of course. Nevertheless during his administration the Dutch holdings on the Gold Coast of Africa were purchased, thus bringing the entire area under British rule, and in 1874 the Governor of Singapore was empowered to make treaties with neighbouring Malay princes whose States were seething with disorder. By these treaties Britain established a virtual protectorate over the Malay peninsula, and within twenty years astonishing progress was made in settling the country, building roads, hospitals, railways, and developing the tin mines. By 1895 the Federation of Malay States had been formed. British intervention in Malaya brought prosperity and order where there had been poverty and chaos.

Yet it was the avowed policy of Gladstone and the Liberals to avoid being involved in any expansion of the empire. Lord Granville, the Colonial Secretary, caused great bitterness in New Zealand by withdrawing British troops at the height of the Maori War. The succeeding Conservative Government under Disraeli has usually been credited with planning the extension of empire. But Disraeli's own personal interest was confined mainly to India and the Near East where he was concerned to resist Russian advances. In 1875 he astutely purchased a controlling interest in the Suez Canal from the bankrupt Khedive of Egypt, and three years later on the Khedive's refusal to pay the interest on his debts, Britain and France as the chief creditors intervened. They set up a commission in Egypt known as the Dual Control to manage Egyptian finances which had been squandered by the Khedive on chorus girls and ballet dancers from Paris. By the Treaty of Berlin (1878) Britain was allowed to occupy Cyprus, thereby acquiring a further base in the Near East for the protection of the route to India. Elsewhere

PACIFIC OCEAN

GILBERT IS.

ELLICE IS.

FIJI I.    UNION I

NEW HEBRIDES

PITCAIRN I.

NEW
ZEALAND

CHATHAM I.

AUCKLAND I.

DOMINION
OF CANADA

NEWFOUN

ATLANT

BERMUDAS

BAHAMAS

OCE

BRITISH     JAMAICA    BARBADOES
HONDURAS                TRINIDAD

BRITISH
GUIANA

FALKLAND IS.

S GEO

Main sea routes  -------

British Possessions        Spheres of Influence

THE BRIT
At its fullest ex

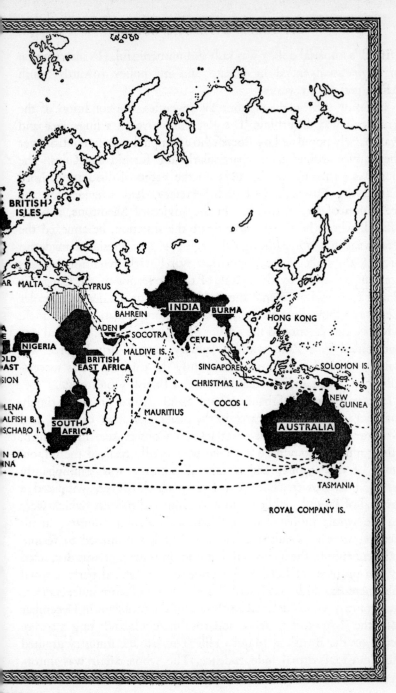

Disraeli's imperial policy was rash and unsuccessful. His intervention in Afghanistan ended in defeat,[1] and his policy towards South Africa met with reverses.

In South Africa, throughout the seventies, the condition of the Transvaal was disturbing. The Republic covered a huge area and was sparsely populated by Boers who attempted to keep control over the natives around them, particularly the formidable Zulus. The Boer Government was by 1875 on the verge of dissolution. Lord Carnarvon, Disraeli's Colonial Secretary, had schemes for the federation of South Africa. On the advice of Shepstone, a Natal official, whom he sent to investigate the situation, he annexed the Transvaal in 1877. Although the corrupt Boer President made no protest, the bulk of the population was bitterly resentful. Matters were made worse by the action of the Governor of the Cape, Sir Bartle Frere, who ordered the Zulus to disarm. Under their leader Cetewayo they chose to fight, and to the consternation of Disraeli, who had not sanctioned the actions of his subordinates, England was committed to a Zulu war. In January 1879 a British force was slaughtered at Isandhlwana but by July the campaign was successfully completed and Zululand became a British protectorate.

The reverses in Afghanistan and South Africa provided timely material for the Liberal party in the general election of 1880, and Gladstone launched a major attack on Conservative imperialism. His arguments convinced a public who hardly realized the importance of the empire, and a Liberal ministry was triumphantly returned to power. The next five years, however, witnessed a reversal of English public opinion on imperial matters, which were on the whole mishandled by Gladstone's second ministry. In his election speeches Gladstone had more or less promised to restore independence to the Transvaal, but once in power, he was distracted by the problem of Ireland. A section of the Liberal party insisted that there should be safeguards for the natives before independence was granted, which delayed a solution of the problem. In December 1880 the Boers lost patience and rose in revolt, inflicting a severe defeat on the British at Majuba Hill. Too late the ministry granted the Transvaal virtual independence. The whole affair was unfor-

[1] See page 265.

tunate in every way and left the Boers and their new President, Paul Kruger, angry and distrustful.

In 1882 a Nationalist revolt broke out in Egypt, led by a discontented colonel, Arabi Pasha, who aroused popular feeling against the foreign interference of the Dual Control. The stability of the Egyptian government was endangered and Gladstone asked France to join in occupying the country. France declined and Britain acted alone, bombarding Alexandria and landing an army under Garnet Wolseley (1833–1913) which quickly overthrew Arabi at Tel-el-Kebir. This unexpectedly easy victory, which gave Great Britain control of Egypt, poisoned Anglo-French relations until 1904. Gladstone declared that Britain had no "intention of occupying Egypt permanently" and Sir Evelyn Baring (later Lord Cromer) was appointed to assist the Khedive's Government to reform the administration. Cromer, who remained in Egypt till 1907, was more than an administrator, he was a statesman who created a nation. There was a tremendous amount to be done in the country and so Gladstone's declaration was not acted on until 1922. Britain stayed in Egypt partly to protect the Suez Canal, but she gave the Egyptians an efficient civil service and a disciplined army, and developed the resources of a land which, except for the Nile Valley, was arid and unproductive.

Since 1819 the Egyptians had governed the Sudan. Their rule was weak, cruel and corrupt. In 1881 a religious leader named the Mahdi won control of the Sudan and rose in revolt against the Egyptian Government. Attempts to put this rebellion down failed entirely and in 1883 Lord Cromer recommended that the Egyptian garrisons should be withdrawn and the Sudan abandoned. The officer chosen by the British Government to carry out this policy was General Charles Gordon (1833–85), an engineer officer with an unusual career behind him. At the age of thirty he had been employed by the Chinese government to crush a rebellion. Brilliantly successful, he had returned to England to build forts at the mouth of the Thames, spending his pay on charity in the East End of London. He was intensely devout and had the same personal consciousness of God which inspired Livingstone on his arduous and lonely expeditions. After six years in England he left to become the Khedive's Governor of the Sudan where he devoted himself to building roads, suppressing rebels and studying the scriptures. In 1879 he left the Sudan and continued his adventurous career in South Africa, China and Abyssinia. It was to this extraordinary, independent-minded officer that Gladstone's government unexpectedly turned in 1884 to complete the evacuation of a province where he had once been the triumphant governor. Gordon, unlike Gladstone, realized that the Mahdi was not the leader of a people struggling to be free but the chief of a minority of war-like fanatics who wished to impose their own tyranny on the Sudanese. He was therefore reluctant to carry out his orders.

In any case he soon realized that the Sudan could not be evacuated without fighting. The government refused to admit this. Gordon's appeals for reinforcements, telegraphed from Khartoum where he was cut off by the Mahdi, were disregarded. In England public opinion suddenly awoke to the situation and demanded that a relief expedition should be sent to rescue Gordon. Gladstone, however, procrastinated. Not until August 26th, when Gordon's danger was already acute, was Garnet Wolseley appointed to command an expedition. Ill-luck dogged its march to Khartoum and when at last it reached the city on the 28th January, 1885, it found the Egyptian flag no longer flying and the town in ruins. The final attack had taken place two days previously and Gordon himself had perished, his head being taken as a trophy to delight the Mahdi. Gladstone faced a storm of reproach, from the Queen down to her meanest subject. He was accused of murdering Gordon, and the accusation coloured the general complaints at his neglect of the empire.

During his ministry the scramble for Africa among the European powers had begun. Italy, Germany, Belgium, Portugal, and France staked out claims, while Gladstone who disliked colonial commitments willingly stood aside. East Africa, which had been opened up by Livingstone and his successor Kirk, was surrendered to German influence. Only in 1887 did England realize that the other European powers intended to close the areas they seized to the trade and missionary activity of other nations. In that year an agreement was made with Germany marking out rough spheres of influence in

East Africa (later to be made exact in 1890 in exchange for the cession of Heligoland). A British East Africa Company was chartered in 1888 and as a result the Government assumed a protectorate over Uganda (1893) and Kenya (1895). In 1886 the Royal Niger Company was founded, largely owing to the enterprise of Sir George Goldie.

From 1885 England pursued a policy of sustained and conscious imperialism. This spirit was most evident in South Africa where it achieved a temporary success until it was checked by the South African War (1899–1902). The relations between the Boer republics and the two British colonies of the Cape and Natal had never been good. In 1871 a diamond field had been found in the angle between the Vaal and Orange Rivers. The ownership of the land was disputed between the Boer States, the British and a native tribe of Griquas. Arbitration awarded the land to the Griquas who surrendered their claim to the British. This surrender was resented by the Boers, but to the colonists of the Cape it opened up prospects of untold wealth. The Kimberley diamond fields, as they were called, were soon thronged with prospectors, some of whom rapidly amassed large fortunes. One of the richest was Cecil Rhodes (1853–1902). The son of an Essex vicar, he had left England for reasons of health at the age of seventeen. By the age of nineteen he had become a man of means and spent the next eight years combining the life of an undergraduate at Oxford with that of a ruthless diamond magnate in Africa. He quickly took the lead in the amalgamation of the diamond mines and with enormous wealth behind him entered the Cape Parliament. He was inspired by a great vision, nurtured during his years at Oxford, of spreading the influence of the English-speaking race throughout the world. In Africa, where the great powers of Europe were scrambling for territory, he saw the most dangerous threat to English expansion, particularly in the belt of country stretching from coast to coast made up of the two independent Boer Republics and the German and Portuguese colonies in East and West Africa. To Rhodes who dreamt of a British dominion stretching from the Cape to Cairo this was intolerable. In 1885 he persuaded the home Government to annex the Bechuanaland territory to which the Boers were already spreading.

"I look upon this Bechuanaland territory", said Rhodes, "as the Suez Canal of the trade of this country, the key of its road to the interior."

Rhodes' ambition and methods were those of a full-blooded imperialist of the new age. Raised in the hard pioneer school of the diamond mines, he had few scruples; self-assertive and determined, he intended to achieve his vision of Empire in Africa: a Dominion of English-speaking peoples with the fullest measure of self-government.

Having saved the road north through Bechuanaland, Rhodes suddenly found himself deeply involved in the Transvaal, for in 1885 gold was discovered in large quantities in a range of hills called the Witwatersrand. Because of the depth of the veins the goldfield could only be worked by elaborate and expensive machinery, for which Rhodes and his fellow diamond magnates found the capital. White settlers, whom the Boers called Uitlanders, poured into the goldfields, and within a few years outnumbered the total Boer population. The country north of the Transvaal was Rhodes' next concern. This was the land of the Matabele and Mashona tribes, ruled by Lobengula the Matabele king. Already white men were forcing their way through and in 1888 Rhodes' agents obtained concessions from Lobengula for the exclusive right to exploit the mineral resources of the land. The following year the British South Africa Company was formed to work the concession and in June 1890 two hundred pioneers under Dr. Jameson, an old friend of Rhodes, set off to form the nucleus of what is now Southern Rhodesia. Before long, Lobengula realized that he was losing his independence and in 1893 war broke out. Lobengula fled and for a while his people resigned themselves to the rule of the white man.

Rhodes had become Prime Minister of the Cape in 1891 and in South Africa his imperial ideas were universally accepted. In England, too, interest in the empire was at its height. In 1887 Queen Victoria's Jubilee was made the occasion of a colonial conference, the Colonial Secretary remarking that "there is on all sides a growing desire to draw closer in every practicable way the bonds which unite the various parts of the Empire". In 1891 the Government made a treaty with Portugal by which that country gave up its claims to a trans-African belt between Mozambique and Angola. Portugal recognized the new British protectorate of Nyasaland, and the British interest in the country between the Zambesi River and the Congo Free State, which was taken over by the British South Africa Company (later it became Northern Rhodesia). Gone were the days when the Government refused to annex. In 1895 a Conservative Government succeeded Gladstone's last ministry which had for its three years of office been exclusively occupied with the problem of Irish Home Rule. The new Colonial Secretary was Joseph Chamberlain, who, like Rhodes, typified the spirit of late Victorian imperialism. Chamberlain had made his reputation as Mayor of Birmingham by reforming the city and clearing slums. He brought to the Colonial Secretaryship the same energy and enthusiasm. To him the colonies were undeveloped estates, particularly in the West Indies and West Africa, and he was responsible for launching many schemes of practical improvement, founding schools of tropical medicine and a department of agriculture for the West Indies, and floating loans for the construction of harbours and railways. The standard of life in the over-populated West Indies was appalling and nothing had been done by the home Government since the abolition of slavery. Chamberlain was keenly aware of the value of the empire and did a great deal to strengthen the relationship with the self-governing colonies and to develop the backward areas. He also promoted the idea of imperial preference to bind the empire with economic links in a world of competitive trade monopoly. It has been his misfortune to be linked with the bombastic imperialism of Rhodes and Jameson, whose activities he regarded with mixed feelings.

In 1895 Rhodes and Chamberlain corresponded when Rhodes received permission to take over the Bechuanaland Protectorate on behalf of the British South Africa Company. This concession would enable him to achieve his ambition; it would strengthen his hold on the interior and give him a strip of land along the western frontier of the hostile Transvaal. Rhodes was already planning a showdown with the Boers. After the discovery of gold, the Uitlanders outnumbered the Dutch in the Transvaal but were allowed no votes, civic rights or educational opportunities, although they paid the bulk of the taxes. Kruger, the Boer leader, defended this treatment of the Uitlanders, whom he claimed were destroying the pastoral character of the country's life. Consequently the Uitlanders plotted against the Boer Government and Rhodes agreed to assist a rising by sending a force to invade the Transvaal. Jameson, his right-hand man, collected a force of 500 on the frontier and on December 29th suddenly crossed into the Transvaal. Of this plan Chamberlain was probably ignorant, although he had heard sympathetically of a suggested Uitlander rising. Jameson's hot-headed action horrified him; even Rhodes at the last moment had qualms and tried to stop Jameson. The raid was a ghastly failure and on January 2nd, 1896, a Boer commando surrounded Jameson's small column.

The entire episode was disastrous and irresponsible, but the action of the German Kaiser in telegraphing his congratulations to Kruger and ordering troops from East Africa to proceed to the Transvaal, gave the British public an opportunity for patriotic demonstrations which diverted attention from the stupidity of the raid. Relations with the two Boer Republics rapidly deteriorated. In 1897 the Orange Free State allied with the Transvaal and Kruger obtained arms and staff officers from Germany. It was becoming clear that Dutch and British could not live together in South Africa in different political units. "It is our country you want", Kruger said, and in a spirit of stubborn defiance the Boers prepared to fight. Kruger appealed to all the Dutch people in South Africa to help expel the British altogether. He relied on European jealousy of Britain to secure the intervention of the great powers. Germany was Britain's rival in trade and on the seas, while in 1898 Anglo-French relations reached breaking point at Fashoda. At this small post on the Upper Nile young Captain Marchand having toiled across Africa faced the British General Kitchener and his victorious army. Britain had at length reversed the policy of abandoning the Sudan, and by the battle of Omdurman (1898) it had been reconquered. Marchand represented French ambitions of an empire stretching from the Gulf of Aden to the Niger; Kitchener stood for British power in Africa from the Cape to Cairo. For a few weeks war seemed certain until the French climbed down.

In this atmosphere of international tension the Boers might well expect assistance. In 1897 Sir Alfred Milner had been sent to the Cape as Governor and High Commissioner and he saw that war must come sooner or later. His negotiations with Kruger were conducted in no conciliatory spirit and the Boer leader merely awaited a favourable opportunity to act. When British reinforcements were ordered to South Africa he protested, and on the British refusal to recall them war broke out in October 1899.

The Boers invaded British territory in great force and inflicted humiliating defeats on the British troops, who were ill-trained for South African fighting and badly led by General Redvers Buller. Only the stubborn resistance of British garrisons besieged in Ladysmith, Kimberley, and Mafeking, prevented the Boers from sweeping through to the sea and provided sufficient time for the British to rally. Fresh troops and better generals (Kitchener and Roberts) came out and in 1900 the sieges of the three towns were raised, the Boer Republics were entered and their capitals occupied. Kruger fled to Europe where he found Germany unwilling to countenance an unsuccessful cause. Although Britain annexed the two republics the war was far from over, and the mobile Boer commandos continued a gallant guerrilla resistance under the leadership of such resourceful generals as Botha, Hertzog and Smuts. The Boers did not wear uniform and turned farmer when defeated, only to take up arms once more when British troops had passed. Kitchener devised a plan to meet this problem by clearing all farms and concentrating all their inhabitants in great enclosed camps. In the early stages the camps were badly run and disease broke out, causing a very high death rate. Not until May 1902 did the Boer generals come to terms and by the Peace of Vereeniging all the Boers became British subjects and were promised representative government as soon as possible. Three million pounds were granted towards the re-stocking of Boer farms. Before the war was over, Rhodes had died but he made a prophecy for the future that "the Dutch are not beaten. The country is still as much theirs as yours and you will have to live and work with them".

## CHAPTER XVI

## INDIA AND THE MODERN EMPIRE

### 1. India: The Last Years of the Company, 1830–1858

INDIA in the nineteenth century was not legally described nor generally considered as belonging to the British colonial empire, and although it was governed in the name of the East India Company, the new charter of 1833 ended for ever the trading activities of the Company in India. Henceforward the Company's directors were no more than a governing body, closely supervised by a board of control under the Cabinet in London. Free trade opened the markets of India to all comers, and the Indian Government under the Governor-General concerned itself primarily with political problems. No longer as in the days of Clive, Hastings, and Wellesley were the Company's demands for dividends to stand in the way of political reform, although action was still limited by the poverty of India's resources. About 40 per cent of the Government's revenue came from the land tax, and land in India was notoriously infertile. Expenditure on the army and civil administration rose in the nineteenth century to 70 per cent of the total revenue. Although an honest and efficient government was provided, there was little to spare for building hospitals and schools.

British activity in India from 1830 to 1858 was dominated by two ideas—the Victorian belief in the superiority of Western culture, and the fear of Russia. Leaving Russia on one side for the moment, let us consider the Victorian approach to Indian civilization. To the evangelical it was pagan, to the believer in progress it was barbaric. The missionaries convinced the Government that the only hope of training an Indian political class was to give them a Christian, and therefore Western, education. Lord William Bentinck (1772–1839), as Governor-General, began this task. His Governor-Generalship, from 1828–1836, saw the beginning of the campaign to stamp out the *thugs*, a secret society who murdered solitary travellers as a sacrifice to the goddess Kali. In 1829 the Hindu custom of *suttee*, by which the widows of dead men were compelled to throw themselves into the flames of the funeral pyre, was prohibited by law. Many women had been brought up to regard *suttee* as a religious obligation, and conservative Hindu opinion was shocked by Bentinck's decision. In March 1835 the Governor-General in Council decided that "the great object of the British Government ought to be the promotion of European literature and science among the natives of India and that all the funds appropriated would be best employed on English education alone". The basis of this decision was the famous Minute on Education drawn up by Macaulay who had come to India as the legal member of the Council. He dismissed the learning of the East with contempt. A knowledge of English became a condition of entry to government service and, though upper-class Indians held aloof, increasing numbers of middle-class *babus* acquired a smattering of Western education. But it was not among them that the British had hoped to educate the leaders who would interpret the West to the Indian masses.

England's industrial and commercial power had more effect in India than religious and social ideas. Every Governor-General was concerned with the material conditions of Indian life but Lord Dalhousie, who was Governor-General from 1848 to 1856, made the most notable advances. He planned the Grand Trunk Road (completed in 1864) which ran from Calcutta to Peshawar "bearing without crowding India's traffic, for fifteen hundred miles—such a river of life as nowhere exists in the world. For the most part it is shaded with four lines of trees; the middle road—all hard—takes the quick traffic. Left and right is the rougher road for the country carts". The great Indian railway system was begun, and the whole country was linked by telegraph. A halfpenny rate for letters aided inland communication while harbour improvements and coastal surveys made navigation easier and safer. Irrigation works and the Ganges Canal were among the achievements of the tireless Dalhousie. He had shown what the West could do for the East.

These improvements in communications raised the Indian standard of life, but their original purpose was strategic. British fears of Russian ambitions in the Near East were confirmed by

Russian activity in Persia and Afghanistan. In 1700 the British and Russians were separated in this part of the world by over 4,000 miles; by 1830 this distance had narrowed to 1,500 miles and by 1873 it was only 400. British penetration of North-Western India therefore had more to do with strategic necessity than economic advantage, although the annexation of Sind in 1843 gave Britain control of the commerce of the Indus Valley. Since the decline of the Mogul Empire three warlike groups had been competing for power in the North-West of India; the chieftains known as the Amirs of Sind, the Sikhs of the Punjab, and the Amir of Afghanistan who held the unruly Afghan tribes in an uncertain grip. The Afghans and Sikhs were foes by religion and tradition, while the Amirs of Sind were little more than bandits, preying on the trade of the Indus. For the British the problem was complicated by geography: military operations were difficult, but with Russian intrigues in Afghanistan it was essential that the Indus Valley should be controlled. Lord Auckland, Governor-General from 1836 to 1842, took the first effective measures to this end. The Punjab under the Sikh chief, Runjeet Singh, was already bound by a treaty of friendship made in 1808, and in 1838 Auckland negotiated a short-lived treaty with Sind. He then decided to replace the exiled Amir of Afghanistan, Shah Suja, on the Afghan throne. The decision was disliked by the Indian army who believed that the frontier of British power should remain in the Punjab. Events justified this opinion. Although Kabul was occupied and Shah Suja installed as Amir in 1839, his power depended upon the British army. In November 1841 Kabul rose in rebellion, Dost Mohammed, the banished Amir, reappeared, and the British commander, completely outnumbered, agreed to withdraw under a safe conduct. In the depth of winter the column set out through the Khyber Pass, harassed by Afghan tribesmen whom Dost Mohammed was powerless—and probably unwilling—to control. From a total force of 4,700 troops and 12,000 camp followers only one survivor, an army doctor, reached safety. The others had either been killed or taken prisoner.

This reverse was a severe blow to British prestige in the North-West and to save what remained of it, the next Governor-General,

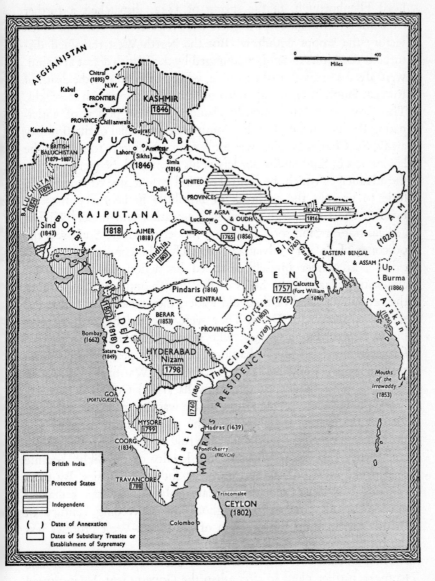

**INDIA**

ILLUSTRATING THE GROWTH OF BRITISH TERRITORY AND SUPREMACY.

Lord Ellenborough, in the spring of 1842, dispatched a further expedition to Kabul. The prisoners were released and after this token victory the troops withdrew. But the North-West remained disturbed; the Amirs of Sind, encouraged by the British defeat at Kabul, were always ready to make trouble, while in the Punjab the death of Runjeet Singh in 1839 had ended our understanding with the Sikhs. The Government temporarily abandoned their policy of anticipating Russian threats, but the Commander-in-Chief of the Bombay army, Sir Charles Napier, was too strong a character to tolerate the lawlessness of Sind on the borders of his command. Napier, realizing the advantages which the control of Sind would give to Britain, did little to prevent the outbreak of hostilities in February 1843. A brilliant short campaign ended in annexation and under Napier's administration Sind soon became a model province. Such was the outcome of "a very advantageous, useful, humane piece of rascality", as Napier himself described his action. In its turn this annexation alarmed the Sikhs of the Punjab and in 1845, without the restraining hand of their old leader, they took the initiative and started to march for Delhi. They were opposed by British forces under General Hugh Gough, who stemmed the invasion after two ferocious and hard-fought battles. The ensuing peace was no more than an armistice and in 1848 the Second Sikh War broke out. Again it was bitterly fought: at Chillianwalla (1848) Gough was nearly beaten, but at Gujerat (1849) his courage was rewarded by a crushing victory which left the Punjab at the mercy of the British. The province was annexed, and under the rule of the two brothers, John and Henry Lawrence, who won the loyalty of the Sikhs, became one of the most orderly and obedient Indian territories. By these campaigns in Sind and the Punjab, only Afghanistan remained outside British control. Throughout the succeeding century of British rule in India the problem of the North-West Frontier was the problem of the Afghan border.

These notable successes undoubtedly encouraged Lord Dalhousie to make further plans to strengthen the Government. He instituted the "doctrine of lapse", whereby he refused to allow native princes, allied by subsidiary treaty, to follow the immemorial Indian custom of adopting their heirs. If they had no sons of their own, the suc-

cession was to lapse to the pa
doctrine was imposed in three
In addition Dalhousie decided
which had been allowed to re
with the life of the then holder
Burma, and in 1856 took ove
order, tyranny, and corruptior
in spite of successive British p
from the same desire for good go
India's transport and commerce, bu
By 1856 there was a feeling of unres
English teaching, English interference,
Rumours circulated wildly and an old pr.......
British rule would last only for a hundred years after Plassey (1757).

Discontent there certainly was, but by itself it would never have produced the Mutiny. This outbreak was confined to an area around the Ganges Valley; all the major princes held aloof, the newly annexed provinces remained calm, and the Indian people as a whole made no move against the British. The trouble started in the Bengal army where the ratio of British troops to sepoys was only 1 to 8 as a result of withdrawals for the Crimean War. Many of the officers were elderly, and the bulk of the sepoys were high-caste Hindus recruited from the recently conquered Kingdom of Oudh. For a long time they had had grievances, and slack discipline allowed these to grow. The crisis came with the issue of a new type of cartridge coated in grease. The soldier had to bite the end off before using it, and news quickly spread that the grease was that of a cow, an animal sacred to the Hindu. Other rumours held it to be pig's grease, which equally affronted the Moslems. To the discontented sepoys the new cartridge appeared as a direct affront to their religion and when officers insisted on the cartridge being used, a regiment mutinied on May 10th, 1857, at Meerut. Probably even then the British could have checked the movement had they shown intelligent leadership, but the mutineers were allowed to march on Delhi unmolested, gaining recruits with every mile. In Delhi they routed out the aged Mogul Emperor from his palace within the Red Fort and by acclaiming him as their ruler, associated Moslem

n the succeeding weeks of summer, death
the Ganges Valley; English soldiers and officials
lieve that the loyalty of the sepoys was broken,
particularly at Cawnpore and Lucknow, might have
ted by quicker action. The conflict from the first was
d bloody: the English felt little inclined to mercy when
ound the bodies of two hundred women and children thrown
wn a well at Cawnpore, brutally murdered by Nana Sahib. This
man was the adopted heir of the last head of the old Mahratta
confederacy and he seized the opportunity of the Mutiny to assert
his claims.

India was saved by the loyalty of other provinces, by the resolution
of John Lawrence in the Punjab, and the uncertainty of the mutineers
who hung about Delhi without a leader to direct them. Lawrence
anticipated mutiny by disbanding unreliable regiments, and sent a
force under Nicholson to recapture Delhi. The Bombay command
remained loyal, and the Rajput princes remained faithful to their
subsidiary treaties. Such conduct did much to justify past British
policy. Meanwhile from Calcutta, Lord Canning, the Governor-
General, had despatched a force under Henry Havelock, a stern,
puritanical soldier, to relieve Lucknow. By September 20th the
Red Fort of Delhi had fallen; within its walls stood the splendid
palace of the Moguls, from which the last Emperor had fled. By
the close of 1857 the worst was over, although a year of hard fighting
was needed to reduce the province of Oudh, and the final sparks
were not extinguished until the spring of 1859.

India was never the same after the Mutiny; the spell had been
broken. The practical consequences were easy to see: a new India
Bill in 1858 transferred the government of India from the Company
to a minister of the Crown. The Company's officials, who had since
1853 been chosen by competitive examination, formed the new
Indian Civil Service, and its troops were absorbed into the armed
forces of the Crown. Precautions against mutiny were taken in the
sepoy regiments. But the hidden effects of the Mutiny were serious
and permanent, transcending these outward changes of organization.
The old confidence was gone and the British grew less and less
inclined to mix with the natives. Hill stations and army cantonments

were filled with "Strangers in India" as one civil servant so aptly named a book on the last years of British rule. Increased speed of transport made communication with England easy. Gone were the days of Lawrence and Nicholson, when the British believed that their mission was to transform India in partnership with the native peoples, who would soon govern themselves. Now it was accepted that East and West must remain separate; the ultimate purpose of British rule was never clearly thought out until too late, and the Government concentrated more and more on providing efficient and impartial administration. The Viceroy[1] lost his independence of action after the invention of the telegraph linked him with Downing Street. He became, for all the pageantry of imperial splendour that surrounded him, an over-worked secretary, for ever on the defensive. British administration increased the material welfare of India, but after the Mutiny the Indians were changed. They remembered the harsh scenes of vengeance, and in face of the new British attitude resentment began to grow among the educated classes. Western education taught them ideas of political democracy and in course of time they started to regard the Mutiny as a national movement for liberty, which, in fact, it had not been.

## 2. *British India, 1858–1947*

The economic development of India after the Mutiny was remarkable. By 1938 over 67,000 miles of canals brought irrigation to millions of parched acres. Railways, financed by British capital, spanned the country, till by 1905 over 28,000 miles of railway track existed. This magnificent system served not only a strategic purpose but the very life of India. In particular it enabled the Government to control the frequent famines which cursed the country. With no wars to kill them off the population grew rapidly and any failure in the food supply could bring disaster. Experience taught valuable lessons and by 1883 a detailed famine code was drawn up. An annual sum in the budget was allotted each year to famine relief, and the railways enabled supplies to be despatched to a starving province without delay. The Government certainly did a great deal for the

[1] The title of Governor-General was changed to Viceroy by the Act of 1858.

Indians but their numbers increased at such an alarming rate[1] that the standard of living did not rise.

The new communications opened up many Indian resources, including jute, cotton, and tea, to private enterprise. The Crimean War, by cutting off jute supplies from Russia, left the field clear for Indian export, and the American Civil War did the same for cotton. Trade increased steadily throughout the century: in 1855 exports totalled £23 million, and imports £13½ million, and by 1910 the figures had risen to £137 million and £86 million. The prevailing doctrine of Free Trade prevented India from imposing protective tariffs for the benefit of her infant industries. Such industries as cotton, jute, and paper mills were established with difficulty and it was not until 1917 that the Government was allowed to impose a tariff, discriminating against Lancashire cotton goods. Undoubtedly British rule brought a marked increase in wealth to India but she could not escape the penalty of her political subordination. It is a purely academic question whether she would have benefited more if she had had political liberty. Independence was not a practical issue in the nineteenth century, and even assuming that it had existed, India would have been helpless without English economic support. It is sometimes said that India was sacrificed to English Free Trade interests, but this argument is unsound. The British Government might have made some concessions but her general policy could not well have been other than it was. In retrospect it is easy to find fault and equally easy to forget the foundations on which Indian economic independence stands.[2] Without roads, railways, irrigation, and British capital, India would have remained a backward agricultural country.

In spite of the industrial and commercial advances of the nineteenth century the bulk of the Indian people became steadily poorer. The increase in population offset increased production. The Indian peasants never escaped from debt to local money lenders, and were therefore incapable of any co-operative effort to improve their land.

---

[1] A census of 1871 gave the figures as 206 million. In 1941 the number was approximately 390 million.

[2] After the Second World War India had become a creditor country; i.e. Great Britain was in debt to India.

The Government was hampered in its turn by lack of revenue, and neither it nor the peasant could break the vicious circle. Only a prodigious expenditure by the British taxpayer would have sufficed. Despite all its good intentions the Indian Government could achieve no more than its funds permitted, and these funds were inadequate. Expenditure on the army and the civil administration accounted for 70 per cent of the Indian revenue, and too little remained for agricultural projects. A large army was undoubtedly necessary for defence of the North-West, but it is questionable whether 150,000 troops were needed. The Government in England regarded these forces as a strategic reserve for the whole empire and Indian regiments were used in Egypt, China, and in South Africa during the Boer War. This burden on India cannot be justified and it provides the most damaging criticism of British rule.

After 1858 the defence of the North-West Frontier occupied most of the Government's attention. Behind the wild tribesmen lurked the power of Russia, a spectre that haunted the minds of British statesmen. The situation was affected by diplomatic as well as strategic considerations and altered according to the state of affairs in Europe. Both Russia and Britain at different times adopted aggressive policies; both were challenged by each other and eventually withdrew anxiously trying to maintain their prestige. In 1876 Lord Lytton, the Viceroy sent out by Disraeli, challenged Russia's penetration of Afghanistan. Europe at this time was deeply suspicious of Russian designs on Turkey, and Disraeli regarded the penetration of Afghanistan in this context. The Amir had accepted a Russian military mission, and on his refusal to receive a British one, Indian troops under General Roberts (1835–1914) invaded the country. This second Afghan War followed the pattern of the first; Kabul was occupied, the pro-Russian Amir fled, and a rival prince was established, bound by treaty to Britain. Two months later, in September 1879, the British Resident and his staff were murdered and Roberts returned to Kabul to punish the murderers. A new pretender Abdurrahman seized power; he was recognized as Amir and Roberts withdrew, having made a memorable march from Kabul to Kandahar to crush a rising which had defeated a second British column. Abdurrahman kept faith with the British and in the years following maintained his position against both the Russians and his own tribesmen. Britain accepted Afghanistan as a buffer State and her confidence was rewarded.

Roberts' exploits during the Afghan War made him a popular hero. His march along mountain paths in extreme temperatures caught the public imagination. After the war he became Commissioner at Peshawar where he built roads and strategic railways to provide rapid transport in the event of an emergency. Later as Commander-in-Chief he reorganized the Indian army, gaining the affectionate loyalty of the private soldier whose interests were his lifelong concern. As Afghanistan became comparatively stable the problem of defending the North-West Frontier consisted more in checking the wild Pathans. From their strongholds in the hills they made periodic forays, spreading terror and destruction. No final solution was ever reached, although Baluchistan was brought to order after a British base had been established at Quetta. After several attempts at coercion, Lord Curzon (Viceroy 1899–1905) decided to form the area between the Indus and Afghanistan into a separate North-West Frontier province. Troops were stationed in large garrisons ready to deal with trouble as it arose. Except for a violent rising in 1919 the frontier thereafter remained relatively tranquil, but it was always a region of active service for soldiers whose exploits have inspired innumerable novels and films.

In military and economic matters the Indian Government had a clear policy after 1858, but its political objectives were confused and contradictory. Before the Mutiny the British had reckoned that within a few generations Indian leaders would be educated to self-government, and Britain could withdraw. This was the faith in which Macaulay had drawn up his Minute on Education. But after the Mutiny there was a subtle change; self-government was no longer mentioned, and Indian leaders were suspect. In 1877 Queen Victoria assumed the title of Empress of India and greater reliance was placed on the Indian princes who, as a class, had remained conspicuously loyal in the hour of crisis. The constitutional rule of the Viceroy was despotic and depended solely upon the approval of the British Parliament, 4,000 miles away. Despite an educational policy designed to produce Indians with University qualifications, almost all of the higher civil service posts were closed to them in practice, and naturally many educated Indians became agitators. In fact for over forty years after the Mutiny the political future of India was obscure; only too late did the British Government formulate a policy for constitutional advance and the result was that when it came it was already too conservative for Indian opinion. This opinion had been allowed full liberty in the popular Press, and nothing could have been more provocative than to deny men access to political power, yet to permit them to champion their opinions in print. With all these contradictions Indian politics were frustrated and bitter.

The achievement of political liberty is necessarily complicated, and in India there were three roads to its attainment: restriction of the Viceroy's power by democratic institutions, the abolition of British Parliamentary control, and the replacement of British officials by Indians. The British were slow and uncertain in dealing with these three matters. A start was made by establishing municipal councils in the larger towns on an English pattern, but they failed to arouse widespread enthusiasm. In an attempt to enlist Indian opinion, the Viceroy gave his blessing in 1885 to the first meeting of the Indian National Congress. This was a gathering of seventy-two representatives from all over India, mainly consisting of lawyers and journalists, and including several well-disposed Englishmen. All the members were brought up in the Western liberal tradition and believed that self-government could be attained by gradual and constitutional means. Their activities were confined to discussion, and they always began their proceedings by singing "God Save the Queen". They continued to meet every year, growing less and less patient with the slow progress of reform. By 1892 Indian representation on the nominated Councils of the Central and Provincial administrations had been increased, but already younger Congressmen were adopting a tone of violence in their criticisms of British rule. They were inspired by a revival of Hinduism, an appeal to the ancient traditions of India, and a reaction against Western ideas. The popularity of such doctrines was ominous for the British. This Hindu nationalism not only rejected compromise with the West but also implied the subordination of the Moslem people of India. These two factors—refusal to compromise and the split of Moslem and Hindu—henceforth dominated the political history of India. The Congress was the scene of a double conflict, between moderate and extremist, between Hindu and Moslem, and in these struggles the eventual partition of India under threat of violence was foreshadowed. From being an intellectual talking-shop the Congress became the centre of Indian nationalism, voicing the growing hostility towards British rule. Terrorism began to spread through Bengal and was intensified by Lord Curzon's decision in 1905 to divide the province into two for administrative convenience. This action encouraged the Congress extremists to demand revolutionary changes. The moderates managed to retain control but in 1906 the Moslems, alarmed at the growing Hindu majority, withdrew from the Congress and formed their own All-India Moslem League.

This turmoil convinced the British Government that terrorism must be curbed. Some of India's political demands had to be satisfied. The reforms drawn up by Lord Morley, the Secretary of State, and Lord Minto, the Viceroy, were temporary rather than long-term, a collection of expedients, not a coherent plan for the future development of India. Their policy was confused because its objective had not been clearly thought out. Indian representation on the Councils was again increased and free discussion of all topics was allowed. The principle of election to these Councils was admitted, but the Moslems were allowed separate electorates to prevent their interests from being submerged by the Hindu majority. But despite these reforms Morley denied any intention of introducing a parliamentary system into India. Time was to show that Britain could not avoid this logical conclusion. Only in 1919 did British statesmen lay down a definite plan for India's future. By then India had emerged as a power which had contributed greatly to the allied victory. Her volunteer army had been larger than that of any of the Dominions and her industry had made rapid progress. She had been accorded representation at the Versailles Conference, and on the successful conclusion of a war "to make the world safe for democracy" she could hardly be denied some measure of it.

Hindu and Moslem political leaders had agreed in 1916 to demand parliamentary government and dominion status for India. Edwin

Montagu, the Secretary of State, accepted these demands as legitimate objectives, and together with Lord Chelmsford, the Viceroy, drew up a report which became the basis for the Government of India Act of 1919. It provided the Viceroy with a central legislature, the majority of whose members were democratically elected. Although the Viceroy remained responsible to the British Parliament, it was hoped that the nucleus of an Indian Parliament had been formed. A chamber of princes was also established as a purely advisory body. In the provinces the principle of ministerial responsibility was developed; each Governor ruled with a cabinet chosen by the provincial legislature. Certain subjects, law, police, and finance, were "reserved" to the Governor, but in time it was expected to transfer these functions entirely to the Indian ministries. The franchise was given to seven million people in all, and the building of a magnificent capital at New Delhi, designed by Lutyens and Baker[1] symbolized a new India advancing on the road to self-government.

Given time the new scheme might have worked, but Indian political leaders were impatient at this cautious progress towards independence. The new regime had a disastrous start: there were riots in the Punjab, where General Dyer shot down 387 people at Amritsar in April 1919. From the first the Congress party boycotted the new Governments and it was the moderates who undertook the unwelcome responsibility. Some useful work was done; Indians entered the Civil Service in increasing numbers and economic independence for India was achieved with the imposition of duties on British goods. But with the bulk of Indian political talent remaining in opposition the atmosphere remained tense and threatening. Indian politicians believed that complete self-government could be achieved at once, and their new leader, Gandhi, known as the Mahatma or "Great Soul", quickened nationalism with a fresh religious fervour. Gandhi had had a distinguished career as a lawyer in South Africa, and on his return to India began to live as an ascetic holy man. After 1919 he set himself at the head of Indian politics with a proclamation of revolutionary pacifism. He urged his followers to pursue a policy of peaceful non-co-operation with the

[1] When Lutyens and Baker quarrelled about the plans, Lutyens at length gave in, remarking "At last I've met my Bakerloo".

Government and prophesied that this would give India self-government immediately. The Mahatma's teaching was misunderstood, and the resulting savage outbreaks of violence horrified him. In 1922 he was imprisoned, and his personality and courage captured the imagination of the Indian peasant. Until his assassination in 1948 he remained the great figure in India, impressing his belief in peace on the world by prolonged fasting. His ambition for India was to free her from the West; he deplored industrialization and saw in simple village life the true destiny of India. Although a Hindu, he deeply valued Hindu-Moslem unity and laboured to prevent the split which Congress extremists did nothing to avert.

This division between Moslem and Hindu was more than a religious one; in numbers and in economic power the Moslems were markedly inferior, and they were naturally concerned to protect their interests in any self-governing India. The Congress claimed to represent the whole country and in 1928 stubbornly refused to accept the idea of Federation advanced by the Moslems. The Hindu Congress wanted a united and independent India, rather than a federation of minorities. In 1928 a commission under Sir John Simon arrived in India to review the workings of the Montagu-Chelmsford reforms, and its report became the basis for a round table conference in 1930. Representatives from every Indian party and interest were invited to London, but Congress refused to attend and Gandhi launched a civil disobedience campaign. Eventually he was persuaded to come to London, but the conference soon revealed the fundamental issues dividing India. The Congress party rejected both the idea of federation and the plan for dominion status. Only a united independent India would do. It is hard not to sympathize with the British Government, who had to help 300 million people to secure self-government, and at the same time to protect the rights of minorities. They moved cautiously, striving to reach the best solution but with every month Indian exasperation increased. In 1935 a new Government of India Act was passed, establishing full responsible government in the eleven major provinces and designing the machinery for setting up a Federation as soon as a specific number of Indian states agreed to join. But Congress would have no compromise with their demands, and refused to take part. Instead they intensified their propaganda among the princely states and towards the Moslems, to convert them to the idea of a united India. Only in 1937 did Congress contest elections with the avowed purpose of undermining the new Act if they got into power. Under Pandit Jawaharlal Nehru, they achieved a striking success and in the summer of 1937 seven Congress ministries took office. But their rejection of the Moslem offer of coalitions in the other provinces was a fateful step.

Nehru, a disciple of Gandhi, was educated at Harrow and Cambridge, and by 1936 had become the leading figure in the Congress party. By repulsing the Moslem offer, Congress generated a wave of fear throughout Moslem communities in India. Within two years Mohammed Ali Jinnah, leader of the Moslem League, had become the head of a major political force. By 1940 Jinnah, who in the past had worked so hard for unity, proclaimed that a separate state, Pakistan, was the Moslem political objective. Congress intransigeance was alone responsible for Moslem unity, and henceforth partition became the paramount issue. The Second World War threw the other questions into the shade. Congress demanded immediate and complete independence as the price for its co-operation in the war: the Moslem League offered its support only if the Congress terms were rejected. In face of this deadlock the Viceroy had to be content with maintaining the administration with his own resources; industry was mobilized and volunteers flocked to the colours, providing eventually an army of over two million men.

When the Japanese invaded Burma the support of the major political parties in India seemed more than ever desirable. Sir Stafford Cripps was sent out with proposals at once realistic and generous. After the war India was to have complete freedom to withdraw from the Commonwealth and any provinces could form a separate union. Congress, however, demanded the immediate establishment of a National Government which the British Cabinet rightly judged as impracticable in the existing emergency. Gandhi described Cripps' proposals as "a post-dated cheque on a bank that is obviously failing" and he launched another civil disobedience campaign, calling on the British to quit India. The Government had to assert its authority, and Gandhi and other Congress leaders were imprisoned.

At the end of the war the only question for the British was how to leave India quickly and successfully. The Labour Government despatched a mission in May 1946 with specific and well-considered plans to preserve Indian unity. In September the first wholly Indian and fully responsible Government was sworn in by the Viceroy. It contained both Hindu and Moslem members which appeared a hopeful sign. But before many weeks had passed it was evident that neither side was genuinely seeking co-operation. Britain did no finer service to India than in these months when by shrewd and tactful negotiation she tried to maintain the hard-won unity of India, whose achievement had been the greatest glory of British rule. But the Indian leaders, trained in long years of factious and irresponsible opposition, did not respond, and they must take the blame for the widespread outbreaks of violence and murder which threatened to end in civil war. The Punjab in fact degenerated into this condition, and Britain took the courageous decision of announcing that she would withdraw from India by June 1948 at the latest. This was an attempt to startle the Indian leaders into some sort of agreement, by making them aware of their responsibility. This courage was rewarded in the last minute willingness of Congress to compromise. Realizing that a United India could only be achieved by force, Nehru and his colleagues informed the new Viceroy, Lord Mountbatten, that they would accept partition. With none of the delays of the past, an Indian Independence Act was carried through the British Parliament in July 1947. Two dominions were created out of the Indian Empire: Pakistan in the north-west and in eastern Bengal, and the new State of India. The position of the Indian princes was left undecided and they could either seek independence or association with one of the new dominions. Divided among themselves and deserted by Britain, independence was hardly a practical alternative, and individual princes very quickly came to terms which left them as titled pensioners deprived of power. The title of Emperor of India lapsed and the new dominions were free, if they chose, to leave the Commonwealth.

By the end of 1947 partition was a reality. Much blood had been spilt, tempers were still high, but civil war had been prevented. Partition had many weaknesses: it ignored the economic and strategic unity of India and left Pakistan, much the poorer of the two, to guard the North-Western and North-Eastern Frontiers. But it solved the immediate political difficulties, and its achievement was a fitting tribute to British statesmanship. Time alone can heal the wounds of hatred, and link India and Pakistan once more in that unity which was the greatest gift of British rule. This rule cannot escape severe criticism; since the Mutiny, short-sightedness and complacency had too often characterized British administration. Decisions were taken too late and so the British lost the credit for their good intentions. They did not mix with the Indian political class on terms of equality, and mutual misunderstanding was the consequence. But, judged by any standards, the British achievement in India was remarkable and it may well be the verdict of history that

> Nothing in his life
> Became him like the leaving it.

### 3. The British Commonwealth, 1901–1950

The South African War ended an epoch in British imperial history. There was less optimism and more awareness of the snags and difficulties in the path of an imperial power. The anti-imperialists and Little Englanders formed a powerful school of opinion which, if it did nothing else, quickened the conscience of England towards her colonies. Tension and conflict among the European powers encouraged Britain to strengthen her links with her empire overseas. This fell into two distinct categories; the old settlement colonies, and the tropical dependencies in Africa and the Far East. The former developed into self-governing dominions, the latter were controlled from London on the new lines laid down by Chamberlain.

The settlement colonies had shown their loyalty during the South African War; Australia, New Zealand, and Canada had sent more than 30,000 men to the front. During the previous fifty years there had been tremendous advances in the wealth and population of these English-speaking peoples. Men, ideas, and money were among Britain's chief exports in this period and through them the links were strengthened. Canada progressed with the aid of great businesses like the Hudson's Bay Company, and in 1885 the Canadian Pacific Railway opened up the interior of the continent. British capital found a ready use in Canada and did much to keep her linked to Britain rather than to her great neighbour, the United States. In 1900 after eleven years of negotiation the various Australian colonies formed a federation and the Commonwealth of Australia Act came into operation on January 1st, 1901. Fear of European competition and colonization in the Far East brought about this Union. In 1907 New Zealand was recognized as a dominion, though this was more a change of title than anything else. Recovery in South Africa was so rapid after the war that responsible government was granted to the two Boer provinces in 1907, and three years later all the provinces agreed to form the Union of South Africa. Thus the dreams of Grey, Rhodes, and Chamberlain were realized.

All these self-governing colonies became increasingly conscious of their own identity and imperceptibly the idea of the empire as an association of equals took root. The colonial conference was re-named in 1907 the imperial conference. In 1902, when Canada was asked to contribute ships to the Royal Navy, she preferred to begin a fleet of her own, and five years later Australia followed the same course. This independent spirit undermined the many schemes for some form of imperial federation which were advanced in these years. Not until the conference of 1911 was the idea decisively rejected by the dominions. The home Government on its side had refused to adopt any form of imperial preference but, despite these failures, schemes for common defence and improved communication were well advanced before the outbreak of war. Dominion premiers were kept informed about the international situation, and plans were drawn up for action in the event of war. A Chief of the Imperial General Staff presided over officers drawn from all the dominions and in 1909 Lord Kitchener made a world tour to give advice on mobilization plans. It was practical co-operation, not legal formulae, which created the Commonwealth.

The centre of strategic importance shifted during these years.

Hitherto British interest in the Middle East was concerned with safeguarding the route to India, but the introduction of oil as a fuel for the Royal Navy in 1911 altered things. The British Government acquired shares in the newly-formed Anglo-Iranian Oil Company, and the Persian Gulf became an area of vital concern to British policy.

On the outbreak of war in 1914 the dominions placed their forces unreservedly at the disposal of the British Government. Surprising demonstrations of loyalty occurred, and though the dominions had been committed to war without direct consultation, they at once identified their interests with those of Britain. This unanimity is a tribute to British policy in the nineteenth century. Even the two disturbed areas of India and Ireland remained quiet and provided hosts of volunteers for the armed forces. The naval units of Australia and New Zealand patrolled the Pacific against German raiders; and South Africa began operations against the German African colonies. But the major contribution of the dominions was soldiers for the Western and Middle Eastern fronts. Apart from India, the dominions sent over a million men abroad. Economically they financed their own war effort and after 1916 their ministers were consulted on all major questions of policy. In 1917 Lloyd George brought General Smuts of South Africa into the War Cabinet as a permanent member. His presence symbolized the new conception of the Commonwealth. The quality of British imperialism had been tested in a mortal struggle and was not found wanting.

At the peace conference of 1919 the dominion Prime Ministers accompanied Lloyd George to Paris, and their nationhood was universally recognized by the admission of the dominions and India as full members of the League of Nations. During the twenties a demand grew up for specific definition of dominion status, in order to regularize the constitutional position. At the imperial conference of 1926 a statement was issued declaring that the dominions were "autonomous communities within the British Empire, equal in status, in no way subordinate to one another in any aspect of their domestic or external affairs, though united by a common allegiance to the Crown and freely associated as members of the British Commonwealth of Nations". Five years later the legal situation was tidied up by the Statute of Westminster. This measure was concerned with legal technicalities, and its importance was largely symbolic. It marked the end of legal sovereignty over the dominions and the end of British imperial expansion.

British imperialism depended upon the export of men and money. Until the 1914 war both had been maintained; in 1913 over 300,000 people left the British Isles and the total figure of profit on external trade and overseas investments was £180 million. Our commercial and financial supremacy was already, before the war, powerfully challenged by the United States and Germany, and the strain of war stretched British resources to the limit. After 1919 we faced in every market the competition of modern industrial production in countries which had once relied on British exports. A few figures illustrate the decline in Britain's relative position: in 1913 Lancashire exported cotton goods worth £98 millions; by 1937 her exports had dwindled to £45 millions. In 1914 Britain built 60 per cent of the world's ships but by 1937 the figure was less than 30 per cent. Between 1913 and 1937 our total exports decreased in volume by 28 per cent, while our total imports increased by 32 per cent. This adverse balance of trade was barely offset by our reduced overseas investments, built up in the prosperity of the nineteenth century. Emigration declined as well as trade; in 1929 only 87,000 people left Britain, and thereafter more returned than departed.

The reasons for this end to emigration are complicated. The old settlement colonies had become nations in their own right, and throughout the East old nations had come to life, rejecting Western culture but adapting Western industry to their own uses. In the Middle East, nationalism turned against the rule of the British, who had brought law and order where once there had been chaos. Economically, politically, and psychologically nineteenth-century imperialism was in retreat. "During the three generations of British supremacy there were five modes of expansion: by settlement, by trade, by finance, by conquest, and by the spreading of ideas. All had reached fulfilment by 1931."[1]

During the great world slump of 1929 to 1931 Britain was forced

[1] C. E. Carrington, *The British Overseas*.

to abandon Free Trade and the gold standard, on which her commercial supremacy in the nineteenth century had rested. The economic links of the Commonwealth were broken, and at the Ottawa Conference in 1932 Britain negotiated new agreements with her dominions. These were bilateral treaties between equals, and provided for preferential trade in certain commodities. On the whole the dominions benefited most by making sure of a market for their raw materials. It enabled Britain to restore a certain stability to international trade but the old days were gone for good. Her income from overseas investments shrank from £230 millions in 1929 to £184 millions in 1938, and her total exports by 1938 were still considerably below the 1929 figure.

If the dominions were economically and politically on their own, Britain still had to administer her wide range of colonial dependencies: African colonies, Malayan states, strategic bases, West Indian islands, and Middle Eastern protectorates. In all of them new problems arose, calling for the finest and most sympathetic statesmanship. The partition of Africa in the nineteenth century had reflected diplomatic rivalries in Europe, and Britain had found herself in control of vast, unmapped areas inhabited by primitive tribes. It is impossible to give details of the individual history of each colony, but certain general principles may be observed. The Colonial Office had adopted a policy of preserving where possible the peasant economy and tribal organization. Nigeria and the Gold Coast are political creations knitting together many tribes, whose chieftains retain their powers under the general supervision of British officials —a system known as Indirect Rule. The trade which the central Government has developed pays for universities, roads, waterpower, and bridges. Kenya and Southern Rhodesia attracted large numbers of white settlers and a policy of segregation has been followed, guaranteeing protection to the natives. Southern Rhodesia was granted self-government; but in Kenya it was decided that: "the interests of the African natives must be paramount, and if the interests of the immigrant races should conflict . . . the former should prevail". The British Government has regarded their administration of Africa as a trust towards the native peoples. Slow, patient, and often thankless work has been required in face of many difficulties. Agitators have made noisy demands for immediate self-government which Britain, as a responsible trustee, cannot grant until her wards have reached years of political discretion.

In South Eastern Asia and the West Indies, Britain pursued a similar policy of introducing self-government by stages. She has also done much to improve social and economic conditions. The eternal problem in the West Indies is poverty; Joseph Chamberlain began the attempt to develop other industries besides the sugar crop and though much has been done the general standard of life of the steadily increasing population remains low. The resources of Malaya on the other hand are extremely rich; she produces a large proportion of the world's rubber and tin. The commercial centre of Singapore was the nucleus of a loose system of states under British control. Native states under their princes had made treaties by which a British Resident exercised control as in India, and in 1896 certain of them were merged into a Federation. The British gave some semblance of unity to Malaya and opened up the resources of the country. Singapore itself was a centre for trade with Asia; together with Hong Kong, on the Chinese mainland, it was the basis of the British commercial empire of the East.

In the thirties the empire was advancing steadily but the shock of the Second World War vastly accelerated the rate of change. In 1939 every dominion, except the Irish Free State, declared war on Germany. But the effect of total war in Europe, the Middle East and Far East was to upset the already wavering balance of forces. The United States of America and Russia emerged as the two greatest world powers, and strategically all the British dominions and colonies were drawn into the American sphere. During the war Burma and Malaya had been occupied by the Japanese, and the Middle East had been a battleground. After 1945 drastic reconstruction was called for; Burma renounced the British connection altogether, while India, Pakistan and Ceylon became dominions. The Malayan Federation was enlarged to include Sarawak, after an attempt to form a united colony had foundered on the opposition of the sultans. After the confusion caused by the Japanese occupation, and the subsequent eruption of nationalism in almost all the countries of the Orient, Britain could not re-establish her commercial supremacy.

In the Middle East the situation was equally dangerous; the Arab kingdoms, particularly Egypt, wanted independence; Persia and Palestine seethed with nationalism. The oil of these regions made their defence of supreme concern to the free world. Since 1919 Egypt and Palestine had never settled down. In Egypt forty years of British rule had provided a sound administration and good order but the time had come to surrender the government to the Egyptians. Certain conditions, however, had to be imposed: namely, the security of the Suez Canal and the continuation of British rule over the Sudan, until such time as the Sudanese could decide their own future. In 1922 Fuad was made King of Egypt and an Egyptian Government took office. It was composed of the Wafd, the nationalist party, which denounced the presence of British troops in the Nile delta and Britain's share in the rule of the Sudan. The Wafd remained truculent and not until 1936 was a treaty signed by which Britain undertook to withdraw her troops to the Canal Zone and Egypt acquiesced in a joint rule (or *condominium*) over the Sudan. Nationalist agitation continued and after 1945 increased to such intensity that the Wafd demanded the renunciation of the 1936 Treaty.

Palestine and the Arab States of the Middle East gained their independence from the defeat of Turkey in the First World War. Britain was vitally interested in the future of the Middle East, and during the war encouraged T. E. Lawrence to promise the Arabs independence as soon as Turkey was beaten. But the British Government played a double game: the Sykes–Picot agreement made with France in 1916 arranged a settlement conflicting with Arab nationalism. The result was anger and distrust in Arabia, which was only allayed in 1920 after skilful negotiation. Two Arab States, Irak and Trans-Jordan, were set up under British protection in the area entrusted to British control by a League of Nations mandate. In 1932 the mandate over Irak was surrendered and in 1946 Trans-Jordan received her full sovereignty.

At the close of the first war Britain was also given the mandate over Palestine which General Allenby, assisted by T. E. Lawrence and his Arabs, had won from the Turks. Palestine, then largely an Arab country, was the traditional home of the Jews. In 1897 the Zionist Movement was founded by Jews of different nationalities to re-establish a Jewish nation-state in Palestine, and, by the Balfour Declaration of 1917 Great Britain promised her support. Nothing was said of an independent nation, and Britain merely envisaged a Jewish settlement without separate sovereignity. However, the Jews meant to have a national state, and their ambitions increased as their numbers in Palestine grew. In 1922 they formed only a ninth of the population; by 1936 they were one-fifth and by 1944 one-third. The Arabs resented this challenge to their position and feared the influence which wealth and international status gave to the Jews. The situation was similar to that of Moslem and Hindu in India, and the British were reviled by both sides. The report of a Royal Commission in 1937 recommended partition but it was rejected by both Jews and Arabs. After the Second World War, Britain no longer felt capable of maintaining the *status quo*. After several attempts at compromise the issue was referred by Britain to the United Nations and in May 1948 she relinquished the mandate. The ensuing war between the Jews and the Arabs supported by Egypt, Transjordan and Syria, resulted in partition and the creation of the independent state of Israel.

After 1945 imperialism was in full retreat. Nationalism swept the backward areas of the world, and, if resisted, it seemed likely to turn to communism. British statesmen appreciated this danger. As a trustee for native rights Britain remains to preserve order and to educate people as quickly as possible to the responsibilities of self-government. The British Empire has come in for a good deal of abuse but, as one historian has written: "Let it be recorded that for several generations the British imposed the rule of law, by the authority of the Crown, upon one-quarter of mankind, while they used its mighty influence for peaceful commerce among all nations."

## CHAPTER XVII

# DEVELOPMENTS SINCE 1945

## The Commonwealth since the Second World War

THE fifteen years since the war have seen momentous changes in every part of the world. The speed of change has been infinitely faster than many would have liked, but insurgent nationalism could only be resisted by a force which Britain neither possessed nor would have desired to apply. The communist powers were not slow to fish in troubled waters, particularly in the early nineteen-fifties, and nationalist leaders were prepared to foster discontent among the masses to reinforce their demands. In face of insistent demands for self-government and independence, often in areas with a mainly illiterate and economically backward population, successive British Governments have had to follow where nationalist leaders have led. Violence has been present in the Mau Mau rebellion in Kenya, the terrorism in Cyprus and Malaya, the Suez intervention of 1956, and in border wars in the Aden protectorates. In Central Africa, the threat of racialism spreading from the Union has darkened the promise of progress.

But it would be wrong to over-emphasize the violence of the post-war years. They have also been years of great advance both politically and economically. As Mr. Oliver Lyttleton, then Colonial Secretary, declared in 1951 in the House of Commons, "certain broad lines of policy are accepted by all sections of the House as being above party politics. . . . Two of them are fundamental. First we all aim at helping the colonial territories to attain self-government within the British Commonwealth. To that end we are seeking as rapidly as possible to build up in each territory the institutions which its circumstances require. Second, we are all determined to pursue the economic and social development of the colonial territories so that it keeps pace with their political development." The danger has been that political development has tended to outrun economic and social progress, but nationalism is always impatient. The record is impressive. Since 1950 the Federation of Rhodesia and Nyasaland, (1953) Ghana (the Gold Coast), (1957) the Federation of Malaya, and the West Indies Federation (1958) have joined the ranks of independent countries of the Commonwealth. An independent Nigeria is likely to be welcomed in 1960.[1]

But in a sense the more impressive development has been the growth in parliamentary government throughout the colonial territories. In 33 of the 40 colonial legislatures there is a majority of elected over official members. There is full adult suffrage in elections in 22 territories, and limited adult suffrage in 16 territories. Only in two territories has no constitutional advance taken place. In Malta, during 1958, the disputes over the level of financial aid to the island and the future of the Naval dockyard led to a breakdown of parliamentary government. The constitution was revoked in 1959, and the recent administration is by a Governor and a nominated Executive Council. In British Guiana, the constitution was suspended in 1953 to prevent communist subversion of the government. Until 1957 the legislative and Executive Councils were wholly nominated; in August 1957 elections were held which reintroduced a majority of elected members to both Councils.

The agitation in Egypt against the 1936 Treaty came to a head after the revolution of 1953, in which Egypt became a Republic, with General Neguib as President. In 1954 Neguib was deposed by Colonel Nasser and a Military Council. Negotiations were then conducted in an atmosphere of tension, as a result of which Britain agreed to withdraw from the Suez Base. In 1956 Nasser unilaterally nationalized the Suez Canal.

The Anglo-Egyptian condominium of the Sudan came to an end in 1956, when the Sudan was recognized as a fully independent republic.

Except for the Middle East, therefore, the evolution of the Commonwealth has been encouraging. The links which bind it together are largely intangible, and direct British influence is mainly confined to trade. Yet it is interesting to see how the demand for

[1] The achievement of full independence does not automatically confer full membership of the Commonwealth, which is a matter of consultation with existing members.

British teachers in every part of the Commonwealth is steadily increasing; it would be foolish to underestimate the influence of English ideas and language in areas where the political connexion has been broken. Britain cannot abdicate her responsibility for leadership in many areas, particularly Africa, where her tradition of tolerance and compromise may be of vital importance in establishing a partnership between the races. The triple impact of war, democracy and nationalism has destroyed within a generation the colonial empire of the nineteenth century, but, as John Stuart Mill stated over a hundred years ago, there remains a great moral influence and weight for the power which "of all in existence best understands liberty".

### Foreign Affairs since the Second World War

British Foreign Policy since 1945 has been conditioned by three facts—the power of Russia, the power of America and the rapid development of nuclear weapons. There are, to be sure, many other important features of the post-war world that have affected our diplomacy; the collapse of the old colonial empires, the sudden emergence of China as a great power, the passionate nationalism of Asia, the Arab world and Africa, to name but a few. All of these have presented or soon will present Britain with situations in which our traditional policies are irrelevant or dangerous. But whatever difficulties may arise from the conflict of these new forces it is most improbable that any major disaster will result unless one of the two giants, Russia or America, becomes involved or unless nuclear weapons are employed. To a great extent the second is dependent on the first since nuclear weapons are so expensive to develop and produce that only the giants can afford them. Britain, and more recently France, have indeed done so and other countries may follow their example. But no one imagines that they or any of their imitators will be able to catch up the giants. The point of these remarks, however, is not to assess the moral and practical implications of a defence policy based on nuclear weapons but to emphasize that the whole nuclear question itself intensifies and makes more momentous the pre-eminent strength of America and Russia.

We have already seen (p. 215) that the high hopes of friendship and co-operation between the victorious allies of 1945 were soon disappointed. Sir Winston Churchill in his famous speech delivered at Fulton, Missouri, in 1946, described Europe as being divided by an iron curtain; east of a line from Lübeck to Trieste communist governments, installed and maintained by Russian troops, set themselves to break every tie with the civilization of the West; south-east, in the Balkans, only Greece, at the cost of a long war, succeeded in keeping her freedom. Yugo-Slavia, the one communist government which did not owe its existence to the Red Army, was for three years as obedient to Russia as any that did. But in July 1948 President Tito was denounced by the Russians as an agent of British and American capitalism. His immediate downfall was confidently expected in communist circles. That he not only survived the abuse and threats of the great Stalin but appeared to thrive on them marked an epoch in Russian diplomacy. Already the policy of direct threat had failed in the Berlin blockade of 1947–48. Now it was thoroughly discredited.

What of the countries to the west of the Iron Curtain? The hostile attitude of the Eastern bloc led to a general and immediate drawing together of nearly all such states into an alliance with the giant power of the West, the United States. Into this alliance, the North Atlantic Treaty Organization, or NATO as it is generally known, the Federal Republic of West Germany was soon admitted. The division of Germany into two states—East and West, formed out of the military occupation zones of Russia and the Western powers—was one of the most important consequences of the failure of the victorious allies to agree on the terms of a peace treaty in 1945.

The policy of Great Britain has been one of warm and consistent support for NATO. During the period between the end of the war in 1945 and the death of Stalin in 1953, a period characterized as "The Cold War", there was little room for manœuvre. Ernest Bevin and Sir Anthony Eden, who held the Foreign Office almost without a break, saw no opportunity of bringing about a relaxation in the strained relations of East and West. Since 1953, however, things have been rather more hopeful. A peace treaty has been signed with Austria; there have been meetings between Soviet and Western leaders which may in time develop into something like the congress system of the period that followed the defeat of Napoleon. Although it is still the first principle of British foreign policy to maintain the closest co-operation with the Americans, both Sir Anthony Eden and Mr. Macmillan have during their service as Foreign Secretary and Prime Minister taken a more active part in promoting these exchanges than their colleagues in the United States. Perhaps the British are too optimistic, perhaps the Americans are too sceptical. On the one hand Soviet foreign and domestic policy has been markedly more liberal since the death of Stalin; on the other hand the risings in East Germany in 1953 and in Hungary in 1956 were put down with a treacherous brutality worthy of the great man himself.

The conflict between Russia and the West has not been confined to Europe. It is as wide as the world, envenoming the rival nationalisms of the Near and Far East and sharpening the antagonisms between the old colonial powers and the people of their empires. The concept of Cold War includes all forms of war except an out-and-out-military struggle between the giant powers. It is thus especially favourable to civil, colonial and guerrilla wars. The Greek civil war, the French war against the Viet Minh in Indo-China, the British war against the Chinese rebels in Malaya—all these were to some extent part of the Cold War. The point at which the Cold War came nearest to warming itself into a world-wide conflagration was the Korean War of 1949-51. North Korea and South Korea were the creations of Russian and American military occupation after the defeat of Japan. After the occupying forces had withdrawn the Communist North attacked the American-supported South. Owing to the absence of the Russian delegate from the Security Council of the United Nations it was for once possible for that organization to take prompt action and to make the cause of the South Koreans its own. The Americans took the initiative and shouldered by far the heaviest part of the military burden, but Britain supported her ally both in the debates of the United Nations and on the battlefield of the Imjin. Later, as the war dragged on, there appeared to be a danger that the Americans might attack China who was openly supporting the North Koreans with troops and equipment. Britain, however, made it clear that she would not support such a policy. At that moment the dividing line between Cold and Hot War was thin indeed.

In the Middle or, as it used more accurately to be called, the Near East there has been constant unrest. The conflict between Israel and her Arab neighbours provides an ideal situation for the tacticians of the Cold War. Britain's past promises to Jews and Arabs place her in a position when she can please neither party. Matters are made yet more delicate by the fact that our principal sources of oil, without which our economy would cease to function, are all in Arab lands. Worst of all during the years from the end of the war to the Suez crisis of 1956 we failed to agree on a common policy with the Americans. There are signs, however, that both countries are now more alive to the dangers of division in this most sensitive and elxposive area.

The Suez episode is still the subject of such strong feelings that there is much to be said for omitting all reference to it. In any case it is likely to be many years before the really important evidence is published. It is therefore perhaps the best policy not to attempt any account of the origins and course of the dispute and to refrain from passing any judgement on the wisdom or honesty of the statesmen involved. But there seems little point in blinking the fact that the result was a heavy diplomatic defeat for our country. For the first time Britain found herself in a tiny minority against the moral opinion of the world as expressed in the voting at the United Nations. For the first time she followed the Soviet precedent of using her veto in the Security Council. For the first time she found both the giant powers openly ranged against her. The limits within which British foreign policy must keep were delineated with humiliating clarity.

# LIST OF PRIME MINISTERS[1]

| | | | |
|---|---|---|---|
| 1830 | GREY | 1892 | GLADSTONE |
| 1834 | MELBOURNE | 1894 | ROSEBERY |
| 1834 | PEEL | 1895 | SALISBURY |
| 1835 | MELBOURNE | 1902 | BALFOUR |
| 1841 | PEEL | 1905 | CAMPBELL-BANNERMAN |
| 1846 | RUSSELL | 1908 | ASQUITH |
| 1852 | DERBY | 1916 | LLOYD GEORGE |
| 1852 | ABERDEEN | 1922 | BONAR LAW |
| 1855 | PALMERSTON | 1923 | BALDWIN |
| 1858 | DERBY | 1924 | MACDONALD |
| 1859 | PALMERSTON | 1924 | BALDWIN |
| 1865 | RUSSELL | 1929 | MACDONALD |
| 1866 | DERBY–DISRAELI | 1935 | BALDWIN |
| 1868 | GLADSTONE | 1937 | CHAMBERLAIN |
| 1874 | DISRAELI | 1940 | CHURCHILL |
| 1880 | GLADSTONE | 1945 | ATTLEE |
| 1885 | SALISBURY | 1951 | CHURCHILL |
| 1886 | GLADSTONE | 1955 | EDEN |
| 1886 | SALISBURY | 1957 | MACMILLAN |

[1] See the list of Cabinets in Volumes XIII and XIV of the *Oxford History of England* for further information.

# GLOSSARY

ANGLICAN, ANGLICANISM. Belonging to, or connected with, the Church of England.

ANCIEN RÉGIME. The social structure of civilized Europe before the changes of the French Revolution. In essence, an aristocratic society based on the ownership of land.

BALANCE OF POWER. A term used to describe a system of diplomacy designed to prevent any one nation, or group of nations, becoming so powerful as to be able to dominate all the others. For example, Germany, after the defeat of France in 1870, threatened to dominate Europe, and the Triple Entente was consequently formed, to preserve a balance of power.

BOROUGH. A unit of Parliamentary representation distinct from the county. For the different types of Borough, see Vol. I, p. 201.

BUREAUCRACY. Government by officials, e.g. the extension of the State's activities towards the end of the nineteenth century led to the growth of bureaucracy, since the Civil Service and local government departments were considerably extended.

CALVINISM. The system of belief taught by John Calvin at Geneva in the sixteenth century. There are many forms of Calvinism but three elements are invariable: (1) a hatred of ceremonial in Church services; (2) a rigid belief in predestination—i.e. we are all going to Heaven or Hell and nothing we can do can change our destination; and (3) the acceptance of the Bible as the only ultimate authority in matters of faith, doctrine and conduct. In England Calvinism has always been violently opposed to the existence of Bishops, believing that the Church should be controlled by laymen, i.e. the elders or "presbyters", to use the Greek term.

CARTEL. An international agreement between industrialists to restrict output so as to keep prices up and avoid competition.

CATHOLIC EMANCIPATION. The granting of full privileges of citizenship to Roman Catholics. It is usually taken to mean the Act for the Relief of the Roman Catholics passed by Wellington's ministry in 1829.

CIVIL LIST. The revenue granted to the Crown by Parliament originally intended to cover all the expenses of government. The gradual transfer of naval and military expenditure and the cost of administration to Parliamentary control has left the civil list with little to provide for beyond the maintenance of the Royal Family and their household.

COERCION. Government by force, e.g. to use troops to disperse a mob is a coercive measure.

COLLECTIVISM, COLLECTIVIST. The opposite to *laissez-faire*. A collectivist state is one in which the Government assumes wide responsibilities for the welfare of the governed. Collectivism involves State intervention in the economic life of a nation.

CONSTITUTION AND CONSTITUTIONAL GOVERNMENT. (1) Simply the form of government of a country. Strictly speaking a constitution may be despotic, aristocratic, democratic, etc.

(2) In the term constitutional government, the idea conveyed by the word "constitutional" implies that certain rights are guaranteed to the citizens or at least to some sections of them. Constitutions may be based on tradition and therefore unwritten like the British, or they may be written as is the American.

CO-OPERATIVE MOVEMENT. In 1844 the Rochdale Pioneers opened the first co-operative shop, the profits of which were divided among its customers, in proportion to their purchases. Tom Hughes, the author of *Tom Brown's Schooldays*, was an ardent supporter of the scheme. In the 1870's there were co-operative shops all over the country, as well as factories to supply them. The real importance of the Co-operative movement was that it brought working men together and gave them experience of business and administration.

DENOMINATIONAL. Denominational religious teaching is the teaching of religion from the point of view of a particular sect or denomination.

DIRECT TAXATION. A tax levied on income or property (e.g. Income Tax or Death Duties). Indirect taxation is levied by imposing duties or taxes on goods (e.g. Tobacco Duty or Purchase Tax).

ESTABLISHED CHURCH, ESTABLISHMENT. A relationship between Church and State, in which the belief and organization of the Church are recognized as part of the civil constitution.

EVANGELICAL. Evangelical means literally "of, or according to, the gospel". The distinguishing characteristic of the Evangelicals was that they were passionately concerned with carrying the teachings of the Gospel into the lives of ordinary men and women.

"Things have come to a pretty pass", said Lord Melbourne on hearing an Evangelical sermon, "when religion is allowed to invade the sphere of private life." Although the Evangelicals had no quarrel with the Established Church, the movement as a whole took place outside it. (See Vol. I, pp. 121, 124.)

FRANCHISE. The right to vote at Parliamentary elections; e.g. to extend the franchise means to give more people the right to vote.

FREE TRADE. The abolition of all protective duties and tariffs, so that foreign goods compete on equal terms with those produced at home.

GOLD STANDARD. A country is said to be "on the gold standard" when it restricts its issue of paper money to the limit of its gold reserves. When England was on the gold standard a pound note could be exchanged for a gold sovereign at any bank.

HABEAS CORPUS. In 1679 the Habeas Corpus Act was passed, which enacted that a judge, under penalty of a £500 fine, must issue a writ of Habeas Corpus, whereby a prisoner was to be brought before a Court, charged, and tried within a specified time. In times of emergency the Act was often suspended to enable dangerous suspects to be imprisoned without trial.

HIGH CHURCH. See pages 217 ff.

IMPERIAL PREFERENCE. A system of tariff privileges granted by the Mother Country to her Dominions and Colonies, giving their goods a lower rate of import duty than that extended to foreigners, e.g. the duty on Empire wines is lower than that levied on French or German wines.

INDIRECT TAXATION. See DIRECT TAXATION.

INTEREST. There is no precise modern equivalent for this word as it was generally understood in the eighteenth and nineteenth centuries. Almost always it implies a personal relationship, generally that of blood. Thus to say of a young officer in the Navy "He has interest with Admiral Brown" meant that Admiral Brown would do his best to help that young officer on in his career, either because he was a relation of the Admiral's or because his father had been a friend of the Admiral's or some such reason. Similarly in politics "the Bedford interest" was a collective name for those members of Parliament who owed their election mainly or entirely to the Duke of Bedford.

JACOBIN. A man of extreme revolutionary opinions.

JOINT-STOCK COMPANIES. These developed in the late sixteenth century to meet the risks and expenses of some trade which was on too large a scale for an individual to manage by himself. Previously merchants had associated together to secure by Royal Charter the grant of a trading monopoly, but they traded as individuals on their own account, with their own ships and money. These companies had been called chartered companies. A joint-stock company, in contrast, consisted of a group of merchants pooling their resources and sharing the profits in proportion to their original investment. The greatest of these joint-stock companies was the East India Company (1600). Shares in such a company were transferable.

LAISSEZ-FAIRE or LAISSER FAIRE. The economic doctrine of "Let Alone", i.e. the State should not interfere with the free operation of the laws of supply and demand by attempting to control wages and prices.

LIBERAL, LIBERALISM. The Liberal party was formed by an alliance of Whigs and Radicals, later joined by some Peelites. Under Palmerston Whig influence was dominant, but after Gladstone became Premier the Whigs drifted over to the Conservatives. See also Unionist. Liberalism in the intellectual sense is defined on p. 218.

LITTLE ENGLANDERS. A name for anti-imperialists.

LOW CHURCH. A Low Churchman relies more on the Bible and his own private judgment than on the tradition and teaching of the Church. He dislikes ceremonial and, as a rule, has little use for the mysterious. His spiritual ancestors are the Puritan and the Evangelical.

MANDATE. Authority to act for another.

(1) In international affairs this generally refers to trusteeship over backward or disputed territories. e.g. the League of Nations granted Britain a mandate over Palestine.

(2) In domestic politics a party which is returned to power is generally considered to have a mandate from the people to carry out the major measures specified in its election programme. Whether it is bound to carry out these measures, or whether, if circumstances change, it may introduce others without giving the people a chance to pass a verdict on them at a general election, are questions much in dispute. The doctrine of the mandate, i.e. that a government is bound hand and foot by its election pro-gramme, is a comparatively new one in English politics and has gained ground dangerously in the last few years.

MONOPOLY. The sole and exclusive right to sell a commodity. Thus, a monopoly in trade means that no competition is permitted, e.g. the Post Office is a State monopoly.

NAVIGATION ACTS. A series of Acts beginning in the Middle Ages and reaching their widest extent in the middle of the seventeenth century. They protected and encouraged the British carrying trade by refusing to admit foreign goods into English or colonial ports unless they were carried in English ships, or in ships of the country from which the goods came, e.g. Dutch cheese could be imported into England in a Dutch or English ship, but not in a French one.

NONCONFORMIST. Synonym for Dissenter. Any Englishman who belongs to any religious body other than the Church of England. The term is not generally applied to Roman Catholics.

PROLETARIAT. That class of society which has no property or stable source of income, and which depends for its livelihood upon wages.

PROTECTION, PROTECTIONIST. The opposite of Free Trade; the policy of imposing duties on imported goods so as to *protect* home industries.

RADICAL. Spelt with a small "r" this word denotes sweeping change (from the Latin *radix* = root), e.g. to advocate the abolition of private property is to advocate a radical policy. With a large "R" the word is the label of a political movement intent on political and economic reform which emerged in the years following Waterloo, mingled with the Victorian Liberal party, and was finally swallowed up in the Labour Movement.

REFORMATION. A collective word for the changes in the teaching and organization of the Church and in its place in society which occurred over most of Europe between 1520 and 1560. In England it usually refers to the series of Acts culminating in the Act of Supremacy (1534) by which Henry VIII refused to acknowledge the authority of the Pope.

REFORM BILL. The Reform Act of 1832 is so much better known as the Reform Bill that it is referred to as such throughout this book. It is dealt with at length in Vol. I, pp. 290–5.

ROYAL COMMISSION. A Royal Commission is a committee of investigation appointed by the Government in order to obtain information upon which legislation can be based. Royal Commissions have been appointed to investigate such varied subjects as Trade Unions, Divorce, Prisons, Gambling, and Public Schools. The Government is not bound to accept recommendations submitted to it by a Royal Commission, but since its members are selected for their knowledge of the subject under consideration, their report naturally carries weight.

SELF-DETERMINATION. The right of the inhabitants of a country to determine for themselves under what sovereignty they shall live.

SETTLEMENT COLONIES are colonies established in virtually uninhabited territory where British customs and law become the basis of society. For example Australia was originally a settlement colony, Jamaica was not.

SOCIALISM, SOCIALIST. Socialism is the belief that individual liberty should be subordinated to the interests of the community as a whole. Although there are many kinds of Socialism, all socialists advocate collectivist action. Karl Marx's book, *Das Kapital*, provides the classic foundation of Socialist doctrine: See p. 173.

SPEENHAMLAND SYSTEM. A system devised by the Berkshire magistrates in 1795, whereby the parish supplemented wages out of the poor rates, up to a minimum wage calculated from the current price of corn. The system was copied all over the country, and encouraged employers to lower wages in the certain knowledge that they would be made up to the predetermined minimum by the parish funds.

STATUS QUO. This is short for "status quo ante bellum" (literally, the position as before the war.)

SUFFRAGE, SUFFRAGETTES. The suffrage is the right to vote at elections. The women who demanded this right for their sex were nicknamed suffragettes.

TARIFF. The collective name for the duties imposed on imports, e.g. a Protectionist believes in a high tariff.

TEST ACTS, RELIGIOUS TESTS. The Test Act was an Act passed in 1673 with the intention of excluding Roman Catholics and Dissenters from political power in local and central government. In order to qualify for any public office (e.g. as a Magistrate, Mayor, Army officer, etc.) a man had among other things to receive the sacraments according to the Anglican rites. Where appointment to office depends upon such qualifications, a religious test is said to be imposed. Until 1854 only members of the Church of England could enter the universities of Oxford and Cambridge; until 1871 none but an Anglican was allowed to take a degree or hold a college or university post there.

TORY. Is an old Irish word, meaning a bandit, and was applied to those members of Parliament who opposed the exclusion of James, Duke of York, in 1678. See Vol. I, p. 40. The party broke up over Catholic Emancipation in 1829, but the greater part of it was absorbed into the Conservative party which grew up round Peel in the early thirties. The opponents of Conservatism continue to prefer the older name.

TRUST. The combination of different industries, or branches of a single industry, under common direction and ownership. The trust is essentially monopolistic.

UNION, ACT OF (1800). By the Act of Union, Ireland was given a hundred seats in the English House of Commons, and thirty-two seats in the House of Lords, restrictions on Irish commerce were removed, and redress of Catholic grievances promised. This Parliamentary Union of the two islands was designed to remedy some of the grievances which had led to rebellion in 1798. It was little more than a temporary solution of the Irish problem, particularly as George III refused to assent to Catholic Emancipation.

UNIONIST. A unionist was a person who wanted to maintain the Act of Union (1800) between England and Ireland. The Unionist party was that section of the Liberal party which opposed Gladstone over Home Rule. Gradually the Unionists were absorbed by the Conservative party, which consequently was renamed the Conservative and Unionist party.

WHIG. The word "Whig" was a nickname for a Scottish Covenanter, and was applied contemptuously to those members of the House of Commons who advocated the exclusion of James, Duke of York, in 1678. See Vol. I, p. 40. The party broke up soon after the Reform Bill of 1832. See also Liberal Party.

# THE HOUSES OF HANOVER AND WINDSOR

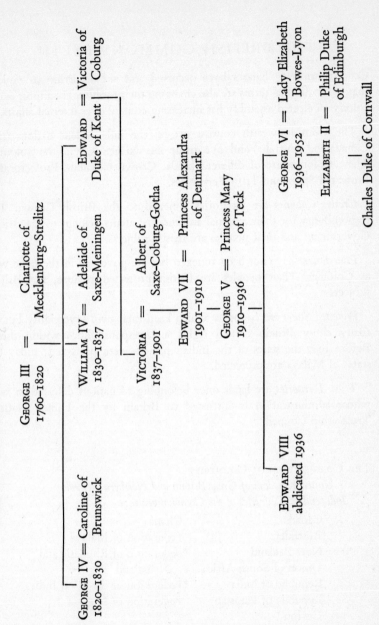

GEORGE III = Charlotte of
1760–1820   Mecklenburg-Strelitz

GEORGE IV = Caroline of
1820–1830   Brunswick

WILLIAM IV = Adelaide of
1830–1837   Saxe-Meiningen

EDWARD = Victoria of
Duke of Kent   Coburg

VICTORIA = Albert of
1837–1901   Saxe-Coburg-Gotha

EDWARD VII = Princess Alexandra
1901–1910   of Denmark

GEORGE V = Princess Mary
1910–1936   of Teck

EDWARD VIII
abdicated 1936

GEORGE VI = Lady Elizabeth
1936–1952   Bowes-Lyon

ELIZABETH II = Philip Duke
of Edinburgh

Charles Duke of Cornwall

# THE BRITISH COMMONWEALTH

CONSTITUTIONAL changes have occurred and are occurring so rapidly that the traditional terms are also changing their meaning. In almost every colony an elected assembly has increasing control over internal affairs.

The Commonwealth consists of: (*a*) the independent nations (like Canada and Australia) and (*b*) a group known generally as the Colonies. These Colonies are of different kinds: Crown Colonies, Protectorates, Protected States and Trust Territories.

*Crown Colonies* are territories annexed to the British Crown. The responsibility for their external and internal affairs belongs to the British Government and their peoples are British subjects.

*Protectorates* have not been annexed but are governed in the same way as Colonies. Their peoples are British protected persons, not British subjects.

*Protected States* are countries which keep their own sovereignty but by treaty allow Britain certain rights and responsibilities within them. Before 1947 the states of the Indian princes were protected; today the states of Malaya are protected.

*Trust Territories* are lands once belonging to nations defeated in war, whose administration is entrusted to Britain by the United Nations Trusteeship Council.


THE COMMONWEALTH COUNTRIES
*United Kingdom of Great Britain and Northern Ireland:*
*Independent Countries of the Commonwealth:*

| | |
|---|---|
| Canada | Ghana |
| Australia | Federation of Malaya |
| New Zealand | *Federation of Rhodesia and |
| Union of South Africa | Nyasaland |
| Republic of India | *Federation of the West Indies |
| Republic of Pakistan | Federation of Nigeria |
| Ceylon | |

* These Federations are made up of colonies and protectorates, in course of time they will become fully independent.

## DEPENDENCIES OF THE UNITED KINGDOM

### East and Central Africa:

| | |
|---|---|
| Kenya | †Colony and Protectorate |
| Uganda | Protectorate |
| *Northern Rhodesia | Protectorate |
| *Nyasaland | Protectorate |
| Somaliland | Protectorate |
| *Southern Rhodesia | Colony with internal self-government |
| Tanganyika | Trust Territory |
| Zanzibar | Protectorate |
| Pemba | Protectorate |

### West Africa:

| | |
|---|---|
| Cameroons | Trust Territory |
| Gambia | †Colony and Protectorate |
| Sierra Leone | †Colony and Protectorate |
| Togoland | Trust Territory |

### South African High Commission Territories:

| | |
|---|---|
| Basutoland | Colony |
| Bechuanaland | Protectorate |
| Swaziland | Protectorate |

### Eastern:

| | |
|---|---|
| Hong Kong | Colony |

### Federation of Malaya:

| | |
|---|---|
| Singapore | Protected State |
| Christmas and Cocos Islands | Colony |
| North Borneo | Colony |
| Sarawak | Colony |
| Brunei | Protected State |

### Mediterranean:

| | |
|---|---|
| Gibraltar | Colony |
| Malta | Colony |

(Britain still retains bases in Cyprus, which has been an independent Republic since 1960.)

* Members of Federation of Rhodesia and Nyasland.
† Adjoining areas administered by the same Government.

DEPENDENCIES OF THE UNITED KINGDOM—*continued*

*West Indies and the Americas:*

| | |
|---|---|
| Bahamas | Colony |
| †Barbados | Colony |
| British Guiana | Colony |
| British Honduras | Colony |
| †Jamaica | Colony |
|     Cayman Islands | |
|     Turks and Caicos Islands | |

| | | |
|---|---|---|
| †St. Kitts-Nevis—Anguilla | Colony | |
| †Montserrat | Colony | Leeward |
| †Antigua, Barbuda, Redonda | Colony | Islands |
| Virgin Islands | Colony | |
| †Trinidad and Tobago | Colony | |
| †St. Lucia | Colony | |
| †St. Vincent | Colony | Windward |
| †Dominica | Colony | Islands |
| †Grenada | Colony | |
| Falkland Islands | Colony | |
| Bermuda | Colony | |

*Western Pacific:*

| | |
|---|---|
| Fiji | Colony |
| Gilbert and Ellice Islands | Colony |
| British Solomon Islands | Protectorate |
| Tonga | Protected State |
| Pitcairn Island | Colony |

*Atlantic and Indian Ocean:*

| | |
|---|---|
| St. Helena (with Ascension and Tristan da Cunha) | Colony |
| Mauritius | Colony |
| Seychelles | Colony |
| *Aden | *Colony and Protectorate |
|     Perim | |
|     Socotra | |

   * Adjoining areas administered by the same Government.
   † Members of Federation of West Indies.

## DEPENDENCIES OF COMMONWEALTH COUNTRIES

### Australia:
Papua
Australian Antarctic Territory
Nauru (Mandated to Britain, Australia and New Zealand.
    Administered by Australia as Trust Territory)
New Guinea (Trust Territory)
Norfolk Island

### New Zealand:
Ross Dependency
Tokelau or Union Islands
Western Samoa (Trust Territory)
Kermadec, Chatham and Cook Islands

### South Africa:
South West Africa (Mandated Territory)

## CONDOMINIUMS
Canton and Enderbury Islands (Britain and U.S.A.)
New Hebrides (Britain and France)

# SUGGESTIONS FOR FURTHER READING

THE following list of books makes no pretence to be comprehensive and does not include most of the books already recommended in the text. For those who require further information, the bibliographies in volumes XIII and XIV of the Oxford History of England cover the period 1815–1914 in detail. These two books (*The Age of Reform* by E. L. Woodward and *England 1870–1914* by R. C. K. Ensor), together with G. M. Trevelyan's *British History in the Nineteenth Century and After* and the relevant chapters of Keith Feiling's *History of England*, are the best general works on the period. The Frenchman Halévy's *History of the English People in the Nineteenth Century* is in a class by itself. Conceived on a scale which its author did not live to execute, its six volumes are as readable as they are learned. The *Cambridge Modern History*, the *Cambridge History of British Foreign Policy*, the *Cambridge History of the British Empire* and the *Dictionary of National Biography* are all useful for reference.

## POLITICAL HISTORY

K. B. Smellie: *A Hundred Years of English Government* (difficult, but especially valuable for the breadth of view).

J. L. Hammond: *Gladstone and the Irish Nation* (though long, this is the best book on Gladstone).

Walter Bagehot: *The English Constitution* (the most brilliant and lucid exposition of the Liberal view of the Constitution).

F. M. Hardie: *The Political Influence of Queen Victoria*.

G. Dangerfield: *The Strange Death of Liberal England*.

G. M. Young and W. K. Hancock (ed.): *Documents of British History*.

## SOCIAL AND ECONOMIC HISTORY

The works of such novelists as Dickens, Thackeray, Trollope, George Eliot, Disraeli, Mrs. Gaskell, Charles Kingsley and Thomas Hardy throw a great deal of light on the social life of their times, as do Memoirs, Biographies and Autobiographies.

G. M. Young (ed.): *Early Victorian England*.

F. Engels: *Condition of the Working Class in 1844* (the author was Karl Marx's most intimate friend).

Sir John Clapham: *Economic History of Modern Britain* (three massive volumes, but surprisingly readable and very easy for reference).

L. C. A. Knowles: *Industrial and Commercial Revolutions*.

G. D. H. Cole: *A Short History of the Labour Movement*.

V. Sackville-West: *The Edwardians* ( a novel).
H. Wickham-Steed: *The Press.*
Christopher Hobhouse: *1851 and the Crystal Palace.*
C. C. Lloyd: *The Nation and the Navy.*
Michael Lewis: *A Social History of the Navy 1793–1815.*

## FOREIGN POLICY

Seton Watson: *Britain in Europe 1789–1914.*
Algernon Cecil: *British Foreign Secretaries 1807–1916.*
J. A. Spender: *Fifty Years of Europe.*
Dwight E. Lee (ed.): *The Outbreak of the First World War.*
Harold Nicolson: *Lord Carnock.*
  *Peacemaking 1919.*
  *Curzon: the Last Phase.*
W. S. Churchill: *The World Crisis* (his four volumes of Memoirs of the
  1914–18 War).
  *The Gathering Storm.*
Carey and Scott: *The Great War* (an excellent short history).
C. R. Cruttwell: *A History of the Great War.*
R. B. McCallum: *Public Opinion and the Last Peace.*
L. B. Namier: *Conflicts* (a collection of essays).
J. W. Wheeler-Bennett: *Munich.*

## RELIGION, EDUCATION AND THOUGHT

G. M. Young: *Portrait of an Age* (by far the best single book).
Edmund Gosse: *Father and Son* (autobiography).
Samuel Butler: *The Way of all Flesh* (a novel).
R. L. Archer: *Secondary Education in the Nineteenth Century.*
S. L. Ollard: *A Short History of the Oxford Movement.*
R. W. Church: *The Oxford Movement 1833–45* (Dean Church was the
  personal friend of the leaders of the movement).
G. Lowes Dickinson: *A Modern Symposium* (an entertaining summary of
  Victorian opinion).
Cyril Garbett: *In an Age of Revolution.*
Michael Goodwin (ed.): *Nineteenth Century Opinion* (extracts from the
  first fifty volumes of *The Nineteenth Century*).

## THE EMPIRE

Sir Reginald Coupland (ed.): *The Durham Report.*
Gibbon Wakefield: *On the Art of Colonisation.*
Charles Buller: *Responsible Government.*

Sir Alfred Zimmern: *The Third British Empire*.
G. Dangerfield: *Bengal Mutiny*.
C. E. Carrington: *The British Overseas*.
W. R. Brock: *Britain and the Dominions*.
A. P. Thornton: *The Imperial Idea and its Enemies*.

### BIOGRAPHY

J. W. Mackail: *William Morris*.
Cecil Woodham-Smith: *Florence Nightingale*.
G. M. Trevelyan: *Grey of Fallodon*.
Lord Ponsonby: *Sir Henry Ponsonby: His Life from his Letters* (Sir Henry Ponsonby was private secretary to Queen Victoria and this book gives one of the most understanding portraits of her).
Lytton Strachey: *Queen Victoria* (very entertaining).
      *Eminent Victorians* (brilliantly unfair).
A. Birrell: *Gladstone* (the best short biography)
D. C. Somervell: *Disraeli and Gladstone*.
André Maurois: *Disraeli*.
Giles St. Aubyn: *Macaulay*.
G. O. Trevelyan: *Life and Letters of Lord Macaulay*.
S. E. Finer: *Edwin Chadwick*.
Walter Bagehot: *Biographical Studies*.
Lord Bryce: *Studies in Contemporary Biography*.
St. John Ervine: *Parnell*.
G. K. Chesterton: *Browning*.
Michael Sadleir: *Trollope*.
Sir Charles Tennyson: *Tennyson*.
W. S. Churchill: *Great Contemporaries*.
G. K. A. Bell: *Randall Davidson*.
F. A. Iremonger: *William Temple*.
Thomas Jones: *Lloyd George*.
Harold Nicolson: *King George V*.
James Pope-Hennessy: *Queen Mary*.

### AUTOBIOGRAPHY AND MEMOIRS

Alexander Somerville: *Autobiography of a Working Man*.
Mary MacCarthy: *A Victorian Childhood*.
E. F. Benson: *As We Were*.
Margot Oxford and Asquith: *An Autobiography*.
Beatrice Webb: *My Apprenticeship*.
    *Our Partnership*.

# INDEX

Entries marked with an asterisk are to be found in the Glossary. Page numbers in heavy type indicate the main reference to an entry in the index. The date of a sovereign's reign is given in heavy type.

## A

INDEX